EPITAPH FOR A DESERT ANARCHIST

The Life and Legacy of Edward Abbey

JAMES BISHOP JR.

Epilogue by Charles Bowden

A TOUCHSTONE BOOK
Published by Simon & Schuster
New York   London   Toronto
Sydney   Tokyo   Singapore

TOUCHSTONE
Rockefeller Center
1230 Avenue of the Americas
New York, NY 10020

First Touchstone Edition 1995

TOUCHSTONE and colophon are registered trademarks
of Simon & Schuster Inc.

Designed by PIXEL PRESS

Manufactured in the United States of America

1   3   5   7   9   10   8   6   4   2

Library of Congress Cataloging-in-Publication Data
Bishop, James Jr.
Epitaph for a desert anarchist : the life and legacy of Edward Abbey /
by James Bishop, Jr.
p.   cm.
Includes bibliographical references and index.
1. Abbey, Edward, 1927–1989.   2. Authors, American—20th Century—Biography.
3. Park Rangers—United States—Biography.   4. Abbey, Edward, 1927–1989—
Influence.   5. West (U.S.)—In literature.   6. Nature in literature.   I. Title.
PS3551.B2Z59   1994
813'.54—dc20   93-47564
[B]   CIP
ISBN 0-684-80439-5

The author and publisher are grateful for permission to use excerpts for the following material: The Estate of Edward Abbey; from "Wildwest," *Collected Poems 1917–1982* by
Archibald MacLeish. Copyright © 1985 by the Estate of Archibald MacLeish, reprinted
by permission of Houghton Mifflin, Co. All rights reserved; from an essay by Barbara
Kingsolver from *The Tucson Weekly*; "Daniel Boone" by Stephen Vincent Benét from *A Book
of Americans* by Rosemary and Stephen Vincent Benét. Copyright renewed © 1961 by
Rosemary Carr Benét. Reprinted by permission of Brandt & Brandt Literary Agents, Inc.;
from "The Quiet Crisis and the Next Generation," by Stewart L. Udall. © Stewart Lee
Udall; from "With Traven and Thoreau: A Narrative Bibliography of Edward Abbey."
Copyright © 1994 by Ken Sanders; from "A Few Words in Favor of Edward Abbey" from
What Are People For? by Wendell Berry. Copyright © 1990 by Wendell Berry. Reprinted
by permission of North Point Press, a division of Farrar, Straus & Giroux, Inc.; from "The
Hollow Men" in *Collected Poems 1909–1962* by T. S. Eliot, copyright 1956 by Harcourt
Brace, copyright 1964, 1963 by T. S. Eliot, reprinted by permission of the publisher. An
excerpt from "Elegy: for Edward Abbey" (1989) by C. L. Rawlins is reprinted by permis-
sion of the author. Pages 205–206 represent an abridgment and condensation of Barry
Lopez's tribute to Edward Abbey. The entire speech is reprinted in the *Journal of Energy,
Natural Resources & Environmental Law*, Vol. XI, No. 1, published by the University of
Utah College of Law, © 1989 Barry Holstun Lopez.

To Edward Abbey's literary forebears, notably Everett Ruess, a vagabond for beauty who roamed the Colorado Plateau in the 1930s, probing for that secret center where there are no bounds; to all Abbey aficionados and to those who have yet to encounter his works.

To Edward Abbey's literary forebears, notably Everett Ruess, a vagabond for beauty who roamed the Colorado Plateau in the 1930s, probing for that secret center where there are no bounds; to all Abbey aficionados and to those who have yet to encounter his works.

VOICE CRYING
IN THE WILDERNESS

This is the dead land
This is cactus land . . .

Between the idea
And the reality . . .

Between the conception
And the creation . . .

Between the potency
And the existence . . .
        —T. S. ELIOT, "THE HOLLOW MEN"

I sometimes choose to think that man is a dream,
thought an illusion, and only rock is real. Rock and sun
. . . belief? What do I believe in? I believe in sun. In
rock. In the dogma of the sun and the doctrine of the rock.
    I believe in blood, fire, woman, rivers, eagles, storms,
drums, flutes, banjos and broom-tailed horses.
        —EDWARD ABBEY,
            A VOICE CRYING IN THE WILDERNESS

CONTENTS

Contents

EDWARD PAUL ABBEY

Born January 29, 1927
Home, Pennsylvania
Died March 14, 1989
Tucson, Arizona

EDUCATION

1951 B.A. in Philosophy and English, University of New
      Mexico
1951–52 Graduate study at Edinburgh University, Scotland
1956 M.A. in Philosophy, University of New Mexico

AWARDS AND FELLOWSHIPS

1951 Fulbright Fellowship, Edinburgh University, Scotland
1957 Wallace Stegner Creative Writing Fellowship,
      Stanford University
1974 Guggenheim Fellowship in fiction writing
1978 Honorary Life Membership, Western Literature
      Association
1987 Creative Achievement Award, American Academy
      and Institute of Arts and Letters (declined)

PUBLICATIONS

1954 *Jonathan Troy.* New York: Dodd Mead (a novel)
1956 *The Brave Cowboy.* New York: Dodd Mead (a novel)
1962 *Fire on the Mountain.* New York: Dial Press (a novel)
1968 *Desert Solitaire.* New York: McGraw Hill (essays)

1970 *Appalachian Wilderness.* New York: Dutton (travel)
1971 *Black Sun.* New York: Simon & Schuster (a novel)
1972 *Cactus Country.* New York: Time-Life (travel)
1975 *The Monkey Wrench Gang.* New York: Lippincott (a novel)
1975 *The Journey Home.* New York: Dutton (essays)
1978 *The Hidden Canyon.* New York: Viking (travel)
1979 *Abbey's Road.* New York: Dutton (essays)
1980 *Good News.* New York: Dutton
1981 *Desert Images.* New York: Chanticleer (essays)
1982 *Down the River.* New York: Dutton (essays)
1984 *Beyond the Wall.* New York: Henry Holt and Company (essays)
1984 *Slumgullion Stew: An Abbey Reader.* New York: Dutton
1984 *The Best of Edward Abbey.* Sierra Club Books
1987 *One Life at a Time, Please.* New York: Henry Holt and Company (essays)
1988 *The Fool's Progress.* New York: Henry Holt and Company (a novel)
1989 *Hayduke Lives.* New York: Little, Brown (a novel)
1989 *A Voice Crying in the Wilderness: Notes from a Secret Journal.* Santa Fe: Rydall Press

PROLOGUE

The year was 1969, and the environmental movement was in its infancy. A young man from New Mexico walked into my *Newsweek* office in Washington, D.C., and handed me a tattered, water-stained book. It was *Desert Solitaire*. He said it was written by a park ranger he knew in Utah. "Forget those documents," he said, pointing to the stacks of government papers and publications on my bookshelves. "Read this instead, if you want to know what's happening in America."

After that, I never missed another book by Ed Abbey. We shook hands once, but I never knew him personally, and I have mixed feelings about that. I would have liked to argue with him over cheap cigars and good tequilla by a blazing river campfire under a sky full of stars. But then, this would be a different kind of book, more of a personal memoir. I agree with B. Traven that the biography of a creative person is less important than his own works. For if that person is "not recognizable in his works, then he is either worth nothing or his works nothing."

So this is neither a definitive biography nor an academic study of Abbey's work. It is my attempt to record the impact of his work on our times and on his admirers who, like him, like all of us, are struggling to exist in a shrinking natural world.

I owe him a debt for raising my consciousness about the importance of individual responsibility and taking action, and about the value of all living things.

I think about him whenever I read that fireflies have stopped appearing in parts of the Midwest and that there are fewer frogs every year in the South. And I feel his words: "Sentiment without action is the ruin of the soul."

ACKNOWLEDGMENTS

Many people helped to make this book possible, from Colorado River boatmen to university professors, from bartenders to artists. Some deserve special thanks, especially Clarke Cartwright Abbey, Ed's widow, and his surviving siblings, Nancy and Howard. And I thank them now for their patience and their willingness to share their memories and opinions.

Without the help of the staff of the Special Collections Department at the University of Arizona, I never would have been able to wade through all the boxes of Abbey's papers. Only their excellent organizational abilities made this possible.

My thanks also go to: David Keeber, Kirk Douglas, Ken Sanders, Rod Nash, Steve Thompson, Bob Lippman, William Eastlake, Scott Thybony, Mary Sojourner, Mike Lacey, Jack Loeffler, Greg McNamee, Jack Proctor, Wendell Berry, Jim and Karin Offield, Ann Ronald, John Mitchell, Roderick Nash, Bob and Sue Clemenz, Roger Clark, Dick Vonior, Donn Rawlings, Edward Hoagland, Bruce Babbitt, Thomas Jefferson Bollinger, Susan Kliewer, Allan Harrington, Dick Kirkpatrick, Geoffrey Platts, Cynthia Bennett, Aliza and Alan Caillou, Terry Gustafson, Stewart Udall, Peter Wild, Elizabeth Rigby, Susan Champion, Clyde Morgan, Bennie Blake, Chuck Bowden, my loving ex-wife, super-proofreader Susan, my feisty literary agent, Jonathan Matson, and Lee Goerner of Atheneum, who provided valuable insights and encouragement along the way.

EPITAPH FOR A
DESERT ANARCHIST

THE MAN AND THE LEGEND

Why the surly hatred of progress, the churlish resistance to all popular improvements . . . Why wilderness?

Because we like the taste of freedom. Because we like the smell of danger.

—EDWARD ABBEY, *SLICKROCK*

Heracles was one of the most popular of the Greek heroes. Often called "the defender of the earth," his crusade took him to the wild places of the known world. And legend has it that wherever he went, he sought to make the land he loved a safer, wiser place in which to live.

Heracles became a legend—and so, centuries later, has a scholarly, disputatious, backwoods country man who decided at a tender age that something was amiss in his native land, that the techno-military-industrial direction it was taking wasn't contributing one particle of beauty, freedom, or dignity to human life.

While the family slept, and the doves sighed in the deep Appalachian woods nearby, he would sit up late at night as a young man and imagine a different kind of country where citizens could still enjoy the best of both worlds—civilization and wilderness—and where they still could be free.

He was one of the fortunate ones, because before he was twenty years old, he had found his Eden in the American Southwest. There he proceeded to make the arid landscape of the Colorado Plateau his special amphitheater, a bizarre and beautiful hundred-million acre expanse of magic and strength the size of New York and New England; prehistoric home to cactus, snakes, scorpions, and vultures; cut by rivers, countless canyons, and pocked by the necks of prehistoric volcanoes standing like guardians on desert floors. "I love it so much," he said, "that I find it hard to talk about." Nothing but desert, nothing but "the silent world . . . both agonized and deeply still. Like death? Perhaps."

Meet Edward Paul Abbey, twentieth-century polemicist and desert anarchist, a character of elaborate contradictions and eccentricities whose words either infuriated or delighted his readers.

In a career spanning four decades, he wrote passionately in defense of the Southwest and its inhabitants, often mocking the mindless bureaucratic forces hell-bent on destroying it. "Resist much, obey little," from Walt Whitman, was this warrior's motto.

While he was alive, attempts to label him in conventional terms nearly always fell short because he was neither left-wing nor right-wing, nor was he an outlaw. Abbey was a genuine rebel who simply did not believe in the modern industrial way of life. He wrote against the grain, always choosing the path of the greatest resistance. Beginning in the 1950s, he depicted the Southwest not as a virgin utopia peopled by rugged individualists, but as a region under siege because of government and corporate greed, its people at risk of being cut off from the primary wellspring of their spiritual strength—the wild places. He's been dead for a while now, but the legend keeps on growing.

* * *

Out in the cinder hills to the east of Flagstaff, Arizona, not long after Edward Abbey's death in 1989, a gathering of curious archaeologists were poking around an old Indian ruin when suddenly, cascading from an alluring cobalt sky, an unexpected shadow fell across the group.

"Look up there," someone said. "There's Ed." Looking up, they saw a single turkey vulture studying them, red head bald, red neck featherless, rocking gently on coal-black wings. "Abbey promised to return as a vulture," another said, "the only known philosophizing bird. He said he wanted to try a different career for a change."

Years after the death of the American West's one true contemporary, and certainly its most controversial literary legend, reports of such sightings are on the rise. For those who valued Abbey, the self-styled desert rat, as mentor and friend, prophet and author, as militant defender of the West's remaining wild places, his passing left a profound void. "Ed was a war horse, a wild horse, and one of a kind," says essayist Edward Hoagland.

Maybe that is why, either out of respect or wish fulfillment, when a vulture is seen soaring above the canyon country, someone will say, "Abbey lives." After all, he did predict it.

> For a lifetime or two, I think I'll pass on eagle, hawk or falcon this time. I think I'll settle for the sedate career, serene and soaring, of the humble turkey buzzard. And if a falcon comes around making trouble, I'll spit in his eye. Or hers. And contemplate this world we love from a silent and considerable height.
>
> —*Down the River*

Reports of such a feathered resurrection fail to strike everyone as great news. "I never wished a man dead before in my whole life," mutters Cynthia Rigden, a fourth-generation rancher in Skull Valley, Arizona. "Because of those damn books of his, people are cutting barbed wire and messing with ranchers all over the place."

Echoes Fred Burke, a veteran Colorado River motorboater, "Abbey was a guru to the hippies, but to me he was a jerk, a mercenary who wrote for the money, a hypocrite who was paid by the Park Service, then he attacked it. You can have him."

Then there are others, such as authors Marc Reisner and Charles Bowden, who sometimes question—half in jest—whether those unflattering eulogies might be premature; whether Abbey really did die on March 14, 1989, and, according to his instructions, buried secretly—and illegally—somewhere deep in the desert he loved.

While sipping wine in a hotel bar on the dusty outskirts of Phoenix, Arizona, about two years after Abbey died, Reisner heard someone mention Abbey's name; his mood darkened, his lips curled under, and he growled: "Everywhere I go people ask me about Abbey. They speak of him as if he were still alive. I'm not sure he's really dead!"

Likewise, whenever Bowden chances into a saloon and scans the mirror behind the bar, he thinks he catches a glimpse of Abbey's bushy gray beard out of the corner of his eye—the vulturine nose and flashing eyes; the furrowed cheeks; the toothy, leering smile—and hears him say in that deep, mellow voice: "I don't believe in doing work I don't want to do in order to live the way I don't want to live." Mutters Bowden: "I know he's dead, but then again, I'm not sure."

Since Abbey's death, a great silence has descended on the Southwest, and his reputation has mushroomed to such proportions that even his closest friends have difficulty separating the man from the legend, truth from fantasy. "I envy those men who become mythological while still living," William Butler Yeats wrote to Oscar Wilde. "I think a man should invent his own myth," Wilde replied.

To some extent, that is exactly what Abbey did, and many of his followers have built him up into a modern savior, making people who knew him well, like Clarke Abbey, his widow and fifth wife, uncomfortable. "Don't make him into a mystical hero," she cautions. "He was damn real, and a very difficult man."

Widespread reports of his resurrection notwithstanding, Edward Paul Abbey did die in Tucson, Arizona, on March 14, 1989, of an incurable and painful pancreatic disease that had played havoc with his body for years.

He was sixty-two.

Only a month before, he had written a dedication in his final novel, *Hayduke Lives,* for his friend Bowden: "Fellow traveler in this fool's journey out of the dark, through the light, and into the unknown . . . "

And it was into the unknown, the man called Cactus Ed did go.

Until a few weeks before the end, he played away on a battered upright Royal manual typewriter: "I pound it. I get excited. I get sweaty, and get emotional. I'm sure it shows." In his last days he had finished his twentieth book, *A Voice Crying in the Wilderness*, in which he had written, "The fear of death follows from the fear of life. A man who lives fully is prepared to die at any time."

Recalls his sister Nancy, a teacher in California: "He died bravely. He never let us know the seriousness of his illness, so we never knew death was so near." But it had been advancing on him for a long time. Seven years earlier, in fact, physicians in New Mexico told Abbey he only had six more months to live. "Well, at least I won't have to floss anymore," he is said to have quipped from his hospital bed.

Old-time dwellers in the often desolately beautiful canyon country that Abbey called his own—haunting, arid, and unforgiving Utah, Arizona, and New Mexico borderlands—pride themselves in their ability to bank their emotions. Many fancy themselves as fierce individualists too tough to cry.

Abbey's death was different.

Readers who had never met him felt that a friend had died. Some wept. Others were like Tucson writer and sometime Abbey confidant Gregory McNamee, who was sure the news on the radio was a hoax, that he and Abbey would meet later that day for lunch at some smoky downtown Tucson dive for good talk and greasy hamburgers (layered with Swiss cheese and mushrooms on rye bread) as they had done monthly for a decade.

There were those who drove into the desert and got drunk or went to the foaming white waters of the Colorado River, which Abbey had spent thirty years of his life celebrating and protecting, and bellowed to the heavens in pain for their lost idol. There were memorial services, some public but many private, marked by flutes, booze, firecrackers, and readings from Abbey's works.

"The Cheshire Cat has now disappeared," mourned Bob Lippman, a friend from Flagstaff, "but his great and powerful and joyous grin remains; his galvanizing expression and gift of Earthiest vision, of courage, of committed action, and of freedom. Resist much, Obey little. Joy and courage, shipmates."

Others shared the experience of Mary Sojourner, the Arizona-based author and a student of Abbey's at the University of Arizona in Tucson: "I went numb. First I was mad at him for taking all that talent away. How dare he leave us! I cried and cried and cried. Then a friend remembered that Ed promised to come back as a turkey vulture. A few days later, I saw a vulture flying high in the sky following me as I drove back East."

For many admirers, it was difficult to believe that Abbey was gone, paradoxes, contradictions, and all; that the last lone ranger, philosophical desert anarchist, and so-called radical environmentalist who threw beer cans out of car windows (he hated paved highways), who advocated population control (yet fathered five children), and who loved the wilds (yet lived in the city), would write no more.

"It sounds silly, but I just didn't think he'd die," recalls his friend, Donn Rawlings, a widely known English professor at Yavapai College in Prescott, Arizona. "Ed created for me a sense of the Southwest. When I heard the news, it struck me that the Southwest might disappear for me, too."

Just who was this man, Abbey, who intrigued and frustrated scholars, critics, and devotees of his writing; and why does the mention of his name still elicit so many contradictory feelings? Depending upon one's companions, he's either revered as the Thoreau of the West, who fought the modern megamachine that is insulting the Great Southwest with bombing ranges, foul power plants, and ugly urban blooms; or he is despised as a xenophobic environmentalist.

"If Mr. Abbey is so in love with wilderness," wrote one reader to a magazine that had published one of Abbey's hit-and-run broadsides, "he should take his beer cans and his warped head and go far back in the hills and stay there. The world would be glad to see the last of him . . . it is obvious he has no place in civilized society."

Abbey relished such letters. They only encouraged him to sound forth a trumpet that would never blow retreat against those who would pillage his paradise. "If we can draw the line against the industrial machine in the West, and make it hold," he contended, "then perhaps in the decades to come we can gradually force industry underground, where it belongs . . . and restore to other parts of our nation, their rightful heritage of breathable air, drinkable water, a democratic industrialism, and a decentralized agriculture. . . .

"What good is a Bill of Rights that does not imply the right to play, to wander, to stillness and solitude, to discovery and physical adventure?"

The key to Abbey, suggests Mike Lacey, executive publisher of *New Times,* is this: "He believed it was important to speak out emotionally about moral issues. In a world so structured and so ordered by laws and regulations, he was a moralist who yowled like a coyote, and we listened."

Most book critics labeled him an environmental radical. But such a label was far too simple, neat, and inadequate. Born of Scotch and German stock, reared by an anti-capitalist, pro-Marxist logger and trapper father and a religious schoolteacher mother, Abbey approached his world with the neo-Calvinist diagnosis of "man, the cracked vessel."

In his teens, he concluded that the Republic was in danger of being mortally wounded by unbridled technology, the cults of growth and consumerism, the growth of huge cities, and the spread of large, unaccountable bureaucracies.

Though more outrageously outspoken than they were in their day, Abbey was an "Old Conservative" in the tradition of William James and Henry Adams, Walt Whitman and Reinhold Niebuhr. The conviction they shared was that true patriotism lay in holding the Republic up to its own highest standards.

Myths about this desert-based dragonslayer aside, friends attest that he was what he always said he was, a boy from rural Pennsylvania who became a ferocious lover of the West, and once aware that it was being lost, told the world. A member of no movement, he was an artist possessed of a visceral hostility for the kind of modern industrialism that would mar and scar the silent, natural world.

"Why write? Speaking for myself," he observed, "I write to entertain my friends and to exasperate our enemies."

And write he did.

Through seventeen years as a seasonal ranger; five marriages; and periods of doubt, dismay, and perplexing illness, he wrote millions of words. They earned him the mantle of a prophet who bore witness in a hostile and mostly uncomprehending world, knowing the odds were stacked against him; knowing too, that not to defend what he loved was dishonorable.

Yet years after his death, even among his friends he remains a puzzle of many parts, with some pieces that don't fit. There was the brazen, romantic public hero and also the shy recluse who wandered the desert alone. With equal ardor, he loved quiet libraries and noisy, dingy bars; tearful country tunes and obscure classical music, which he knew so encylopedically that he could have become a composer of music instead of a writer. His favorites were anything by Mozart, Brahms, Mahler, or Ives.

At once opinionated and open-minded, he loved parties, yet was a loner who disliked crowds. He was a liberal who opposed gun control, and although he was a descendant of European immigrants, advocated stopping Latinos at the Arizona border. (He favored handing them rifles and sending them back to finish their revolution.)

In his heyday, he relished expensive bourbon and cheap cigars— and still cheaper burgundy wine (though his illness curtailed, some say ended, his drinking). And he adored nubile young women, even though he aspired to be a family man and even though he often drew insulting caricatures of such women in his writings.

Among twentieth-century authors, he respected Lewis Mumford, B. Traven, Cormac McCarthy, Annie Dillard, Thomas McGuane, Thomas Pynchon, Jim Harrison, Joan

Didion, and Larry McMurtry, but detested John Updike and other chroniclers of suburban soap opera.

Unlike most of them, Abbey was a coyote and trickster, a curmudgeon who tried to unmask our individual and collective follies and petty, destructive pursuits. A few critics say that is romantic poppycock, that he was a phony, a poseur, who wrote irresponsible hyperbole about the Southwest because he knew it would sell.

His message didn't waver: Oppose the industrialization and militarization of the American West by alien forces from places like Houston, Tokyo, Manhattan, and Washington, D.C.; if opposition isn't enough, resist; and if resistance isn't enough, and other means fall short, subvert.

And his politically incorrect views ranged far and wide:
On feminism:

How can women compete with men, share power with men, without becoming much like men? Facing this distasteful prospect, the feminists demand that men meet women halfway. In other words men should neuter, geld, caponize themselves by becoming as much like women as possible.

On immigration:

It would be wise for us as American citizens to consider calling a halt to the mass influx of even more millions of hungry, ignorant, unskilled, culturally, generally impoverished people. At least until we have brought our own affairs under control ... Yes, I know, if the American Indians had enforced such a policy, none of us pale-faced honkies would be here. But the Indians were foolish, and divided, and failed to keep our WASP ancestors out. They've regretted it ever since.

In any case, authors dream of being read widely, and Abbey fulfilled that dream. One critic was moved to recommend that he be neutered and locked away for life, and another to suggest that Abbey find a garage, turn on a truck engine, and breathe the foul fumes.

What is indisputable about Abbey's thirty-eight-year career is that, through his graceful and musical prose, he called citizens to the beauty and sacredness of the desert—that fragile, unyielding web of life that he loved and feared.

"Walk upright," he challenged readers, "into the ancient blood-thrilling primeval freedom of those vast and democratic vistas. You will never understand the secret essence of the word freedom until you do."

"I hate cant and sham," Abbey declared just before he died. "That's why I'm neither a good liberal nor a good conservative.... I take great pride, in fact, in being attacked by both ends of the political spectrum."

At career's end, he had a lot to be proud of.

"Arrogant, xenophobic, dopey, puerile, and stupid," charged the left-leaning magazine *The Nation,* of one of his novels. "A terrorist . . . guilty of intellectual thuggery," counter-blasted the right-wing magazine *Reason.*

Legend is often grounded by fact, and what lies beyond dispute is that Ed Abbey set his own rules, thought for himself, and lived his truth. These qualities were already very much in evidence when Ed, then nicknamed Ned, was just ten years old, living on an Appalachian farm near the village of Home, Pennsylvania.

Ned's hand rose when the local Sunday-school teacher had finished reading about Moses parting the Red Sea. "Is that supposed to be true?" he asked incredulously. "Everything in the Bible is true," the teacher replied. Ned stalked out of the church.

A few years later, he was walking with his brother Howard toward a busy intersection in a nearby town. When the light turned green for them, a car pulled up and blocked the crosswalk. Howard started to walk around the narrow space left by the car, as the average person might do. Not Ned! The lean youngster strode toward the car, and with his long legs bounded onto the hood, leaving a large dent. Leaping to the street on the other side, he continued on his way.

"That was my brother," Howard recalls. "Very high and mighty. He really thought he was superior. He did things his way. He never changed."

In one of Abbey's last interviews, with *Outside* magazine in 1988, Ned, now Ed Abbey, confessed he'd be a liar if he didn't admit that he enjoyed being a troublemaker.

> I like provoking people. I've been willing to be dismissed as a crank and a crackpot simply for the pleasure of saying exactly what I really do believe. Then I leave it to others, you see, to take up the more moderate approach. I lead the attack and then once contact is made with the enemy I quickly retreat, and let more moderate people start compromising, explaining, and maneuvering while I go off and do something else.

Besides hiking and running rivers, that "something else" was writing, including eight published and several unpublished novels and twelve works of nonfiction. Cactus Ed, as he was called, took his writing seriously; despite widespread reports of his wild and erratic ways, he was the most disciplined of writers. And he told the world what he was about so often in the introductions to his books that he wondered why so few understood him in the "literary world."

"The voice crying in the wilderness," he wrote in the introduction to the posthumous book *A Voice Crying in the Wilderness*, "with its righteous assumption of enlightenment, tends to grate on the nerves of the multitude. But it is mine."

As Clarke Abbey recalls of their early days together, "After reading his books I expected a more jovial and talkative man. But he was ever so shy and used words minimally. Ideas were his life, and he was a full-time writer. I used to tell him he was married to his mind, he lived in it so much.

"It was difficult for him to relate to others, but he was always true to himself and was never afraid to say what he felt and to say it well. It was not a perfect marriage, but he tried."

Try as he did, Abbey had difficulty reconciling the life of a married family man with that of the solitary writer, because to him, a literary career must not be just a job but a passion, a life, fueled in equal parts by anger and love. "How feel one without the other?" he asks in his book of essays, *One Life at a Time, Please.*

This passion, fused with a clear, silky writing style, helped turn him into a legendary figure to his followers, who came to regard him as a prophet and a visionary. Truth was the hero in his writings, because truth, he often said, is an indispensable commodity in a world the Hopi Indians term *Koyaanisqatsi,* a world out of balance, life in turmoil.

Perhaps most of all, Abbey is remembered for the way he saw the land. To him, the despoliation of the Great Southwest, the very centerpiece of the American Dream, was not just a heinous crime against nature; it also threatened America's spiritual resources and its freedom.

Once the wilderness is gone, he warned, freedom will be endangered, too: "We can have wilderness without freedom; we can have wilderness without human life at all; but we cannot have freedom without wilderness."

"True human freedom, economic freedom, political freedom, social freedom," he said a year before he died, "remain basically linked to physical freedom, sufficient space, enough land."

As an artist, Abbey's self-appointed mission was to rise in defense of America's last wild Eden, even resorting to violence if all else failed. "I wouldn't actually push the plunger," he once joshed to some students at Northern Arizona University about a particularly sacrilegious dam on the Colorado River called Glen Canyon, "but I'd hold the flashlight."

Another of his major contributions was to the world of political action. Early in his career, he found a way to take the philosophy of anarchism beyond political and social conditions to the natural environment. He coined the phrase "monkey wrenching," or crippling what he regarded as tools of terrorism—the bulldozers and draglines that tear up fragile lands and dam rivers—but without injuring people.

This was the basis for *The Monkey Wrench Gang*, a hilariously outrageous novel about a gang of half-crazed radicals who set out to destroy the $750-million, 792,000-ton Glen Canyon Dam by filling houseboats in Lake Powell behind it with high explosives. "I hoped it would stir people into action to do things I am too cowardly to do myself," he said.

To many critics, the acts of civil disobedience in that novel were stupid and shocking. To Abbey they were nothing of the sort, but rather an integral part of the American mainstream, part of the American tradition, beginning with the Boston Tea Party, then Ethan Allen's Green Mountain Boys. Like Thoreau before him, Abbey saw nothing radical in committing patriotic acts against machines and technology run amok—as long as no one got hurt.

Unlike other authors who wrote about the Southwest—Mary Austin, Oliver La Farge, and Joseph Wood Krutch—Abbey not only aroused readers to the region's beauty and mystery, but went beyond reverence to actions in defense of the region. "Sentiment without action," Abbey contended, "is the ruin of the soul."

Always the coyote, Abbey refused to accept credit for launching the practice of monkey wrenching. When questioned by the press, he claimed, with a wicked glint in his eye, that he was only reporting what he saw happening around him; besides, *The Monkey Wrench Gang* was only fiction. Even when fiction became fact—and added to the Abbey myth—in the form of Earth First!, a Tucson-based organization of self-styled militants inspired by his writings, Abbey insisted that the organization would have been created anyway:

"MWG was a useful, convenient device, a symbol for them," he said.

Far more than symbolism was involved, however, when Earth First! fell into serious legal trouble for allegedly cutting power lines and ski tows that marred some of Arizona's natural landscapes. After Abbey's death, several members went to jail.

Even though Earth First! has been mostly disbanded, years after Abbey's death there are reports of sabotage, dubbed "ecotage," in the Southwest: bulldozers immobilized by sand and Karo syrup in their crankcases, billboards felled by chain saws and dynamite, and barbed wire slashed on public cattle ranges. Whether Abbey should be held accountable for popularizing monkey wrenching will always be debatable. But there can be no debate that he felt individuals had the responsibility to fight back against technological and industrial developments that insulted their souls.

Another aspect of Abbey's legacy is that he wrote of fears people could not express for themselves. And he wrote with the "stinger of a scorpion" said the late Wallace Stegner, who regarded Abbey as a "gadfly, the most effective publicist of the West's curious desire to rape itself since Bernard DeVoto."

Beginning with *The Brave Cowboy* in 1956, and throughout his later writings, Abbey gave artistic form to those feelings of dread festering in the hearts of countless individuals. And because of Abbey's words, people recognized that the relentless march of techno-military-industrialism into the West's wild places, unless thwarted, would not just destroy those places, but threaten their own freedom.

Perhaps Abbey learned how to sting from his father, an old "Wobbly," or by absorbing Thoreau and Twain. But by his early twenties, he had developed the style of the provocateur and the iconoclast that never lost its romantic and sardonic zing— and contributed to his legendary stature among Western authors.

His skill at playing the provocateur first became evident when he was fired as editor of the student newspaper at the University of New Mexico in 1951 because of an article titled "Some Implications of Anarchy." What enraged authorities was the quote on the cover that was mockingly attributed to Louisa May Alcott: "Man will never be free until the last king is strangled with the entrails of the last priest."

There was an uproar. Copies of the paper were seized and Abbey lost his editorship. But that didn't matter. He was at work on his first novel, *Jonathan Troy*. The scholar with a ravenous appetite for irony and paradox was on his way.

Although he was often portrayed as an angry man, raging at the forces of industrialism rampaging across the Southwest, more accurately he was a frustrated lover whose affair with the planet, as he once put it, was never consummated.

Abbey's humor undercut his serious thoughts and tempered the outraged, indignant tone of his words. He perfected the timing of his fusillades, and unlike so many others who had written about the Southwest, he called for counterattacks.

Abbey depicted it not as virgin country ripe with industrial potential, but as a holy place to be defended, where all living creatures, including scorpions, vultures, and lions, are vested with equal rights. "Humans have rights, too," he contended, "but we have to respect the right of other living creatures to live in their own way, their own style and at their own pace."

Responding to friends who had returned from a trip to a canyon ruin, saying they'd been changed forever and now understood why the ancient Indians got religion, Abbey replied: "You don't understand. That land, those mountains, those canyons and rivers. You don't get religion from them; they are religion."

In Abbey's world, the Southwest was neither the unblemished endless vista of the Hollywood screen nor vast lonely reaches of uninhabitable heat-scorched wasteland that airline passengers glimpse from the sky. It was his dreamland, but it was under attack by forces from his own native land: Big Energy Companies and Big Government.

In this New West, the image of the noble and rugged individualist, engraved in our cultural memories by virtue of Owen Wister's moralistic classic, *The Virginian,* had no chance of survival against modern odds. In the twentieth century, the loner as embodied by *The Virginian* was now engulfed in a tempest of change, lost and confused in a world out of balance.

Koyaanisqatsi.

It was Abbey's self-appointed task to demythologize the West, to illuminate the fact, in tones of humor and anger, that the West of the imagination barely lasted for a single lifetime; that it wasn't won by mountain men, Indian fighters, and prospectors but by Big Business and Big Government. And they were on their way to creating an awful catastrophe—if left unmatched and unopposed.

In his writings, Abbey depicts the individual—whether as cowboy, hiker, artist, or river-runner—as being trampled by renegade bureaucrats whose legacy is senseless damage to many wilderness and recreational areas.

And they wear no masks.

They are the leaders citizens once regarded as "the good guys," who so eloquently profess their love for the Southwest. Now, thanks to Abbey, they are widely regarded as gutless, pliant politicians and administrators with oversight over federal and state agencies who mouth the right words but encourage strip-mine shovels, animal trapping, air-fouling power plants that feed thousands of miles of power lines that stalk like supernatural beings over sacred habitat.

Upon hearing that Arizona Governor Bruce Babbitt was running for president in 1988, for example, Abbey pronounced that he was "nothing but a flunkie for the developers and industrialists who are rapidly destroying what's left of Arizona."

For Abbey, ever the romantic moralist, the only solution was to return to an earlier America, to a nation of self-reliant farmers (though he personally despised farming), craftsmen, hunters, ranchers, and artists; only then would the rich and the greedy be disempowered and no longer be able to dominate others. Neither to serve nor to rule. In Abbey's mind, that was the true American dream. His mission was to fight for its return and in the process, kindle similar fires in his readers' hearts.

Until Abbey came along and pumped some passion into it, the nation's conservation movement in the post–World War II years had been gentlemanly, its leaders having been lulled into believing that fair play would work successfully in corporate boardrooms and in Congress. When that view proved to be dangerously naive, Abbey, virtually alone in the fifties and sixties, loudly denounced the industrial invasion of his beloved canyon country.

To draw attention to the region's plight, he painted word pictures of neon wilderness and sprawling reaches of asphalt in which "New Age man, eyes hooded, ears plugged, nerves drugged cannot even get a decent night's sleep."

While others stood on the sidelines, fearful of the fallout if they spoke from their hearts, Abbey encouraged citizens to fight back, not to surrender their sovereignty to the state, or to Exxon, or to Peabody Coal, even if the struggle appeared to be a losing one. Every individual had that responsibility; not to struggle was dishonorable.

As early as 1968, when most Americans were still unaware of the tragedies unfolding in the New West, Abbey conceded, in his introduction to *Desert Solitaire,* that the cause of defending the Southwest might be lost: "This is not a travel guide but an elegy. A memorial. You're holding a tombstone in your hands. A bloody rock. Don't drop it on your foot—throw it at something big and glassy. What do you have to lose?"

His words shocked readers in the East. What was this ranger writing about? Was he on drugs? The Southwest was as clean and pure as ever, they insisted. After all, didn't *Arizona Highways* magazine and American Automobile Association tourist brochures say it was? Why was he being so downbeat, so pessimistic?

For one thing, Abbey was no armchair adventurer. He lived in the middle of the battle. Along the way, his artistic vision was nourished by people he met, and later was reflected in his nonfiction essays. For example, in a piece titled "The Second Rape of the West" in *The Journey Home,* Abbey describes meeting up with a rancher named Mrs. Cotton, a silver-haired, windburned woman whose Montana ranch lay in the path of Peabody Coal's towering strip mine shovels.

Although both the U.S. government and the coal company had told her they wanted the coal under her cattle ranch, and promised to pay her well, she had decided to fight. "We cannot keep moving on," she told Abbey. "No matter what the price, where could we find another place? This is our home. We always used to think it didn't matter, that when you mined one area, or farmed it out, or overgrazed it, you could move to new country beyond the hills, keep moving West. But there are no new places to go anymore. The land is full. We have to stay where we are, take care of what we have. There isn't going to be anything else."

Those were Abbey's sentiments exactly. "The ideal society," he wrote, "can be described, quite simply, as that in which no man has the power or the means to coerce others."

In time, Abbey—a potent blend of anti-establishment Lone Ranger, Samuel Adams, and Natty Bumppo—became the literary point man for several generations of citizens who needed inspiration to fight against the national passion of growth for growth's sake, which Abbey said was "the ideology of a cancer cell."

And Abbey, as early as the 1950s, a time when many Americans believed the American Dream was about to come true, said the cancer was spreading. And he kept up that drumfire for years. "Keep it like it was," a character pleads in *The Monkey Wrench Gang*. "If the wilderness is our true home," Abbey argued in his essay "EcoDefense," "and if it is threatened with invasion, pillage, and destruction, as it certainly is, then we have the right to defend that home, as we would our private quarters, by whatever means are necessary . . . we have the right to resist, the obligation."

When reviewers found his books to be raw and bawdy, Abbey retorted that they were meant as antidotes to despair for citizens feeling afraid and helpless in the onrush of technocrats, bureaucrats, and fast-buck charlatans intent on transforming the remaining wildness of the Southwest into a kind of urbanized national sacrifice area.

Brushing critics aside, Abbey blasted away on the theme that creeping industrialism, whether capitalist or socialist, with its oil fields, coal and uranium mines, transmission lines, and dams, was not the savior of the modern age, but an unforgiving tyrant. "Our modern industrial economy," he wrote, "takes a mountain covered with trees, lakes, running streams and transforms it into a mountain of junk, garbage, slime pits."

Novelist William Eastlake *(Castle Keep, Go in Beauty)* based in Bisbee, Arizona, was an old Abbey pal, and recalls a day when the two of them did something about creeping industrialism.

It was the summer of 1963, and Abbey was a ranger at Sunset Crater near Flagstaff, Arizona. Upset by a huge Las Vegas "girlie" sign that was, in Eastlake's wry remembrance, "hiding the West," together, outside the law, they sawed it down, billboard posts in those days being made of wood. It is also outside the law to rip up survey flags in the desert, to throw beer cans from a truck window, to put molasses into the crankcase of a bulldozer, to attack a power line with a jeep, or to even talk about blowing up a federal dam on the Colorado River. "I pounded survey stakes before I ever got the notion to pull them out," he once quipped to the *Los Angeles Times,* refusing to confirm various other acts of monkey wrenching.

In his best writing, whether one considers his fiction or journalistic essays, Abbey was at once sarcastic, absurd, and funny. "No more cars in national parks," he trumpeted in *Desert Solitaire,* an account of two summers in the late 1950s spent as fire lookout and ranger in Utah's Arches National Monument: "Let the people walk. Or ride horses, bicycles, mules, wild pigs—anything—but keep the automobiles and all their motorized relatives out. We have agreed not to drive our automobiles into cathedrals, concert halls, private bedrooms, and the other sanctums of our culture; we should treat our national parks with

21

the same deference, for they, too, are holy places." Forty years later, park management officials are harkening to Abbey's words, and are drawing up plans to ban cars from such landmarks as the Grand Canyon National Park.

Another irresistibly fat Abbey target was cattle ranching on public lands. How his fans loved it when he attacked rich ranchers, when he lashed out at their reckless grazing practices that savaged the public range. At the same time, he loved the beefsteak those he called "welfare cowboys" raised on those lands, particularly when cooked thick and bloody over a mesquite fire, far from city lights.

Although reviewers often thought otherwise, Abbey insisted that he wasn't writing to inspire people. "I am a comic writer," he told one interviewer, who was probing to get at Abbey's true purpose. "The generation of laughter is my aim. My books should be read for fun, not inspiration. One good laugh is worth a thousand homilies." But ranchers, land developers, federal bureaucrats, and other targets of his ire didn't think his attacks were funny, and he lost a few good friends over the years.

As time went by, many observers gave up trying to figure Abbey out, becoming lost in what they saw as his contradictions: the backwoodsman with the gentle, resonant voice who read Schopenhauer while listening to Mozart; the reclusive philosophical anarchist who, although he detested the industrial system, drove wildly around Tucson in a shiny, old red Cadillac convertible with a plastic flower on the hood.

Most ignored the fact that Abbey kept telling them who he was, and what he was doing: he was an Appalachian mountain boy who had a love affair with the West, and told the truth about what was really out there, that it was fast becoming like the raped and plundered land he had escaped, the pillaged hills of Appalachia.

It was an affair of the heart that caused him to be hailed, jailed, and railed against. Yet he delighted in it and seemed to change his persona, and cover his tracks at will: desert hermit, river rat, scholar, lover who was irresistible to women, drinker, hiker, and mountain man—but always the disciplined writer.

In person Cactus Ed defied easy labels. In private he could be friendly but reserved, not unlike talking to an old cowboy. Speaking to a group, he could also be brash, outspoken, loud, outrageous, and anti-establishment. In either guise, he was Lincolnesque, possessed with the kind of charisma that caused people to line up to touch him.

Nearly always he was shy and aloof, but the quality that fueled his writings was hardly shyness. "If there is one word to capture his central writing quality, it is that he was sardonic. By that I mean derisive, ironic, mocking, sarcastic, contemptuous, scornful, wry and skeptical," reports Peter Wild, sometime friend and colleague on the faculty at the University of Arizona in Tucson. "Ed would take an anti-establishment stance, no matter what the establishment was. He had a high school dropout mentality. He did not have a plan to fit in."

Others who closely observed Abbey's kaleidoscopic ways believe the key to understanding him is that he was a traditionalist. Indeed, what is more traditional than an American taking a stand, as Ethan Allen and his Green Mountain Boys did when the wildness that defined their lives was endangered by the Redcoats?

"I'm a stranger and afraid in a world I never made," Abbey once wrote. Afraid? Not Ed, says his longtime friend, novelist Allan Harrington, a New Yorker transplanted to the Sonoran Desert. Harrington is one of the proud survivors of numerous nocturnal adventures with Abbey.

From time to time, says Harrington, Abbey could seem estranged from his own life, and from the lives of others, and "this could bring on an ironical detachment, occasional savage humor and mockery, and also solitary retreats and renewals into the desert. At first it could be imagined that he didn't believe in love at all. But later, it was clear that he believed so much in love among us, and its saving of all of us, that he could become jokingly furious and testy and mean and not especially faithful when love disappointed him."

Abbey was keenly aware of this aspect of himself, writing in *Abbey's Road*, "So many of my journeys have been made in pursuit of love, in pursuit of pain. And in flight from both." For all his quirks and eccentricities, however, there's nothing detached about fellow writers' remembrances of him as a deeply generous person who was never conceited or overbearing, always willing to help with a book jacket quote, counsel, or professional contacts.

Remembers Tucson writer Gregory McNamee, "Ed was absolutely unsparing of his time, his money, his intelligence, and himself. He thrived on thunderous arguments, and, although God knows he could be gruff, he was never discourteous in waging them. I cannot recall a conversation with him from which I did not walk away changed just a little. He despised fakery, cowardice, the usual pieties. He applauded deliberation, honorable action, the unfettered mind. He held little sacred, and he vigorously tested the convictions of his friends and opponents alike, probing, questioning, arguing."

Author Mary Sojourner also had direct exposure to Abbey's less-publicized side when she took his University of Arizona writing course a year before he died. "I came to his class ready to do battle," she recollects. "I knew of him as a man who had a lot of judgments, who treated women as boobies, and who kept searching for younger and younger women as he grew older.

"I thought he stood for a lot of the qualities in men that make women so angry, all the macho bullshit. But he turned out to be a most compassionate man. We became comrades. He listened to me. He honored my writing. He never responded negatively and was very deferential to all the students."

Once, when Sojourner won an important southwest regional fiction award but was disqualified because she was still a student, Abbey came to her defense. He wrote letters and at one point threatened to lead a march to Phoenix to secure justice. In the end, she got her prize.

Sojourner, who feels his death deeply, offers the view that the problem with Abbey was that he was a *Bodhisattva*, a spiritual being that delays its own enlightenment to advance others'. Perhaps, but then there's also the man's powerful physical side to consider, and the indisputable fact that he lived a very full life—beginning with his days as a modern version of a real mountain man.

One day during his college years at the University of New Mexico in the 1950s, Abbey journeyed to find author William Eastlake at his ranch in Cuba, New Mexico, near the Colorado border. He went seeking an autograph and brought with him some home brew as an offering. After several other visits they became friends, and Eastlake tried, with only partial success, to teach Abbey how to ride a horse.

Eastlake was a better rider than Abbey, but his young friend was better able to cope with the harsh environment. "Abbey had the ability to start a fire out of nothing," Eastlake recounts, "and he could cook a meal in the wild out of rabbits and herbs. Once he told me that he wanted the reputation of a mountain man. And he worked hard at it."

One evening, Abbey decided to round up some stray steers, though Eastlake cautioned him that it was getting dark and that he might get lost on a mountain trail. Abbey rode off regardless, with a wave of his hand. After he had been gone for more than five hours, Eastlake was concerned enough to saddle up a bronc and ride out to track him down in the black New Mexico night.

Hours later, on a trail up to a high mesa, Eastlake saw a light and rode toward it, thinking he'd never seen light up that high. It turned out to be a fire burning in a cave, and when he got there he found Abbey grinning at him: "What are you worried about, Bill? I'm happy here just waiting for the dawn to come."

One of the principal sources of the Abbey legend is that from an early age, he deliberately chose to make things difficult for himself. During one college summer in the 1950s, he took a job on the local newspaper in Taos, New Mexico, and tended bar at the famed Taos Inn at night. One afternoon, Lady Dorothy Brett, the famous English writer, artist, and friend of D. H. Lawrence, took a seat at the bar and ordered her favorite drink from the dashing young student. "I don't know how to make one of them fancy drinks," Abbey retorted, though he had made them many times. "You'd better make me a grasshopper," she said. "If not, I'll get you fired." And she did.

This contrariness was a life pattern that began early and seemed to compound itself as he grew older. Two years before he died, Abbey received the kind of letter an author dreams about. It was from Irving Howe, then-chairman of the Awards Committee for Literature of the prestigious American Academy and Institute of Arts and Letters. Howe was writing to inform him that he had been chosen to receive one of eight five-thousand-dollar awards for his career of writings. In order to pick up his check, Abbey's attendance was required at a special ceremony two months hence.

Abbey's reply, to put it mildly, sent a jolt through the Academy's senior ranks as well as among some of his writer friends who had been lobbying for the award for him behind the scenes:

I appreciate the intended honor but will not be able to attend the awards ceremony. I'm figuring on going down a river in Idaho that week. Besides, to tell the truth, I think that such prizes are for little boys. You can give my $5,000 to somebody else. I don't need it and don't want it. Thanks anyhow.

Edward Abbey
Oracle, Arizona

Abbey apparently thought this so clever that he sent his reply on to friends, including Connecticut-based editor and writer John Mitchell, who had worked with Abbey on Sierra Club books in the early 1970s. This note was scrawled at the bottom: "'There's a time and place for everything—including arrogance,' as Mother Teresa once said."

Both Abbey's response and the fictional aphorism, which recalled the Louisa May Alcott episode three decades earlier, surprised Mitchell. "It struck me then and it strikes me now as revealing a darker side to Abbey. Gawd! What anger he had stored up against the establishment. I prefer to remember the guy as I knew him best—under a straw sombrero, somewhere back of beyond."

Abbey's life-style and behavior evoke an interesting parallel to those of the elusive B. Traven, author of *The Treasure of Sierra Madre* and *The Night Visitor.* The comparison becomes more intriguing with the discovery that Traven's prose and mysterious life-style had a major influence on Abbey and his work.

Writing from obscure, often imaginary redoubts in Mexico between the 1930s and '60s, Traven also was a romantic who crafted many faces for himself, generating various biographical smoke screens, taking anarchistic stands against the establishment. Like Abbey, he delighted in creating enigmas and puzzles for earnest scholars in the future by exaggerating or omitting facts of his life. As more than one frustrated literary historian has complained, Traven would tell people outrageous and impossible things and watch closely for their reactions.

Ed Abbey did that well, too, writing from such totally nonexistent places as Fort Llatikcuf (spell it backwards), Arizona, calling for revolution and yearning for simpler, pre-industrial times.

And, like Traven, Abbey painted sentimental pictures of the world after the revolution:

> I hope that somewhere out there on the far fringes of the future, deep in the surviving jungles, high in the isolated mountains, far out on the forgotten deserts, little bands of free men and liberated women may still be roaming, hunting, fishing and gathering, begetting, and mothering human children, awaiting their opportunity to attack the corrupt cities, to sack the temples of technology, to ravish and raze once again the leaning tower of babble.
>
> —*One Life at a Time, Please*

If there was a thread that tied these two men of many guises together, it was that Abbey, like Traven, was an anarchist with the gallows humor of a revolutionary, not a bomb-thrower advocating bloodthirsty acts. He was the philosopher-kind who made rebellious statements for effect, and whose true mission was to defend the individual against the State and to advocate liberty: No one may transgress against another.

To make his point, Abbey often quoted Thomas Jefferson, the last American president he respected: "The tree of liberty is nourished by the blood of tyrants." It was a figure of speech, because neither Jefferson nor Abbey truly believed that killing was required to mount a revolution. On Abbey's road, anarchism was a positive moral force, as it had been in Europe before events in nineteenth-century Russia gave it such a dark and bloody connotation. In this perspective, it meant following the path of the Jeffersonian dream through which the individual can be resurrected as the foundation of civil society; nothing more or less than "democracy taken seriously," as Abbey put it once, meaning "no rulers," not "no rule."

For his models he chose leaders of the Boston Tea Party, like Sam Adams, who struck back against abuses being inflicted by bureaucrats and tax collectors. Underlying much of Abbey's major work is the conviction that governments are evil by nature, carrying murder and mayhem in the form of war, and outright theft in the form of taxation.

Seen this way, his best-known novel, *The Monkey Wrench Gang,* is less of an environmental tract, as most critics contended, than an anguished plea for the return of individual liberty. This was the basis, too, for his second novel, *The Brave Cowboy:* "Don't have none. Don't need none. I already know who I am," says cowboy Jack Burns when he's arrested after a bar fight and asked for identification.

Burns's words still strike a chord with anyone familiar with B. Traven's *The Death Ship,* written in the 1920s, in which the character Gales says to the authorities about his lack of papers, "I do not need any papers. I know who I am."

Abbey's writings can be read on many levels, and on one level they are a call to arms. "Do we need another revolution, people wonder?" he asked in a 1979 essay. "What do you mean another? We have yet to see the first. But it's coming." In Abbey's world, during his boulder-strewn journey, the true patriot's task was clear: to defend his country against the Government.

A centerpiece of the Abbey legend is that he was an anarchist. Theoretically, he certainly was: "In the ideal realm, yes," he candidly told an interviewer in the 1980s. "[But] I am not a practicing anarchist. I am very much a member of our society, willy-nilly, like it or not, don't have much choice. I have to pay taxes. I own property and I'm putting two kids through college. I'm pretty bogged down in the whole catastrophe like everyone else."

He did take anarchistic actions during his life. In the June 7, 1965 issue of *The Nation*, around the time the Vietnam War was escalating out of control, Abbey declared in a letter to the editor that he no longer would pay taxes to the U.S. Government: "Since letters, marches, proclamations or protest have all proved futile, I have decided at the very least that I shall no longer help finance Johnson's war."

Though the IRS garnished his earnings for the amount due, Abbey never ceased his campaign against Big Government, inflamed by the belief that every word in the Bill of Rights was true; someone had to fight back—and Abbey's weapon was irreverent humor and the polemic.

If there was anyone he had failed to insult, he liked to say, he would be happy to apologize for the oversight, and as for "growth maniacs," those who want to urbanize the Southwest, all they needed was some psychiatric care.

In common with Walt Whitman and B. Traven, Abbey wrote from the wild places in his own heart, using nature as the setting, reasoning that nature was the only place where man can be whole and free. And in his many guises, he came across variously as biblical prophet, mountain man, Pancho Villa, and The Lone Ranger.

Did he succeed? That question will always be the subject of debate, but in the closing decades of the twentieth century, Peter Wild asserts, "We needed Abbey to show us how preposterously the nation had become tangled in the century's glitter. He often spoke the truth that lay in our hearts, unrecognized until he brought it to the surface from his."

As a writer, Abbey was free to challenge his readers to rise up: "New dynasties will arise, new tyrants will appear—no doubt. But we must and we can resist such current aberrations by keeping true to the earth and remaining loyal to our basic animal nature. Humans were free before the word freedom became necessary. Slavery is a cultural invention. Liberty is life: eros plus anarchos equals bios. Long live democracy. Two cheers for anarchy."

Critics often described him as a radical ecofreak, but what is not generally appreciated is that this ornery iconoclast fired just as many verbal barrages at the bureaucracies of large environmental organizations as he did at federal agencies and corporations. Indeed, he protested that he didn't know what the word ecology meant, that he was too lazy to be a conservationist, and that he sure as hell wasn't a nature writer.

Of course, Abbey did write about nature, and just as well as Joseph Wood Krutch or Annie Dillard. So it is not surprising that most critics automatically pegged him as a nature and environmental writer. A stronger case can be made that he was a singular member of a vanishing breed, the independent social critic, his primary subject being himself—and human nature—against the backdrop of deserts, rivers, and canyons. Read in that context, the essence of much of his work is that he was writing in defense of himself as part of nature. This is what separates him from such nature writers as John Muir and Henry Thoreau, august company with whom he has often been compared.

One who argues for this distinction is Wendell Berry, the distinguished Kentucky farmer-poet who, like Abbey, took one of Wallace Stegner's writing classes at Stanford University in the late 1950s. In later years, Abbey and Berry corresponded and Berry spoke at Abbey's memorial service in Utah in May of 1989.

Berry has made it clear that he disagrees with most reviewers of Abbey's writings in that he regards Abbey as an autobiographer, not an environmentalist at all. Certainly Abbey wrote on one or another of what are now called environmental issues, Berry acknowledges, but he always remained Edward Abbey, speaking as and for himself, fighting, literally, for dear life.

"This is important," Berry has argued, "for if he is writing as an autobiographer, he *cannot* be writing as an environmentalist, or as a specialist of any other kind. As an autobiographer, his work is self-defense."

As a conservationist, says Berry, Abbey was working to conserve himself as a human being: "But this is self-defense and self-conservation of the largest and noblest kind; for Mr. Abbey understands that to defend and conserve oneself as a human being in the fullest and truest sense, one must defend and conserve many others and much else.

"What would be the hope of being personally whole in a dismembered society, or personally healthy in a land scalped, eroded, and poisoned, or personally free in a land entirely controlled by the government, or personally enlightened in an age illuminated only by TV?" Berry asks.

Berry looms as one of the few critics of Abbey's works to penetrate the mists surrounding Abbey. Without the benefit of having read the personal journals Abbey kept for more than forty years, Berry concludes correctly that Abbey was fighting on a much broader scale than any single "movement" such as environmentalism.

His was a fight for the survival, not only of nature, but of human nature, of culture, as "only our heritage of works and hopes can define it," Berry asserts. "He is, in short, a traditionalist, as he has said himself, expecting, perhaps, not to be believed ... the trouble is then—a trouble, I confess, that I am disposed to like—is that he speaks insistently as himself. . . . My own notion is that he's going to become harder to ignore."

In his Nobel acceptance speech, Ernest Hemingway declared that a truly good writer is driven far out, past where he can go, out to where no one can help him.

In Abbey's writings, notably in the essay collections *Beyond the Wall, The Journey Home, Abbey's Road,* and *One Life at a Time Please,* Abbey was indeed struggling "out there" where there was no help, defending the diversity and freedom of humankind from the forces destined to reduce nature, him, and everyone to the status of subjects, to the rank of slaves and mere statistics.

"Out there" for him, however, was also a powerful physical inspiration, the Sonoran Desert. Once, while contemplating a landscape of buttes and mesas, Abbey saw not just rock and sand but enchanted ships "floating on a lilac purple sea." He then speculated about the scene unfolding before him:

> I feel again the poignant urge to grasp it, embrace it, know it, all at once and all in all; but the harder I strive for such a consummation, the more elusive that it becomes, slipping like a dream through my arms. Can this desire be satisfied only in death? Something in our human consciousness seems to make us forever spectators of the world we live in.
>
> Maybe some of my crackpot, occultist friends are right; maybe we really are aliens here on earth, our spirits born on some other, simpler, more human planet. But why were we sent here? What is our mission, comrades, and when do we get paid?
>
> A writer's epitaph: He fell in love with the planet earth, but the affair was never consummated.

More than any writer of his generation, Abbey did get "out there," refusing to pretend to know natural reality without fully participating in it. This aspect of his life, whether floating down foaming rivers or hiking the deserts, his cathedrals, is the principal link between the man, his character, and his art.

The well-known writer Edward Hoagland, who corresponded regularly with Abbey for two decades—often stormily—surmises that Abbey slept out more nights under the stars than all other writers of his time combined. Jack Loeffler, a Santa Fe–based environmental activist, figures that if all the miles Abbey hiked across the Southwest were toted up, they would equal the distance between California and Maine.

Abbey was part river rat, having run the Colorado River, the Green, the Rio Grande, and the San Juan dozens of times. He would do almost anything to go down a river, including jeopardizing his job as a ranger at Lee's Ferry on the Colorado River.

One brilliant June morning in 1962, he left his superiors agog by ripping off his ranger shirt and jumping aboard a rubber raft at the invitation of some pretty young women floating by. The raft was headed into white water, and that was all anyone saw of the young ranger until the next morning when he walked back along the bank upstream with a toothy grin on his bushy face. "Shall we gather by the river?" Abbey wrote on Independence Day, 1981. "On with the river, day by day, down to the ultimate sea. Shall we gather by the river? Why not? One more river one more time. And then no more. And then that ancient river must flow right on down without me."

And if it wasn't an invitation to go down some river, a chance to trek the desert could pull him from his writing room, a one-room shack not far from his modest two-bedroom frame house ("no pool, no horses, no color TV, no microwave, no computer, no lawn mower") on the edge of the desert within Tucson's city limits.

Among its contents were an outmoded manual Royal typewriter atop a worn wooden desk (he despised electronic writing contraptions); bookcases lined with works by Bertrand Russell,

Joseph Wood Krutch, B. Traven, and Lewis Mumford; an ammunition box stamped *High Explosives;* a wooden shoe on a windowsill (the word "sabotage" is derived from the French noun *sabot,* meaning wooden shoe); and on one wall, a blood-red monkey wrench painted on a field of black cloth.

In those surroundings he wrote about the desert: "In my case it was love at first sight. The desert, all deserts, any desert. No matter where my head and feet may go, my heart and my entrails stay behind, here on the clean, true, comfortable rock, under the black sun of God's forsaken country."

As often as he could, and at the risk of eroding his status as a responsible family man still further, Abbey would hike alone for miles into the seldom-traveled reaches of the Sonoran Desert. New country can only be seen on foot, Abbey believed, "erect like a man—on my own legs, under my own power. There's immense satisfaction in that."

He made a point never to tell anyone but his family exactly where he was headed. No more "Californicating" of the last good country, was his motto. And besides, he'd say, no one should go out into the desert anyway, because it is a dangerous place. Everything in the desert either stings, stabs, stinks, or sticks, a hell-hole alive with rattlesnakes, Gila monsters, conenose kissing bugs, scorpions, centipedes, and javelinas.

Despite obvious danger and doubt about what lay beyond the next horizon, that was where Abbey wanted to be. "Out there is a different world," he wrote in *Desert Solitaire,* "older and greater and deeper by far than ours, a world which surrounds and sustains the little world of man as sea and sky surround and sustain a ship. The shock of the real. For a little while we are again able to see, as the child sees, a world of marvels."

American literature has never been short of writers who long for quiet, holy places where, for a few moments, the spiritual and the incarnational meld together: Thoreau's *Walden Pond* in New

England; *Huckleberry Finn*'s raft on Mark Twain's Mississippi; Nick's northern Michigan camp in Hemingway's *Big Two-Hearted River;* the mystical forest clearing in William Faulkner's *The Bear;* and the South Seas in Herman Melville's *Moby Dick.* With *The Brave Cowboy, Desert Solitaire,* and scores of essays, it is fair to say that Edward Abbey's desert has earned a rank in that company.

Although he described himself as an "earthiest"—not an agnostic like his father—one detects a vibrant religious sense underlying his writings; an influence attributable to his childhood when the Bible was staple reading for Ned and siblings Howard, John, Bill, and Nancy.

Taking the religion tack, we can regard Abbey's books as jeremiads that call citizens back from their lives of "quiet desperation." Like the Puritans, Abbey was concerned with morality and righteousness, but he was not out to try to save the world, which he perceived as a hopeless wasteland of "overcrowding, squalor, misery, oppression, torture, and hate." It wasn't the world he was trying to save. No, his self-appointed charge was to save the chosen people, that is, the Americans; the Bill of Rights; the Constitution; and that special land—America.

Employing metaphor, allegory, and shocking images as well as any writer living or dead, Abbey often thundered on like an old preacher in his writing, renouncing the backsliding of the masses away from the utopian ideal into a world of slavery:

> We are nearly all slaves. We are slaves in the sense that we depend for our daily survival upon an expand-or-expire agro-industrial empire—a crackpot machine, that the specialists cannot comprehend and the managers cannot manage. Which is, furthermore, devouring world resources at an exponential rate. We are . . . dependent employees.

What will be our salvation in such a land, Abbey asks, then quotes directly from his version of Scripture, Thoreau's *Walden and Civil Disobedience*: "In Wildness is the preservation of the world."

Abbey's love of wildness led him to his true home, the Great American Desert. Where most people see only bleak, lifeless, and ugly terrain, Abbey saw mystery and beauty. In his writing there is sensual delight in the names of shrubs, trees, animals, insects, rocks, dry gullies, and washes. What he loved was the very emptiness, the vast desolate nothingness of the deserts he trekked.

> I am——really am——an extremist, one who lives and loves by choice far out on the very verge of things, on the edge of the abyss, where this world falls off into the depths of another. That's the way I like it.
>
> —INTRODUCTION TO *ABBEY'S ROAD*

Wildness and contrast were what he sought in the desert, and he would go off at a moment's notice, usually wearing a faded blue Levi's work shirt, chinos, and scuffed size-eleven jungle boots, shouldering a worn army-green forty-five-pound Kelty pack containing maps, a flute, and maybe some bourbon. He would also bring along enough food for ten days, his old black cooking pot, a faithful gnarled wooden spoon, aspirin, a poncho, matches, small spiral notebooks, and a one-gallon canteen of water. With that on his back, the search for beauty and danger could begin.

He had many favorite desert haunts, few of them on any tourist map; places like Two Tanks and Heaven's Half Acre, Skull Valley, and Tamale Flat. And then there was the Cabeza Prieta National Wildlife refuge, south of Phoenix on the

Mexican border, a vast arid sea of sand—barren, hot, and dry—one of America's truly forbidding areas.

Abbey loved this place. He loved it for the legends of its ancient people, for the Gila woodpeckers and ash-throated flycatchers, for the blue paloverde bush and the mesquite, for the catclaw acacia and ironwood, for the creosote bush and the saguaro cactus.

"Why do I do this sort of thing?" he once mused. "I don't know. I've been doing this sort of thing for . . . years and still don't know why. Don't even care why. It's not logical. It's pathological."

On one such trip into the Cabeza, he was on the verge of running out of water when he discovered a fifteen-foot-high water tank with a clanking windmill on its top that was disconnected from the pump shaft. He didn't see how he could tap that tank.

Abbey knew that the next water source was thirty miles of arid desert ahead. He also knew he could backtrack to a known source four miles back. But that wasn't Abbey's way. It was the wrong direction. Meantime, he was certain there would be water in the tank in front of him; the problem was how to get at it. It was the sort of challenge he went to the desert to find.

From the wreckage of a nearby cabin, he grabbed a two-by-four, set it against the tank, and then stood on it to reach the steel ladder riveted to the upper section of the tank. Once on top, he wrestled with the rusty hatch that guarded the water, finally twisting it free to reveal rainwater glistening ten feet below. But now there was a new problem. He had nothing to collect it with.

Back in the cabin, he lifted two stove lids from the ancient cast-iron cookstove, wired them with some baling wire he found, then attached his canteen to the contraption to weigh it down. Climbing back onto the roof of the tank, he lowered it into the water. His canteen gurgled, sank, and filled.

Though the water tasted strongly of sodium and calcium, he now had two gallons of it. Soon he was happily on his way again, only to discover a buried trough fifty yards from the tank, bubbling with water. "You're a clever fellow, Abbey," he would write later, "but not very bright."

Resuming this adventure, he trudged onward across lava fields past graves of gold-seekers and outlaws. The temperature being well over a hundred degrees, if he lingered too long in one place, the next passerby would have little choice but to cover him with rocks and sand.

Soon, he heard the tromping of large feet, and the sound of heavy breathing. He tromped on and then stopped. The heavy breathing stopped. The sound of tromping stopped.

He was alone. And he loved it.

In the evenings, coyotes yipped and howled nearby. The coyote chorus recalled the cry of a loon on a lake of his youth, and this made him thirsty, but his water was running low again. He thought of mountain lions, bighorn sheep, grizzly bears, javelinas, pronghorn sheep, golden eagles, the California condor, the gazelle, ibex, Siberian tigers, and back to the American bison, most of them threatened with extinction, if not extinct already.

Too bad, people say. Human expansion requires it. Human progress and well-being are more important than preservation of obsolete and uneconomic species, they say. "False!" charged Abbey. "The defense of wildlife is a moral issue. All beings are created equal, I say. . . . Who speaks for the Bengal tiger? For the Mexican grizzly, for the desert tortoise? . . . It is a man's duty to speak for the voiceless . . . all are endowed by their Creator (call that God or call it evolution) with certain inalienable rights; among these are rights of life, liberty and the pursuit—each in his own way—of reproductive happiness. I say these things because far too many say the opposite."

For Abbey, those hikes were not just getaways from family responsibilities, or from the stress of crossing swords with editors and agents; nor were they mere escapes to watch rare birds and fiery sunsets. While alone, he could search for deeper truth, if there is such a thing. There, he contemplated the possibility that the desert will breathe a sigh of relief when man has vanished and the desert can return to "ancient procedures, unobserved and undisturbed by the busy, anxious, brooding consciousness of man."

Often, he would reflect that the finest quality of the wild places where he trekked was their absolute indifference; whether man lives or dies was of no consequence. "Let men in their madness," he contended in *Desert Solitaire,* "blast every city on earth into black rubble and envelope the entire planet in a cloud of lethal gas . . . the canyons and hills, the springs and rocks will still be here, the sunlight will filter through, water will form and warmth shall be upon the land, and after sufficient time—no matter how long—living things will emerge and join and stand once more, this time perhaps to take a different and better course."

Abbey argued passionately for the defense of this kind of wild nature because it stirred the romantic idealist in him, and stimulated the beast lurking there, too. In his writings, there's a particular fascination with solitude and silence—and death—a ferment that likely explains his wish to be buried in the desert.

Over time, he made hot, dry deserts the setting for his outrage. As distinct from his experiences with most humans and their modern institutions, he found there was a natural world that was faithful, never disappointing—even though at times, it could be intense, even fearsome.

Abbey nearly met his maker one summer day in 1950, when he was twenty-three years old, a junior at the University of New

Mexico. He decided to hike alone down into Havasu Canyon, also called Havasupai, located toward the western end of the Grand Canyon. For weeks he climbed, fished, and made notes in his journals.

On an especially long solo hike one afternoon, he realized that he had climbed too far from his camp to get back safely before dark. While pondering his plight, he spotted a small side canyon, steep, narrow, and dark with shadows. Without a rope, with only a gnarled juniper walking stick and an almost-dry canteen, he started down, hoping he'd find a route to the canyon floor where there would be drinking water. Instead of an escape route, he found himself in more trouble.

Ahead lay a series of descending, scummy pools through which he had to swim to the next rocky lip. Gambling that when he climbed out of the last pool, there would be an easy way out, he swam them. Instead, he came to a cliff that overhung a pile of broken rocks at least eighty feet below. Starting in the back of his mind but moving swiftly enough so that it became his only thought, was the real prospect of a flash flood cascading down through the narrow canyon wall and then death.

Then, far above the steep, vertical walls, Abbey spotted a small, rainless white cloud puffing by, "so lovely and precious and delicate," he was to write fifteen years later, "that it broke my heart and made me weep like a woman, like a child. In all of my life, I had never seen anything so beautiful."

The cloud's inspiration gave him a new idea, and his walking stick was the key. With water-soaked boots dangling from his neck, Abbey started to climb the steep overhang inch by inch, then used the stick to stand on until he could get a fingerhold. Somehow he found enough niches in the soft red sandstone for his fingers and toes, and slowly climbed to the rim amid artillery salvos of summer thunder exploding in the distance.

Finally safe again, Abbey stretched out in a coyote's den, hot tears of victory spilling down his cheeks. Later, he wrote in his notebook that it had been the happiest day of his life, mostly because he had done it all alone.

Alone he was happy. Around people Abbey often was not at his best. Recognizing this, he often resisted invitations to speak in public, even though it might be a chance to sell books. Author Lawrence Clark Powell sums this up well: "Like Robinson Jeffers, Abbey prefers nature to most people."

Against his wishes, nevertheless, he was often pulled into the world of the quasi-celebrity and became much in demand as a speaker at conservation clubs and writing workshops. Being diffident and nervous as a speaker, there were times when he was unable to bank the furnaces of his basic orneriness.

In the spring of 1985, some friends prevailed upon him to give a reading at a Sierra Club meeting (which Abbey liked to satirize as the "Sahara Club") near Phoenix. A few hours before he was to appear, he called his friend Dick Kirkpatrick, director of Southwest Studies at Arizona's Mesa Community College to complain: "They want me to take them on a goddamned nature walk! Don't they know that I'm a f—— writer, that's all I've ever wanted to be." Soon he calmed down, kept the date, but refused to take his disciples on a nature walk, for which some senior members have never forgiven him.

There were times when Abbey's rebellious side emerged full-blown during appearances in front of people who regarded him as the modern Moses destined to lead them into the wilderness—after he had saved it. On such occasions, whenever he felt that an audience expected him to say the right code words, to act in a certain way, he liked to shock them.

Several years before he died, Tucson's poetry center invited him to spend a week sharing his experiences with a number of fledgling literati. Topping off the week was supposed to be a serious reading by Abbey. But it was not to be. He walked onto the stage and proceeded to do the exact opposite of what the audience expected, by spinning stories of sexual hijinks with willing women during his days as a college student at the University of New Mexico. "He went on and on," recalls Charles Bowden, "poem after poem. A kind of Abbey version of *The Joy of Sex* danced through the air as people began streaming out of the auditorium. And another brick was added to the bad boy legend."

Sometimes Abbey definitely went out of his way to be belligerent and to create controversy. One of the most memorable examples centers around an essay called "Free Speech: The Cowboy and His Cow," based on a speech he delivered at the University of Montana some four years before his death. (He suffered bleeding attacks on that occasion, the inevitable concomitant of pancreatitis, which had begun to thin the walls of his veins and arteries, and eventually caused his death.)

Abbey opened his talk by pulling a .44-caliber revolver from his briefcase and waving it around, saying he'd be pleased to answer questions. It was unloaded, but his audience didn't know that. Thus armed, he proceeded to accuse ranchers, who made up most of the audience, of being "welfare parasites." Then he referred to their cows as "ugly, clumsy, stupid, brawling, stinking, fly-covered, shit-smeared, disease-spreading brutes."

At the climax of that infamous appearance, dusty boots were stomping the hardwood auditorium floor, and ranchers were shouting crude epithets at the speaker. Some said they heard a pistol go off in the parking lot.

Abbey ended his talk with this prescient observation about the Western rancher: "They've had their free ride. It's time they learned to support themselves." His manners notwithstanding,

Abbey had struck a controversial chord that most other writers had ignored by addressing the U.S. government's program of doling out subsidized land and water for ranchers, while averting its eyes from damage being caused by their sheep and cattle to public land.

Radical talk then, but by the early 1990s, growing numbers of politicians, including President Clinton and Interior Secretary Bruce Babbitt, were trying to defy the political power of Western ranchers by not only becoming advocates of higher grazing fees, but even mulling the notion that public ranges should be cattle-free. Some mainstream newspaper columnists have picked up Abbey's theme by comparing ranchers, who have long boasted of their conservative principles, to welfare mothers in New York City.

The speech, first printed in *Northern Lights*, the Montana magazine, and then in *Harper's* Magazine, attracted one blistering letter that Abbey was to treasure. It was from the writer Gretel Ehrlich of Shell, Wyoming, who called him "nonsensical, nasty and unconstructive." Nasty and unconstructive. Abbey loved that.

This is the same Abbey who asserted in "A Writer's Credo" that he knew he had been harsh at times: "rude, cruel, offensive, even unkind. I hate that. I believe in good manners."

Another essay that blackened his reputation was the one he wrote on immigration, on assignment for the *New York Times* Op-Ed page. It never ran, due to "lack of space," or so an editor told him. Subsequently, the same piece was rejected by *Harper's, The Atlantic, The New Republic, Rolling Stone, Newsweek's* "My Turn" column, and *Mother Jones.*

Giving up on the national press, Cactus Ed mailed the piece off to Mike Lacey, then editor of *New Times,* a Phoenix weekly, who proceeded to publish it. It was an audacious decision, bringing a hailstorm of outrage down upon Lacey and, of course, on Abbey. "It was pure Abbey," Lacey recalls. "Few dared to touch the subject of overpopulation then . . . Abbey put all the arguments together into a bomb, then lit the fuse."

Widely denounced as a misanthrope, an elitist, and a racist in the wake of the essay advocating a limit on further immigration by Mexicans, Abbey retorted that he didn't think it was elitist but simply common sense. Who could disagree, he asked, with the fact that Americans have not, so far at least, been able to solve their own problems of poverty, unemployment, crime, and racial conflict?

Therefore, the prospect of taking in the surplus populations of Latin America would only increase America's economic and social troubles—without really doing anything to help Mexico.

Ten years later, others, including California Governor Pete Wilson, were registering the same concerns—without being accused of racism. And even the editorial pages of the *Wall Street Journal,* in the aftermath of the Los Angeles riots in 1992, sounded the alarm by printing an article warning of the dangers posed by Latino immigrants moving into California—dangers to the state's huge deficit and a high unemployment rate—and about the lack of opportunity available for migrants.

That *Wall Street Journal* article raised the frightening prospect that there may never be enough money to rescue California from insolvency as long as millions of immigrants keep pouring in uninterruptedly. Yet when Abbey expressed that concern in 1985, the only politician who came to his side was then-Colorado Governor Dick Lamm.

By any measure, Abbey's words often moved people to anger, not just liberals advocating open borders regardless of the consequences, but also women who felt that Abbey was the classic male chauvinist in the way women were depicted in his books as often loopy, insultingly sexy caricatures.

Did he do this to be provocative, simply to capture attention? Did he really believe what he said, or was he a poseur, doing it for the money? Unquestionably, Abbey delighted in the put-on, the adolescent nose-tweaking, the hoodwinking, "the cartoonish pyromaniacal characters," as Peter Wild calls them, darting through the shadows of his novels.

In studying Abbey's works, it isn't always apparent where the disgruntled romantic idealism leaves off and the leg-pulling mischief starts. It just may be, as some students of Abbey have suggested, that Abbey didn't know—and maybe didn't care. Old Ed was just writing from his gut, anyway.

Some observers have contended that Abbey had a "dark side." His close friends have no quibble about their late friend's aloofness, conceding that it often gave the wrong impression, but they disagree on the existence of a "dark side" that drove him to pick fights with feminists and ranchers, and to be gruff and distant in the company of people.

According to Dick Kirkpatrick, for one, Abbey was deeply introspective and did not want people to know just how sensitive he really was, so, as a cover, he developed a super-macho personality.

Arizona author and balladeer Marshall Trimble experienced the Abbey "act" up close in the late 1970s at Scottsdale Community College, where Trimble was on the faculty. Scheduled to speak in the evening, Abbey arrived exhausted. In those days Abbey did imbibe, and after a short nap, he had a few beers to revive himself. When they got to the auditorium, Abbey requested another beer. Impossible, Trimble replied, because they were on the Salt River Pima Indian Reservation, where alcohol was prohibited. Abbey said he wanted a beer anyway. He needed it to overcome his shyness.

Against his better judgment, Trimble found him one, and they talked quietly in an anteroom until Abbey's turn to speak came. On stage, Abbey became a different person, bellowing about the damage the U.S. government and corporations were causing in the Southwest.

When the time came for questions, several students asked him to attack certain specific agencies, like the National Park Service, for which Abbey had worked. Abbey refused, saying that he had friends in those agencies and didn't want to insult them.

Even today Abbey is resented for his attitude toward women—and his skirmishes with feminist leaders such as Gloria Steinem. Was this just another disguise? Once, using the pseudonym Cactus Ed, he wrote a letter to Gloria Steinem at *Ms.* Magazine beginning with "Dear Sirs." His complaint? Her magazine was upsetting the rural balance: "Out here a womin's place is in the kitchen, the barnyard and the bedroom in exactly that order and we don't need no changes." Did he really appreciate women as equals, but just liked to poke fun, and stir up the pot?

Yes, said Abbey. As for charges that he was a male chauvinist pig of the first magnitude, he told an interviewer a few years before he died: "I love women. I've been misinterpreted. I've got a good wife and two daughters, and none of them were denied anything on account of their sex. I am absolutely, wholeheartedly, one hundred percent in favor of equal opportunity. It is perfectly consistent to love the differences between men and women, and even to exaggerate them, and at the same time to support the notion of equal opportunity. . . . "

However, says his friend Allan Harrington, "Ed wanted to become an artist, but in my opinion, he was a flawed artist, due to his inability to write about half the human race—namely women. In his work, his view of women tends to be crude, cynical, and shallow. There is very little tenderness in evidence. Instead, he gave his readers caricature."

In earlier years women flocked to Abbey, and he to them. For most of that time, friends concede, he had the maturity of a teenager in sexual matters. Dick Kirkpatrick contends that his friend Ed only got beyond the pubescent stage in his final years, "but I'm not sure that he ever understood women." Perhaps that was because of the kind of women he attracted, suggests Allan Harrington: "Ed kept getting involved with environmental groupies, but down deep he didn't respect them. Perhaps this is why he disliked being called an environmentalist, for that's what drew women groupies to him."

Other friends say that Abbey's conquests were vastly exaggerated—by many women themselves because they desperately wanted to be part of the Abbey myth. "Maybe they are lying. Maybe they're not," says Dick Kirkpatrick, "but the women keep coming forward. It's the equivalent of all those people in the 1880s bragging that they'd shot Jesse James and Billy the Kid."

Mary Sojourner compares women to nature in Abbey's world: "He liked women as long as they were like a mysterious back-canyon, dangerous. He kept trying to tame that canyon, and when he did, he was bored. Unlike real canyons, women to him were an absolutely unsolvable mystery. At least he could go out on the land, be in it, and make a little sense out of it."

Abbey's reputation as a man who regarded women as little more than sexual toys irked reviewers, not to mention women, including his wives. On occasion, women who had expected to meet some kind of Neanderthal had a different experience. That was surely the case with author Barbara Kingsolver.

In 1988, when she learned that she would be meeting Abbey about the judging of a Tucson writing contest, she complained to a friend: "Me and Abbey in a restaurant, trying to agree on something? Sounds like a blind date from hell!"

Plainly, Abbey was a man she had no interest in knowing. While she admired his ferocious reverence for the land, much of what he said about people sounded to her like bigotry; his proscriptions for Latino refugees were brutal, and on the subject of women, he was given to remarks "so anachronistically patronizing that they were either annoying or absurd."

To Kingsolver's astonishment, their meeting was far from a disaster. She found Abbey to be gracious to the point of deference and wonderfully guileless. And she discovered that she and Abbey both had failed careers as musicians before they became writers. Abbey reminisced about his beatnik days as a flutist in an Albuquerque coffeehouse, and about the night he was fired after some incensed townsfolk shot out the windows with pistols because they didn't like his artistic music.

It dawned on Kingsolver that the revolution of Abbey's youth was not at all like hers: "While Abbey was inspiring the ire of cowboys with his black turtleneck and beret, Steinem and Malcolm X were still awaiting conversion, and I hadn't yet learned to walk. His language came out of a time I never knew. I decided to lighten up on Ed."

As the pleasant evening wound down, Kingsolver and Abbey exchanged phone numbers and addresses. As they parted she asked him: "Do you just do the Old Bastard image so that people will leave you alone?" Abbey gave her a radiant smile and said, "Yep." She went home that night—her home turned out to be across a deep desert gulley from Abbey's—assuming she would have all the time in the world to cultivate her new acquaintance. "I didn't, and I regret it," she said after his death.

To Abbey goes the last word: "Women are truly better than men. Otherwise, they'd be intolerable." To this day, people still argue about Abbey and women, but it is not his failings or glories in that area for which he will be remembered. It will be for his writing, for his humanism in trying to shock readers into recognizing their actual place in nature and becoming interested in their own survival.

For what he was about was so precisely fixed in his own mind that he could write about it coherently in the essay "A Writer's Credo" published in *One Life at a Time, Please:*

> That is all I ask of the author. To be a hero, appoint himself a moral leader, wanted or not. I believe that words count, that writing matters, that poems, essays, and novels—in the long run—make a difference. If they do not, then in the words of my exemplar, Alexsandr Solzhenitsyn, the writer's work is no more important than the barking of village dogs at night.
>
> The hack writer, the temporizer, the toady, and the sycophant, the journalistic courtier (and what is a courtier but a male courtesan?), all those in the word trade who simply go with the flow, who never oppose the rich and powerful, are not better than, in my view, Solzhenitsyn's village dogs.
>
> The dogs bark, the caravan moves on.

Decades before Abbey emerged as the eloquent anarchist, Aldo Leopold, the heroic conservationist, peered into the future: "The major premise of civilization is that the attainments of one generation shall be available to the next."

And it was that proposition that Abbey, the writer and the man, always kept in the forefront of his consciousness. Despite the black humor evident in his writings, he offered up hope against the villains—the land-killers and the charlatans in suits—that there was still time to meet Leopold's challenge.

If citizens refuse to accept that challenge, and pursue the path of power and materialism, where the pleasures of life can be obtained without effort, they are certain, he predicted, to find "a world of insufferable boredom, degrading humans to the sloth and torpor of swine in a luxury sty; unworthy of us, the death of our nature." The planet will survive, he was saying, it is human nature that is in the greatest jeopardy.

Abbey sought to be an artist, but when he saw the land he loved under attack—the paradise he had left the wounded Appalachians to find—he was transformed into the advocate. "Leave it like it was," he pleaded.

Near the end, his face became a road map of all the arid, dusty places he had lived and hiked, deeply lined and bushy-bearded, with mischievous blue-gray eyes that squinted even in shadowy places. Never one to take care of his health, friends say, Abbey ignored the advice of physicians and made fun of vegetarians, instead eating greasy eggs, hot chiles and pig meat—going his own way, down Abbey's road.

"I've suffered my share of personal disasters," he told a writer shortly before he died. "The loss of love, the death of a wife, the failure to realize in my writing the aspiration of my intentions. But those misfortunes can be borne. There is a certain animal vitality in most of us which carries us through any trouble but the absolutely overwhelming.

"Only a fool and idiot will let grief and sorrow ride him down to the grave. So, I've been lucky, as most people are lucky; the animal in each of us has a lot more sense than our brains."

He must have known he was going to die, for in the fall of 1988 he turned down a lucrative literary reading for the following March, telling the organizer of the conference, "I won't be around."

In the next few months, he said a series of quiet farewells to many people with hugs and final hikes. He knew how close death was, but most of his friends never suspected they were seeing him for the last time. This is why, when it struck so suddenly, many who knew him personally, or knew his work, were left in a state of shock.

Despite all his contradictions and controversial qualities, Abbey left behind a prodigious legacy. As Charles Bowden sums up, "Ed taught us how to see the Southwest as something besides real estate to butcher. And now we have to learn to see it without him." Gregory McNamee measures the loss of his dead friend this way: "Ed reminded us of absences, of open lands, of wilderness, of the human freedom we deserve but do not have, of societies responsibly organized. And he reminded us of the joys and the hard duties of living well. And now we have another absence, that of Ed himself; everyone who cares about the wilderness, about the American West, about our freedom, about our future, feels that loss."

No one has filled the void left by the desert crank's demise. Meantime, the news is getting heavier in the Southwest; public lands are under siege by the forces of industrial tourism, the very kind of motorized tourism Abbey feared, and the Cold War isn't over, not with billions of dollars worth of nuclear weapons and toxic waste dumps pocking and leaking into the land Abbey showed people how to love.

Because of his words, nonetheless, hope still runs high; many thousands have come to love the land as passionately as he did—and are fighting back in many different ways against what Abbey saw as "our contemporary techno-industrial greed-and-power culture." This now includes President Clinton's new Interior Secretary, Bruce Babbitt. Breaking ranks with his former gubernatorial constituency of ranchers and developers, Babbitt is determined to recast federal management of public lands in the West, to bring to an end to the massive public subsidies received by powerful interests for grazing, water, and minerals. Babbitt's motto: Tread lightly on the land. No one expects him to say "leave it like it was," because in many places in the Southwest, it is too late for that.

In many of Abbey's obituary notices, he was labeled as a cantankerous, misanthropic curmudgeon with many enemies. Abbey would have appreciated that, for his definition of a curmudgeon was anyone who hates hypocrisy, sham, dogmatic ideologies, the pretenses and evasions of euphemism—anyone who has the nerve to point out unpleasant facts, who takes the trouble to string those facts on the skewer of humor and roast them over the fires of empiric truth, common sense, and native intelligence. In this nation of bleating sheep and braying jackasses, he said, "it then becomes an honor to be labeled curmudgeon."

He also enjoyed disputing that label, insisting that he was as far from a radical crank as he could be. Indeed, the Abbey of most of his books he riposted in *Abbey's Road*, "bears only the dimmest resemblance to the shy, timid, reclusive, rather dapper little gentleman who, always correctly attired for his labors in coat and tie and starched detachable cuffs, sits down each night for precisely four hours to type out the further adventures of that arrogant blustering macho fraud that counterfeits his name."

Sure, Ed!

THE EARLY YEARS IN APPALACHIA

I am a redneck, born and bred on a submarginal farm in Appalachia, descended from an endless line of dark-complected, jug-eared, beetle-browed, insolent barbarian peasants, a line reaching back to the dark forests of central Europe and the alpine caves of my Neanderthal primogenitors.

—"In Defense of the Redneck," *Abbey's Road*

I longed for the warm green hills of Pennsylvania, for the little wooden baseball towns. . . . I thought of the winding red-dog road that led under oak and maple trees toward a creaking old farmhouse that was our home . . .

—"Hallelujah on the Bum," *The Journey Home*

Many creative artists pass through various cyclical stages of development before their character and ideas form and crystallize. Not Ed Abbey. By the time he was in his mid-teens, many of the convictions he was to hold throughout his life had begun to harden, thanks to his strong-willed parents, his romantic perspective, and his own sense of place in the mountains where he was born.

While other aspects of Abbey's later life may seem murky at times, the facts of his early years are beyond dispute. He really was born in the backwoods of Appalachia in 1927, the eldest of five children; and he really did grow up in a two-story house on a submarginal farm down a lonely dirt road near some ancient woods, once teeming with Indians.

It was a beautiful, though ragged, farm community where people were connected to the earth in a way that today's agribusiness magnates can never be. People knew the wildflowers by name, tending and appreciating them as they grew. They watched the trees for signs of the changing seasons and loved them for their summertime shade.

Many of today's armchair, born-again environmentalists like to portray nature as a peaceful, idyllic experience in contrast to the brutal harshness of urban America. But Abbey learned something early that was to affect his later writing, that the natural order is not peaceful or safe, but interdependent and sometimes violent, with a rhythmic harmony incorporating conflict and death and a food chain in which only the fittest survive. This knowledge gave him a marked edge during his desert wanderings in later years.

Called Ned by his family, he showed a rebellious streak at an early age that almost always surpassed that of his three younger brothers, John, Bill, and Howard, and his sister, Nancy. "I don't see why you have to do these things to me," he wailed at his mother, Mildred, while she was trying to wash his hair. "I'm a big man and don't cry when I get my head washed."

He was four years old.

His sensibilities, to a considerable extent, were shaped by his father, Paul Revere Abbey—a logger, trapper, and farmer, and an anarchist and agnostic of Swiss and German extraction. In the evening, after the work was done, he would read lines to the family from Walt Whitman such as "stand up for the stupid and the crazy." The hands that held the book were large and leathery.

"Dad was anti-capitalist, anti-religion, anti-prevailing opinion, anti-booze, anti-war, and anti-anyone who didn't agree with him," recalls Howard Abbey, Ed's surviving younger brother. Paul was also a fierce and self-centered idealist who often put his idealism ahead of the family's needs. This is one characteristic Ned definitely inherited from his father, though the son is reported to have been more aware of this shortcoming than Paul Abbey ever was.

Ned's character was influenced, too, by his mother Mildred, whose Presbyterian ancestors, the Postelwaites, had emigrated from Wales and Scotland in the seventeenth century. She is remembered as a pretty, artistic, intelligent woman who never weighed more than 100 pounds. As a schoolteacher and organist for the local choir, she walked five miles a day until 1987, when she was killed in an auto crash. It was from Mildred that Ed Abbey inherited his writing, musical, and artistic abilities.

And then there was his birthplace, nestled in the Allegheny Mountains of Pennsylvania, near a tiny town called Home, the kind of burg where weathered tobacco advertisements from years gone by still decorate the fading red walls of many old barns.

In his adolescent years during the Great Depression, roaming untamed places was the crux of Ned's life. He dug and splashed in a swampy paradise called Crooked Creek, shot birds with a BB gun (only once), and built his first tiny boat (his last).

There was also a tract of ancient forest that Ned and his brothers and sister used to call the "Big Woods." It was a wild and spooky place, luxuriously overgrown with poplar, white oak, maple, hemlock, and hickory, still safe then from loggers because its slopes were so steep. Thick vines of wild grape trailed down the limbs of primordial oaks into musty, hidden places, "dank glens of mystery and shamanism," Abbey was to write of this woodsy playground.

Although the Abbey children knew little of primitive mythology, they sensed that magic was glimmering in and around those trees. And they learned some of the lore of the people who once lived in those woods: Delaware, Seneca, and Shawnee. Like them, the Abbeys relished scampering down the deer paths through fern, moss, yarrow, and mayapple, "among the massive trunks in the greengold light of autumn, from spring to stream and marsh," Abbey remembered more than forty years later.

Although the Indians had vanished more than one hundred years earlier, finally driven out in the eighteenth century by Colonel George Rogers Clark, the children believed that Indian spirits still lingered there, and now had risen back to life through their own pale skins for a few transcendent summers.

Abbey later remembered those early years as the time of "our idolatrous mimicry." Sometimes he would tell interviewers that he, too, had Indian blood, but if he did it wasn't much more than a few drops. Swiss, German, Scottish, and Welsh blood is what pulsed through his veins, but the possibility of Shawnee ancestry added to his mystique.

The children knew about feathers and moccasins and bows and arrows, and they relished the game of running up and down the old trails without stepping on a single twig so they wouldn't alert the creatures or frighten the spirits. That their knowledge came from children's books and stories didn't matter, for the deep forest and their imaginations made it all so very real.

Brother Johnny had a special talent. He could talk to trees. And he could skin a squirrel, start a fire without matches, and spot the eye of a sitting rabbit. As for young Ned, he was best at listening to doves; of all the melodies in the Big Woods, he loved most that of the doves, which he described as "the ancient voice of one whose voice I heard first and forever in the humid mists of home; the gray dove always mourning, crying its lonesome call to silence into the emptiness of all nature's longings, saying 'Who are you? Where do you go? And why? And did we not know each other long ago in the dark forests of Germany?'"

Years before, the wolf had departed the woods, and so had the puma, but there were still bobcat, deer, raccoon, and gray fox. It was good country then, the country of Abbey's childhood, even though every family in those parts suffered through their share of hard times during the depression. Paul Abbey got the family through by driving a school bus, shooting in marksmen contests, and selling magazines. And the children always had the Big Woods to retreat to, the boundless green forest that guarded so many old mysteries.

It was a fine place in which to vanish, and when Ned didn't want to do farm work, he hid there, smoking corn silk–stogies until someone smelled the smoke, and he was found out. Of those woods Abbey wrote: "It was a sultry sullen dark-massed deepness of transpiring green that formed the theatre which made possible our play. We invented our boyhood as we grew, but the forest, in which it was possible to get authentically lost, sustained our sense of awe and terror in ways that fantasy cannot."

Home for much of Ned's early years was on a sixty-seven-acre farm the family called *Old Lonesome Briar Patch* because it *was* one of those hilly remote and run-down places, rocky but beautiful in its way. For years, the family was without a telephone. Then, when party lines arrived, the Abbeys had to shout to be heard above the neighbors who were trying to use the line at the same time.

Nancy Abbey recalls those days with her brother Ned: "I don't remember him as an environmental writer as so many people do. He just was a very fine writer who cared about the environment. The 'environment' was part of who he was.

"It was part of who we all were; our parents taught us the many different trees, and about all the wildflowers. It was a very important thing to know. Mother cultivated the wildflowers, and gathered up the seeds." It was truly a rural mountain culture in which neighbors helped neighbors through the bad times when the mines and mills were shut down. No one wanted the shame of going on "relief."

"There were a lot of people who truly loved everything that was there," Nancy continues, "and they, like our family, would gather hickory nuts and walnuts and make maple syrup." The Abbeys had five varieties each of maple and oak on the farm, and in the spring the dogwood would billow like white clouds everywhere.

One of their neighbors had a wildflower farm and they would ship the flowers, together with wild plants from the Big Woods, to customers all across the country. The Abbeys' food came from the land, everything except salt, pepper, and sugar. Paul Abbey kept the family in meat, and also trapped mink, skunk, and muskrat and then sold their furs.

"This is anathema now to environmentalists," Nancy observes, "but you see, my father loved the animals. He knew all the tracks in the snow and he taught them to us. It was a matter of living in the environment. Looking back, I feel we really lived in harmony. We used the animals as part of our sustenance and lived lightly on the earth so that they thrived around us."

Not for sport or trophy did Paul Abbey hunt in the deep woods and meadows. He saw it as a matter of survival in the universal order of things, and his skill at stopping rabbits in their tracks created many stews during the winters. Mildred Abbey canned the excess in Mason jars, as she did peaches, pears, sweet corn, tomatoes, and pork sausage.

By every measure, Mildred was a powerful influence over Ned and the other children and is remembered as the stronger parent, but for sake of harmony she usually took a back seat to her more gregarious, outspoken husband.

As Abbey wrote of her in his final, mostly autobiographical novel, *The Fool's Progress:* "She was a beautiful woman . . . she had fine flaxen hair that fell to the small of her back when she let it down; we loved to watch as she washed her hair. She had bright hazel eyes, widely spaced—a sign of intelligence—a thin fragile-looking hen's beak of a nose and a narrow but expressive mouth trembling most of the time on the verge of laughter. Or of grief."

Normally, Nancy recalls, the family took the evening meal together. They were traditionalists. After supper, the family would listen to radio programs such as "I Love a Mystery" or to their mother playing the piano.

Stephen Foster songs were everybody's favorites, especially Paul Abbey's. With a powerful tenor voice, he would be accompanied by Mildred on the piano while the children convened around them, enjoying every song.

When these gatherings ended for the evening, Ned—from the time he was just six or seven years old—would go to his room to read, and write down his thoughts. After all the dishes had been washed, the children would go to bed, falling asleep to the strains of Chopin, Debussy, and piano classics like "The Old Rugged Cross."

Sundays! After a week of school, working the gardens, and helping with barn chores, the Abbeys truly cherished Sundays. After church, Nancy and her mother would set up a card table near the fireplace, and neighbors would come by for peanut butter, cheese and crackers, and tea. As the kids munched, they would listen to their neighbors' stories about travels to foreign lands, especially delighting in the tales of one who had lived in the Middle East. They were also intrigued by stories of the American West, none more than Ned, who loved to hear his father talk of his days as a cowhand in Montana.

During those Sunday-afternoon get-togethers, Paul Revere Abbey would often sound forth on the virtues of Soviet Communism, Socialist leaders Eugene Debs and Norman Thomas, and about the time he once shook the hand of "Big" Bill Haywood, leader of the International Workers of the World and the most radical Wobbly of them all.

Though less strident than her husband, Mildred would join in the discussion of politics, religion, and literature and usually "cooled" the temperature by talking about neighborhood matters when things got too hot.

All the while, the children listened—and remembered.

It was during those evenings, and in those woods, that Ned Abbey began to wonder about "something else out there," and off by himself he would scribble down his dreams, ideas, and stories. During the fifth and sixth grades, he launched his first publishing experiment by creating a tiny newspaper, hand-printed, featuring cartoons and stories about local marble tournaments and baseball games.

Abbey would rent his only copy to his siblings for one penny. When he had collected enough pennies, he would walk down to the local market with his brothers and sister to buy popsicles for his subscribers. Soon thereafter, he created his own comic book, *The Adventures of Lucky Stevens*, the story of a little hillbilly boy who could break open whiskey bottles with his teeth.

"Ed also was an incredible cartoonist," Nancy Abbey recollects. "If he hadn't gone into writing, he easily could have been an artist. He was a remarkable person to remember. For one thing, whenever he'd complain after a bad review, he'd say that he wished he'd been a farmer; he loathed farming."

The story is told of a day when he was a teenager, working in the garden with his father. "Bring me a hoe," said Paul Revere Abbey. Ed replied: "A hoe? Where do you keep hoes?" His father, a tall, swarthy, handsome man said, "You mean you don't know after all these years?" "Yup," Ned replied, "and I'm proud of it." To understate the case, physical activities like farm work were not Ned's forte; Howard remembers that "he especially hated the 'w' word. Work was for more primitive creatures."

Paul Abbey, who had done hard manual labor from an early age, was a traveling salesman during Ned's early years, always looking for a bonanza to ease pressures at home. As a result, he left much of the farm work to the boys, plowing (with one horse), planting, digging out the cellar, and gouging out a space for a garage with pick and shovel, as well as milking cows and chopping wood.

"Because Dad wasn't there to supervise," Howard recalls, "Johnny and I did the work. Ned always had other things to do, things more fitting to the family genius. He spent his time reading, writing, drawing pictures, and communing with nature. This is where his 'high and mighty' attitude began."

For her part, Mildred Abbey is remembered by her surviving children as a loving mother, open to new ideas, still taking college courses when she was eighty years old. Though she was a good Presbyterian, she never pushed her views on the rest of the family, preferring to concentrate on teaching the children good table manners and proper English. Behind her back, Ned called her "The Old Crone" in loving jest.

"Our whole family stuck out like a sore thumb because we were so politically radical," Nancy recollects. "I mean my father in the 1950s supported Soviet Communism. He and my mother were two of three people in the county of coal miners and loggers and farmers who voted for Norman Thomas and the Socialist ticket all the time."

Paul Abbey was gifted with an inquiring mind and was also possessed with a determination to be different, characteristics Ed inherited full-blown. His father could recite every line of the works of Walt Whitman by heart. One of his favorite passages, from the preface to the 1855 edition of *Leaves of Grass*, was to stay with Ed Abbey all his life:

> This is what you shall do. Love the earth and the sun and the animals. Despise riches. Give alms to everyone that asks. Stand up for the stupid and the crazy. Devote your income and labor to others, hate tyrants, have patience and indulgence toward the people, take off your hat to nothing known or unknown, or to any man or any number of men, go freely with powerful uneducated persons and the young and with mothers of families . . . Re-examine all you have been told at school or church or in any book and dismiss whatever insults your soul.

When Paul was eighteen years old, he hitchhiked west and worked for a time as a Montana cowhand. On his journey, he saw sorry working conditions almost everywhere and soon realized that they were not any better than they were in the steel mills and coal mines of Pennsylvania, Indiana, and West Virginia, close to home. That experience only fueled his contempt for Wall Street financiers who, he was convinced, were bleeding the working man and causing wars.

Another of his heroes was John L. Lewis, boss of the United Mine Workers, the bushy-eyebrowed curmudgeon who had forced the coal companies to improve working conditions in the mines and to build better housing in the company towns that dotted Appalachia. "Our father talked a lot about justice," Nancy remembers. "It was ingrained in us as children." When talk around the dinner table didn't center on the farm and community matters, it was about politics, usually anti-establishment politics.

Ned claimed that one of his first memories of his father was riding on his shoulders, his bare legs clamped around his father's small, muscled waist; his small hands holding tightly to his father's thick black hair. He had to hold on tightly because both his father's hands were on the plow while he talked to the work horses, their bridle lines looped over the plow handles.

"The only noise," Ed Abbey was to recall in his novel *The Fool's Progress*, "was that of the yielding soil, the strain of horses and harness leather, the rattle of metal, the cries of robins in the brush along the fence."

Politics, logging, hunting, and farming were Paul Abbey's interests; religion was not. He prayed to no God and was never a churchgoer, pronouncing that he was an agnostic because it took as much faith to know there is no God as to believe there is one.

Outliving Ed by three years, he is remembered as a kind man who took life's tragedies in stride, including the death of his wife and two sons before he himself died in 1992, chopping wood almost until the end.

Except for the fact that Paul Abbey never touched liquor, his surviving children believe that Ed provided a fairly accurate portrait of their father the anarchist in *The Fool's Progress:*

> . . . my father was a vain stubborn self-centered stiffnecked poker-playing whiskey-drinking gun-toting old son of a gun. He was a good hunter, a good trapper, a poor farmer and a hot-shot but reckless logger.
>
> He was hard on himself, on trees, machines and the earth. He never gave his wife the kind of home she wanted or the kind of life she deserved.

He was cantankerous, ornery, short-tempered, and contentious, probably the most contentious man that lived in
Shawnee County. He was so contentious he never even realized
how contentious he was.

He had strong opinions on everything and a neighborly view
on almost nothing. He was a hard man to get along with. But
I'll say this for him: he was honest. He never cheated anyone.
He was gentle with children and animals. He always spoke his
mind, and he was a true independent—independent, like we say,
as a hog on ice. I mean he really believed in self-reliance and liberty. He was what some call a hillbilly—but we call a mountaineer. The mountaineer is a free man.

Is it any wonder then that Abbey's own character took form at
such an early age and that, according to both Nancy and
Howard, he could be a very rebellious, obnoxious young boy?
"He really had a sense of superiority over the rest of us," Nancy
recalls. "He was high and mighty when he was just a kid," adds
Howard, the only Abbey still living in the vicinity of the Big
Woods of their youth. "He thought he was better than every-
body else."

By all accounts, this attitude created some tense moments.
One day, Howard came home and was on the verge of proudly
announcing to the assembled family that he had been placed in
charge of the school library reading table. "Don't bother," Ned
told him. "They won't even know what a library is." Remembers
Nancy Abbey, "Ed thought the rest of us were stupid, and his
parents definitely so."

As the children grew older, moments of friction at the evening
supper table became more frequent. "Dad was well read,"
Nancy recalls, "but I think he felt threatened by the fact that he
had only a sixth-grade education, that mother was a school-

teacher, and that we were learning new things in school. When we began questioning all the things he had to say, we made him uncomfortable."

At times, Ned thought his father was an uneducated country bumpkin. But there were other times when he felt a deep fondness for him, particularly when poetry and baseball were involved. When he and his brothers were small, his father organized a baseball team of all the local boys. "Ned became the leader of the ball team," Howard Abbey remembers. "We were the 'Home Hellions,' and Dad would haul the whole team in his little Willys automobile. This is where Ned got the idea for his semi-factual baseball game in *The Fool's Progress*. We played teams like Canoe Ridge and Blacklick.

"Ned was a fine pitcher, a southpaw, because he had broken his right arm when he was little. But, after a while, he lost interest. I think he thought it was too small-time for him."

After Ned, now Ed, went west to the University of New Mexico in 1947, he came to admire his father again the way he had when he was younger. Frequently, Ed invited Paul to join him during fire lookout assignments, and Paul once spent a whole summer in the 1960s with his son at a fire ranger outpost at the north rim of the Grand Canyon. Then nearly seventy, Paul hiked with Ed——seven miles down into the Grand Canyon, and nine miles back up on a different trail. Rain fell the entire time, but he hardly complained, and only became angry when Ed offered to carry his pack for him. It was on that trip that Paul discovered rocks, the ancient sandstones of the Canyon, and upon his return to Pennsylvania, talked incessantly about their age and beauty.

Although relations between father and son grew closer over the years, to those around them the relationship remained an enigma. There was the time in the 1970s when Ed, even though he knew his father was a puritan when it came to women, took the older man to a movie in Tucson. Paul Abbey, then in his eighties, could hardly believe his eyes at one tepid love scene and promptly stalked out of the theater. Ed remained in his seat until the end.

Later, Ed went back East for his mother's funeral and to promote *The Fool's Progress,* the ribald account of a young hillbilly anarchist who goes west from Appalachia. It's filled with sexually explicit details that turned many women readers and reviewers off. But they weren't alone.

At the family front door in Home, shortly after his wife was buried, Paul Abbey confronted his oldest son by barking: "Why? How could you?" His question had nothing to do with the fact that the father character, who so closely resembled him, dies in the novel. Rather, the gratuitous sex and the obscenities angered and shocked the old man.

From the romantic perspective of a besieged, modern city dweller, it could appear that the Abbey family lived an ideal kind of life close to the earth. There were strong blood ties, to be sure, and a powerful kinship with the land, but there appears to have been little true intimacy. Mildred Abbey is said to have been bitter about having five children and two miscarriages in ten years——she always wondered what the children she lost might have been like——and was also resentful about their living conditions. She yearned for better food and clothes so that her "nubbins'," as she called her children, could be better off.

By all accounts, Mildred was a tender, gentle, loving person, but she was not very happy——occasionally venting her frustration. Most of the time, she concealed it behind a busy schedule of homemaking, teaching, and church, and beneath a stoic mask. Perhaps this is why Ed Abbey, having grown up aloof, could love others only begrudgingly much of his life, rarely wholeheartedly, and was unable to express himself well with people unless he had known them for years, and often not even then.

Santa Fe–based writer and environmentalist Jack Loeffler, for one, contends that he knew Abbey for nearly a decade before they had heart-to-heart talks. "It was worse than pulling teeth at first," says Loeffler, perhaps Abbey's closest male friend, and the person with whom Abbey developed the idea for *The Monkey Wrench Gang*.

Abbey's lack of much intimacy in his childhood may explain why his novel *The Fool's Progress* is about love for his roots back in the hills, tinged with a certain degree of regret that he and his family hadn't had closer, warmer personal relationships. After Abbey met Clarke Cartwright in 1978 (she would later be his fifth wife), he wrote to Nancy that the Cartwright family was the way a family really ought to be—very close. "He was beginning to change before he met Clarke," says Nancy Abbey, "but I give her lots of the credit. My brother was in his forties before he really began to look carefully at himself and the way he related to women."

The Abbey of later years, some of his close friends sensed, was a far more sensitive person than at times he appeared to be on the surface. But even during the early years there were moments when that caring side came to the fore, like the day he rode on the bus with Nancy on her first day of school. "He came to visit during recess, and then made sure to get me on the bus at day's end. I think it was the fact that he felt that was his responsibility and that he did care," she recalls. "He knew what it was like to go to school for the first time, and he was the big brother."

Later in the school year, when a boy shoved in front of Nancy in the school cafeteria, she stood her ground and punched him in the eye, creating a big, black shiner. Seeing his sister throw the punch, Ed was furious. "My brother was so embarrassed," she recounts, "that all the way home he berated me with 'Is that the way a young lady should act? Don't ever do that again.'"

By the time Ed was in high school, his sensitivities were aroused in another direction. The ugly head of progress reared up in his beloved woods. It would scar him forever. As he grew older, even visiting those woods was painful. The wild places, which had seemed to be so vast, turned out to be tenuous and vulnerable, merely innocent prey for the dragline shovels and bulldozers tearing into the land for timber and coal. "We have connived in the murder of our own origins," he would write.

At an appalling rate, the woods Abbey had thought were eternal were logged, and the mountainside upon which the Big Woods grew was laid to waste by the coal strippers. The legacy of bobcat tracks and day lilies was erased and a new one was created: spoilbanks, mangled, unnatural escarpments, festering pools of stagnant water, and the once crystal-clear creek that now bubbled yellow with pollution.

Abbey wrote about that man-made mayhem in *The Fool's Progress,* in the form of a conversation between the characters Henry, or himself, and Will, who in life was his brother Howard.

". . . What's that mess down there?" Henry pointed to the valley below, past the recontoured slope of the strip mine toward a vast cleared area beyond. The yellow bulldozers and earthmovers were at rest now, for the weekend, but it was plain that their work wasn't completed.

"What the hell are they up to? Isn't that Ginter Hollow?" Will smiled again. "You been away too long, Henry. The Ginters are in real estate development these days. They live in town and spend their winters in Florida. What we're a-lookin' at down there is what they call Sylvan Dell Lake. Dam the crick, make a little lake, clear off the woods, sell five-acre homesites. Might even be a golf course down there someday. God knows what they are up to and I don't want to know. Might make me sick."

In the summer of 1944, with one more year of high school ahead, Abbey decided to travel west. It was the logical thing for him to do because his father had done it. All the kids wanted to go and eventually did. "The only thing that kept me from thumbing my way out there," says Nancy today, "was that 'girls' didn't do that. I tried to find a friend to travel with. My parents said no."

Before departing, Ed's father warned him that his trip would be far more successful if he didn't behave like an arrogant jerk. Then he handed him a twenty-dollar bill. About then, brother Howard said he wanted to go along. "Not a chance," Ed barked. "Why?" asked Howard. "Because frankly you bore me."

As he set off on his first adventure, Abbey saw himself as a "wise, brown, ugly, shy, poetical . . . bold, stupid, sun-dazzled kid out to see the country before giving his life in the war against Japan. A kind of hero, by God!"

With some dollars in his pocket, the skinny seventeen-year-old hillbilly kid from Old Lonesome Briar Patch took to the road. He rode the rails and hitchhiked to Seattle and down the coast to San Francisco; took a side trip to Yosemite National Park; and then, in a boxcar across the desert from California, went through northern Arizona to New Mexico.

On that journey, during which he earned money picking fruit and working in a cannery, it wasn't the Pacific Ocean, nor the California orange groves that stole his heart. It was the

Southwest, whose freshness and innocence reminded him of his first sight of an undressed girl. The brief summer adventure would forever shape his life, for he had seen "the very picture of things which are free, decent and sane," he would later write.

In Needles, California, in early August, Abbey had his first glimpse of the Colorado River, veritable lifeblood of the West that he would spend much of his life enjoying and defending from the kind of progress that was dismantling the Big Woods back home.

He later wrote of that day:

Across the river, waited a land that filled me with strange excitement; crags and pinnacles of naked rock, the dark cores of ancient volcanoes, a vast, silent emptiness smoldering with heat, color, and indecipherable significance, above which floated a small number of pure, clear, hard-edged clouds.

For the first time, I felt I was getting close to the West of my deepest imaginings—the place where the tangible and the mythical become the same.

Reality hit him like summer lightning when, soon after the Santa Fe freight train stopped in Flagstaff, Abbey was arrested by the local police for vagrancy. A quarter of a century later he described the first night he ever spent in jail.

Cold steel, cold cement, a rabble of coughing, drunken, sick bums sprawled on the floor, curled up in the corners. The smell of vomit and urine, the fumes of sweet wine, the peculiar stale and bitter odor of old sweat-soaked rags.

There were no benches, no bunks, nothing but this tank of steel and concrete, and in the center of the ceiling, protected by wire mesh, one yellow light bulb.

As the moment of his arraignment approached, Abbey was sure the police would find the forty-some dollars he had hidden in his left shoe, but somehow it escaped their attention. After looking the scruffy teenager over, the judge announced that Abbey's trial date would be in 100 days unless he could come up with fifty dollars. "But, I have only $1.40, Your Honor," Abbey lied.

That plea touched the judge, so he consulted with the court clerk and then asked Ed, "Are you a draft dodger?" "No," the young vagrant responded. He asked to see Abbey's draft card, and Ed told him that he was only seventeen and therefore not registered. He reduced the bail to one dollar and told Ed to get the hell out of Flagstaff and never, never come back.

A soft-hearted policeman, moved somehow by the ragged youngster, treated him to a meal and drove him to the eastern edge of town, where state route 89A cuts through the vast ponderosa pine forests and heads east toward New Mexico. Before the policeman bade him farewell, he gave Abbey one final warning: Stay off freight trains, because many of them carry military equipment and armed soldiers who wouldn't mind shooting anyone who has all the earmarks of a possible saboteur.

After sleeping among the yellow pines, Abbey disregarded the policeman's warning and hopped the first freight to New Mexico. Through the open door of a boxcar, he saw the dusty, red rangelands of the Navajo, the fiery fringes of the Painted Desert, and the distant pebbled mesas of Hopi land.

"Sometimes," he recollected, "I would catch a glimpse of a hogan under a scarp of sandstone, a team and wagon hitched by the door, a couple of Indians sprawled in the shade of a juniper tree. It all looked good to me."

The beauty of the desert and the plateaus moved Abbey, but by the time the freight rolled into Albuquerque, he was yearning for his family. So he used the emergency money he had earned picking fruit in California, still hidden in his shoe, to buy a bus ticket home.

"I was sick for home," he wrote, for the old farm house where "father and mother sat inside in the amber light of the kerosene lamps, listening to their battery-powered Zenith radio, waiting for me."

Safely home, he had no choice but to momentarily abandon his dreams of the Southwest. There was high school to finish—and there was a war on. Neighbors' sons were going, and soon his turn would come. Between picking fights in the schoolyard with boys who were stronger, he edited the school paper and earned the reputation of being a fine debater. "He'd call one of the top athletes a mental nonentity," Howard remembers of those fights, "or a cerebral microbe."

Mostly, he was liked by fellow students and regarded by his teachers as a boy who could go far in life. He graduated in 1945, despite flunking a journalism course twice and refusing until the last minute to take grammar tests, insisting that he already knew the subject well enough.

Abbey graduated as a top student, but it is doubtful that anyone suspected that the stage was being set for a writing career that would reveal the real West, stripped of its Hollywood mythology and government propaganda, or that Abbey would emerge in the 1960s as the Southwest's most outspoken and passionate defender.

After graduation, Ed went off to war—reluctantly by all accounts—beginning a two-year hitch with basic training in Alabama. The Japanese surrendered on the very day training was over, but the war wasn't over for Abbey. The army sent him abroad to Naples, Italy, where his first job choice was clerk typist. He reasoned that he might get some writing done that way.

No such luck. Instead, his superiors gave him a white helmet liner, a red scarf, and a .45 automatic. His job was patrolling the streets for trouble on a huge Harley-Davidson. All went well until the day he crashed the Harley through a fence and was demoted. "To the vice squad, Abbey, back to the whorehouse for you," the sergeant screamed at him.

In Italy, Abbey was always in some kind of trouble for failing to salute officers. "'You're saluting the uniform, not the man,' they taught us in basic training," Abbey recalled. "Really! I'll salute a *man* anytime, but damned if I'll salute an officer," was his usual reply.

Overall, his wartime service, from 1945 to 1947, wasn't exactly a memorable experience, except that it steered him into becoming an anarchist. In addition to his MP work and the vice squad, most of his time was spent mopping miles of floors and peeling tons of potatoes in the mess hall until the day he was discharged at Fort Dix, New Jersey.

Unlike other authors who went to war, such as James Jones and Norman Mailer, Abbey never got to be a corporal, though not because the army didn't try. He was promoted twice and twice demoted. All he salvaged from his military career was one Colt automatic, chrome-plated by an Italian craftsman, which he smuggled past the guards when he was mustered out as a private.

As he saw it later, his military years were not a complete waste of time, because he became more persuaded than ever to distrust large institutions and their regulations, and to believe, as his father did, in self-rule. True to form, as soon as he received his honorable discharge papers, he promptly mailed them back to the War Department with these words across the top: *Return to Sender.* The FBI took note. Unbeknownst to Abbey until years later, he had already attracted the FBI's interest for an act of civil disobedience on Abraham Lincoln's birthday in 1947.

On the bulletin board at nearby Indiana State Teachers College in Indiana, Pennsylvania, he had posted a notice on unruled white paper that called upon students and faculty members to mail their draft credentials to President Truman, or burn them. "This sounds like a foolish, crackpot scheme," proclaimed the notice, "but it is not. It is much more than that. It is much worse than that—it is a form of civil disobedience.

"That's something rather old-fashioned but in times like these, when America's government is diverting the major portion of its expenditures to armaments and our military leaders are trying to fasten permanent peacetime conscription on the nation, then, as Thoreau said, 'It is not too soon for an honest man to rebel.'" While such an act seems like a minor provocation today, in the patriotic years after the war, it was a considered ultra-radical.

Besides Abbey, the other signers of the campaign to burn draft cards—the real organizers—were the Reverend Donald Harrington of the Community Church in Manhattan, Professor Milton Mayer of the University of Chicago, the economist Dr. Scott Nearing, and Professor Paul Schlipp of Northwestern University. Presenting themselves as honest and sincere, they said they were rebelling, not just against what they considered a violation of personal liberty, but "the slow and deadly drift towards World War III, an international armament race, and universal conscription."

The next day, an FBI agent based in Pittsburgh filed the following report on the incident to headquarters in Washington, D.C.: "Abbey hates the army and all things military." It was the FBI's first report on Abbey, but not the last.

Abbey remained on their watch list for years after that incident, though he didn't know it until shortly before he died. "I'd be insulted if they weren't watching me," he quipped to a reporter when a Freedom of Information request elicited a fat file in the early eighties.

For a few months after being discharged, he toyed with some odd jobs near his family home, took some courses at Indiana State Teachers College, and tried to figure out what to do next. Meantime, dreams of heading west were stirring. Like Henry Thoreau, he dreamed of going there for good. "Eastward I go by force," wrote the Bard of Walden Pond. "I must walk to Oregon and not to Europe . . . every sunset which I witness inspires me to go West."

Thoreau never got there, and young Abbey wasn't about to repeat the mistake of growing older and longing for deserts, mountains, and rivers he had never seen. In his heart, he knew what had sustained him during those two dreary military years were the vivid memories of what he had seen on that first trip west—"the very things that are free, decent, sane, clean and true, what I had seen—and felt—yes, and even smelled—on that one blazing afternoon on a freight train rolling across Northern Arizona."

While his high school contemporaries settled down and found jobs, Abbey decided to return to those haunting places. Within him, the seeds of anarchy were sprouting. More than any of his friends, at the age of twenty he was already an anti-establishment true believer in the Bill of Rights. It was to be a passion that would seethe in him until the end.

When the time to go west was at hand, Ed didn't find it easy to leave the family at Old Lonesome Briar Patch, though he disliked many aspects of life there. Abbey's mother wept when he left for "what was out there," but not in front of him. Never in front of anybody. That was an unwritten Abbey code.

Relishing the notion of being a born-again Westerner, Edward Abbey had to leave, as did Henry Holyoak Lightcap, a thinly disguised Abbey in *The Fool's Progress,* roaring westward at evening, red sun of Texas burning in his eyes. The smoke of El Paso—city on fire—smeared across a yellow sky. Barbed wire. Windrows of dead tumbleweed piled on the fence, range over the rocky desert, munching on cactus, on the dried seedpods of thorny mesquite. Newspapers yellow with lies, bleached by the sun, flap like startled fowl with ragged wings across the asphalt road. Welcome to the West.

As he had anticipated, the Southwest set his imagination ablaze, and it remained ablaze until he wrote his last published words in a book of aphorisms, *A Voice Crying in the Wilderness*, published after his death:

> This is an honest book. (Never mind the occasional self-contradictions.) It warns you at the outset that my sole purpose has been a private and egocentric one. I have no thought of serving others; such ambition is beyond both my intention and my powers. I am myself the substance of my book . . . Farewell then, from Abbey, on the parapet of the tower at Fort Llatikcuf, Arizona, in this windblown, dust-obscured midday twilight on this third day of March in the year 1989 anno Domini.

Toward the end of his life, and knowing death was near, Abbey returned to Pennsylvania more often. He returned to visit with relatives, to listen to the doves, to think of his origins, and to remember the sights and sounds of his childhood. And he came to hear the wail of the iron locomotive on the C&O line, to see the moon beaming down on the ice floes in Crooked Creek, and to call on the Big Woods, or what was left of them, perhaps still visited by the spirits of the past.

And he would always find time to spend with Howard. "Were we friends?" asks Howard. "I hated him at times when he showed his contempt for me. I disagree with much of his philosophy—'I'd rather kill a man than a snake,' as he said when he was trying to prove his love of nature. He was the epitome of selfishness most of the time. But were we friends? He sent me fifty dollars without question one time when I was stuck in New Orleans. He welcomed me happily in New Mexico one winter when I was between jobs. And I always reciprocated when he came back to Pennsylvania. I would have crossed the country for him, and I did a couple of times. Were we friends? Hell no. We were brothers."

Though Abbey had gone west for good, he had left his imprint in the hills of Home, and on the people there, and they had left theirs on him. "He always wanted to go west once he made that first trip," says Nancy Abbey. "But Appalachia was always a part of who he was. He spent much of his life trying to pull the different environments and cultures together. When I remember our early years, I remember that we fought. We cried. We laughed. We were a pretty sad lot."

Until the end, Ed Abbey's heart was torn between memories of the rolling hills of his youth, and fantasies of what his childhood might have been, fantasies that developed when he was marooned on a fire lookout tower in the scorching desert of the Southwest.

Unlike Thoreau, who insisted on one world at a time, Abbey lived in two worlds, and his feelings for both knew no bounds. Reconciling them in his mind, in his heart, and on sheets of paper in his Royal typewriter was the basis for much of his literary legacy.

THE ANARCHIST EMERGES

Anarchy is Democracy taken seriously.
> —"THEORY OF ANARCHY," *ONE LIFE AT A TIME, PLEASE*

We cannot entrust the management of our lives to kings, priests, politicians, county commissioners.
> —*A VOICE CRYING IN THE WILDERNESS*

Abbey arrived at the University of New Mexico in 1947, armed with little more than some GI bill money and the desire to become a writer. Now twenty years old and painfully shy, he waded into a college career that would last off and on for ten years, climaxing with a master's degree in philosophy. His thesis was "Anarchy and the Morality of Violence."

"What I remember about him the most," says Joe Ferguson, a fellow student and now a retired book salesman in Flagstaff, Arizona, "is that he always wore an old brown coat that looked like it had been wired together, hung out with the beatniks, played the flute, and wandered around on the fringes of things. He had a scraggly beard. My mother, who had him for a student in an art class, said he looked like a bum. But that was OK with her because maybe he was a thinker."

Other students remember him as a tall, fuzzy-bearded, gray-eyed youth with a hawklike visage whose shabby dress and withdrawn demeanor reminded them of weathered photos of the young D. H. Lawrence. Years later, Abbey confessed to a friend that he was kind of a schlemiel, the sort of kid who hugs the walls at large gatherings, hoping a beautiful woman will walk up and tell him she loves him, but also hoping, just as much, that people will leave him alone, letting him observe from shadowy places.

He often tried to date black women, because it was then a cool and rebellious thing to do, but when he asked them they would laugh at him, all except for one who went out with him—once. Fellow students recall that he didn't just try to be unlike them. He was. And for such a reserved young man, he was almost always in trouble. One of his professors, Dr. Hubert Alexander, remembers the evening when Abbey and a friend, having been ejected from the lodgings of some ladies, were caught by campus police for bringing a quart of bourbon whiskey onto university property.

Soon after the arrest, Alexander was summoned to the dean's office where the whiskey and Abbey and his cohort were taken for resolution of their egregious crime. "We don't need people around like these two," Alexander recalls the dean saying, "and now what are we going to do with the whiskey? It's illegal for us to have it, too." Abbey and his friend, sensing they were out of danger, smiled from the back of the room, as the two professors hid the bottle in a filing cabinet.

"It was a ludicrous scene," Alexander recollects. Of the young Mr. Abbey, to whose defense he came that night, Alexander says, "He never talked a lot. But he was quite emphatic when he did. He was an interesting young man, different, very different."

As for Abbey's general attitude, Archie Bahm, one of his philosophy professors, says, "Temperamentally, Abbey was already an anarchist by the time he arrived here. He was a lover of nature and antagonistic to people who were officially destroying it."

If there's a cardinal characteristic that set Abbey's life apart from the vast majority of his contemporaries in the sleepy 1950s, it was that he never took the easy road. He always seemed to choose the one that offered the most resistance. He called it Abbey's Road, and the motto was: "Sentiment without action is the ruin of the soul."

Once, while exploring Big Bend National Park in west Texas during his student days, or so the story he told goes, Abbey and a young lady arrived at a fork on a dusty dirt road. According to his well-worn 1948 Texaco map, the road that forked right was unpaved, ungraded, and hooked and curved for fifty miles through desert wasteland to the southwest corner of the park.

Politely but firmly, the resident ranger advised them that the road was so unfit for travel that it was closed and marked with a sign saying No Road, and that the left fork was the safer route. Abbey took the road to the right.

Pulling up the No Road sign, Abbey drove his companion's brand new convertible down the bad road, then stopped and replaced the sign. All went well for about half a mile, then the road got rougher. His girlfriend insisted on turning back, but Abbey kept on driving through dry gulches and steep drops; enduring flat tires, sprung doors, bent tie rods, a steaming radiator, and a burning clutch plate.

By the time they arrived at Rio Grande Village three days later, the car was a wreck, and the woman, who hadn't spoken to him for most of the trip, left town on the first bus. "Determination is what counts," Abbey was to write of the adventure. "I had to see what lay beyond the next ridge."

Those qualities—obstinacy and determination—which often got him into difficulty in his personal life, were also what fired his literary efforts in striking back against the industrialization of the Southwest. Even though the struggle might be hopeless, he had no intention of surrendering; someone had to fight back.

And, from his redoubts in Utah, New Mexico, and Arizona, "a playful jolly sunny land in the 1950s," he called the region, fighting back is exactly what he did. Broke most of the time, and living on about $150 a month compliments of the GI Bill, he complained that he couldn't afford a good horse, let alone a decent car: "The best I could do in 1947 and 1948, was to buy a third-hand Chevy sedan and roam the West on holidays and weekends."

For the first few years in New Mexico, Abbey lived with a bronco rider he called Mac. They rented a cinderblock house on about forty acres in the lovely Sandia Mountains east of Albuquerque, the "Duke City" of *The Brave Cowboy*. "We were both crude, shy, ugly, obnoxious—like most college boys," Abbey reported.

By all accounts, he and Mac had some unbridled times together, beginning nearly every day when they would roar down rough dirt roads to classes some twenty miles away, making the trip in less than fifteen minutes. Usually, Mac would be far too hungover to drive, so Abbey would take the wheel while Mac slumped in the front seat, clutching a big .44-caliber pistol, shooting in his waking moments at road signs, rabbits, anything that moved.

Mac was a cowboy, and Abbey wanted to be one, too. He was always trying to prove that he could do it.

"I'd be on this crazy, crackpot horse going up, down left, right, inside out. Hanging on to the saddle horn with both hands.

The Anarchist Emerges

While Mac sat on the corral, throwing beer bottles at us and laughing. Every time I got thrown off, Mac would say: 'Now get right back on there, Ed. Quick, quick. Don't spoil 'em.'"

—"FREE SPEECH: THE COWBOY AND HIS COW,"
ONE LIFE AT A TIME, PLEASE

What Abbey learned from Mac, and also from William Eastlake, on whose ranch he tried to learn to wrangle, was that he would never make a cowboy, but he could be a scholar, perhaps a writer. Indeed, old hands on the university faculty remember that Ed was always sketching ideas for books, polishing his first novel *Jonathan Troy* (published in 1954), and plunging into the history of anarchy to find its relevance for him.

While Abbey found many of his researches into anarchism fatiguing, they were also intriguing. Early on he studied the works of an ancient Chinese philosopher named Chuang Tzu, whose allegorical essay written in 300 B.C. about a man and horses, according to Abbey's private diaries, etched a permanent imprint on his consciousness.

As the parable begins, Chuang Tzu observes that horses have hooves to carry them over frost and snow, and hair to protect them from the wind and cold. They eat grass, drink water, and show their spirit by flinging up their heels as they gallop over the plains.

Such is the real nature of horses, Tzu observed. Then one day a man appeared who convinced the local people that he truly understood the management of horses better than they did. So they stepped aside as he branded the horses, pared their hooves, slipped halters on them, tied them up, hobbled their legs, and locked them in stables. Before long, three of the horses died. But that failed to deter the man, who told onlookers once again that he understood the management of horses better than they.

Day after day, he kept the horses on short rations of food and water, threatening them with the whip and alternately galloping and trotting them whether they required exercise or not. When half the horses had died, some of the local people began to criticize the man's way with horses, but he told them that it was for their own good, that he truly had a superior understanding of the management of horses.

Then one day, all the horses died.

Abbey grasped the allegory; the man represented the State, and the horses were citizens. After a few months in the Southwest, Abbey had become angrily aware of what the State was doing there: woodlands were being destroyed by the U.S. Forest Service; industrial tourism was invading the National Parks; cattle grazing on public land was, in effect, ruining recreational experiences for countless hikers and wanderers. And he refused to look the other way.

In addition to studying Chinese philosophers, Abbey delved into Plato, James Joyce, the Greek anarchist Diogenes, and Thoreau. A pledge Thoreau had made a century earlier became Abbey's own, that he "did not want to belong to any incorporated society which I have not joined."

In his philosophy classes, Abbey had difficulty picturing what an anarchist even looked like. Were they slightly absurd people who went around wearing beards and muttering to themselves? he wondered in a 1951 notebook entry. Did they carry sticks of dynamite in their pockets? If he were to become a serious, practicing anarchist, he speculated, what kind would he choose to be? A solidly objectified anarchist, a libertine, possibly a licentious edition, a dixiecratic anarchist, a somewhat truculent or contraceptual one, or a barefoot ironical version?

Unable to decide, he ducked the question. "Anarchism is a ridiculous business," he wrote in a notebook one evening. "It's possibly a pathetic business, certainly not to be taken seriously—like philosophy."

Nevertheless, his explorations never lagged. "Perhaps anarchists aren't the only ones who throw bombs," he speculated. "Look at Hiroshima, Guernica and Rotterdam!" An aspect that appealed to him was that an anarchist cannot satisfy the virtues politicians and bureaucrats hold most high, namely order, safety, and tidiness.

In a significant evolutionary step in his thinking, he concluded that anarchism wasn't really about bombs, as the Bolshevik revolution had been, but about opposition to the coercive power of government, what Tolstoy called the "organized violence of the state."

How could one recognize this brand of anarchy? Abbey felt that he saw flashes of it in Gary Cooper's eyes as he waited for the train in the film *High Noon* and in the secret shame on Burt Lancaster's face on film as he went about caricaturing an Apache warrior. He thought that he heard it, too, in the silence that followed Private Prewhitt's bugle call in *From Here to Eternity*.

It was Abbey's task to parley that subtle quality with what he saw happening in the world around him. "The worst part of the nostalgia hanging over our cities, is that it is a justified nostalgia," Abbey reflected. "We have made a sorry mess of things. I don't care what *Time, Life* or *Fortune* magazine says."

Now the young Abbey, in the late 1940s and early 1950s, had struck upon the theme that was to dominate his writings: the true dream of the anarchist was the Western frontier—its deserts, mountains, and rivers—with dependence on space and wilderness, courage, self-reliance, and self-rule. "Now it is gone," he concluded in 1950, "foreclosed, outmoded, fenced out, smothered under the progress."

Looking back, it is difficult to dredge up the name of an American writer in those days, save perhaps Bernard DeVoto, who was recognizing the West for what it really was, for what it was becoming: no longer a comfortable place for the liberty-loving individual. No wonder that Abbey decided early that he had no interest in emulating the escapist adventure writing of Zane Grey, John Van Dyke, or in later years, Louis L'Amour.

And he refused to identify with Hollywood-created, cinematic myths of the Old West, deciding instead to be guided by poet e. e. Cummings's observation earlier in the century that "Buffalo Bill's now defunct."

Much, if not all, of the escapist writing Abbey abhorred echoed familiar themes of the past—the Indian wars, famous gunfighters, Sitting Bull, Geronimo and Buffalo Bill, the virgin frontier. Abbey got a different message, and began to fashion a writing career that went "deeply against the grain of our precautionary times," says Yavapai College Professor Donn Rawlings.

Day by day, resentment welled up in Abbey because the region where he lived, which he felt embodied holy qualities, was being targeted as a national sacrifice area for an "energy crisis" fabricated by the government and the energy industry to raise prices.

The real outlaws, he decided, were Wall Street financiers, politicians, energy company oligarchs, and the Pentagon for creating nuclear messes and building secret missile sites hidden away in remote mountains. That was Abbey in the early 1950s: feeling trapped in a crossfire between the Hollywood-created nineteenth-century myth and shocking twentieth-century reality. Exposing the existence of that gap, and trying to close it, would be the basis of his lifework.

Before he was twenty-two years old, he knew this was an accurate perspective and was now certain that America must take an entirely different direction. Whenever doubts arose, which they sometimes did, he always had Walt "Resist Much, Obey Little" Whitman and Henry Thoreau to strengthen his resolve. Echoes of their thoughts and sentiments ricochet through his writings in word portraits of resistance against the State—of individuals fighting back when their rights as citizens are threatened.

So we see him virtually alone, first in his student body—and then in American literature—grappling with the meaning of anarchism. To Abbey, anarchy was not interesting merely in the academic sense; he believed it might develop into a serious movement to save the country he loved from going down the greed-paved, dead-end road of techno-industrialism. That would mean recapturing a certain old-American sensibility—lofty national ideals and contempt for betrayers of those ideals. Flying the black flag of anarchism, the Old Conservative was emerging.

Millions of Americans had no such concerns, being far too busy moving from cities to the suburbs under the benign leadership umbrella of President Eisenhower. It was the greatest eruption of apparent tranquillity and materialism yet seen in America. That vision was not Ed Abbey's. He suspected that something was very wrong in his native land.

Recalls classmate Joe Ferguson: "People made fun of Abbey because of his beatnik look but, in fact, he was ahead of his time, willing to sacrifice things other students did for fun in order to write."

When he wasn't writing, challenging authority at the university, or chasing women, Abbey went out to explore the desert, determined to immerse himself in the Southwest of his profoundest imaginings. He saw himself as a prospector on a search, not for gold but for "revelation," in "the rust red sea, the lilac purple sea, the wave-wrinkled but static sea of the desert," remote places where few dared venture alone in "red mountains like mangled iron."

His love for the Southwest kept deepening, for the wildness and unpredictability, for the searing, purifying heat, open spaces, scorpions and vultures, rattlesnakes and lupine.

It had to be spared the industrialism and urbanization sweeping like mechanized Roman legions across the rest of the United States. Most of Abbey's friends thought he was a foolishly romantic Don Quixote, flailing at the windmills of mindless, selfish growth. Nobody could singlehandedly stop progress, they advised him; progress was what America was all about.

In reply, Abbey learned to argue that progress as measured by economic statistics alone was not really true progress. He was only in favor of progress defined as a change for the better. If national leaders meant population growth and increasing pollution quotients, then what they termed progress would inevitably be seen decades hence as a tragic joke.

When he was not hitting the books in order to graduate in 1951, Abbey toiled at various odd jobs, including newspaper reporting and bartending in Taos, New Mexico. Due to his reserve, he made few real male friends, but he loved the company of women, and in 1950 he began a marital career that would end after five wives and five children. He also produced a miniseries of tumultuous relationships. Asked by a friend why he married so early, and so often, Abbey cracked, "I thought that you had to get married before you could get laid."

It was shortly before he graduated with a degree in Philosophy and English that Abbey launched into his first marriage to a fellow student, Jean Schmechal. He expanded his horizons still further by going to Edinburgh, Scotland, with the enthusiastic support of his professors, as a Fulbright Scholar. Jean went with him but remained only a few weeks, during which time the marriage collapsed. It was such a failure that in later life, there were times when he refused to even acknowledge it.

Young Ed had become bored with Jean. Boredom was a quality, if not an emotion, that he was to display toward women often in years to come.

Now alone in Edinburgh, Abbey delved into Hume, Reid, Boswell, Scott, and Burns within the dank, antiquated walls of the university. Studying metaphysics and moral philosophy, he also wrote for hours every day. These were reflective, quiet days of reading; relishing tea, scones, sausages grilled over charcoal; and taking occasional trips to Austria and other parts of Europe, usually with German and South African female companions.

Besides skiing and learning to drink schnapps, Abbey fell for several young women who didn't discourage his advances. He had become an attractive young man with more than his share of animal magnetism. He was also rewriting his first attempt at a novel, *Jonathan Troy*, the tale of a Pennsylvania boy who longs for the American Southwest but is hopelessly entangled in a series of destructive relationships. He planned to mail it off as an unsolicited manuscript as soon as possible.

Unbeknownst to Abbey, when the snowy Swiss Alps began melting into record spring runoffs in 1952, the FBI began an investigation into the question of his loyalty to the United States. This aberrant surveillance, which lasted for years—probably until he died—began when U.S. agents based in Salzburg, Austria, observed him at a five-day April meeting in Vienna billed innocently as The International Conference in Defense of Children.

Moving expeditiously, an agent cabled the FBI's regional office in New York City to request a full field investigation on this young American who had attended a "communist-inspired meeting." To Abbey, it was no such thing, just something diverting to do for a few hours. But the possibility that Abbey was an innocent student obviously did not occur to U.S. security agents.

The return cable reported another item of interest for the FBI. It described an earlier Abbey provocation, the letter Abbey had posted on the college bulletin board five years earlier.

No one knows whether his master's thesis, "Anarchy and the Morality of Violence," submitted to professors Bahm and Alexander, might have contained a more vengeful bite had Abbey known that J. Edgar Hoover and his minions were watching his every move, but it's an interesting speculation. He won honors as it was.

Ironically, Abbey's principal theme was the excess of the State. In the introduction, he recounted that after World War II, anarchism was enjoying a revival; he cited writers such as sociologist C. Wright Mills, critics and poets such as Kenneth Patchen and Sir Herbert Read, and the novelists Aldous Huxley and George Orwell.

"Perhaps none of these writers," Abbey speculated, "would be willing to call himself an anarchist; but each, in his own way, has attempted to draw attention to the excesses of the nation-state and advocated, in one way or another, the decentralization of the State's political, economic and military power."

Meantime, FBI agents in Albuquerque, Pittsburgh, and later in Washington, D.C., where he worked as a clerk typist for the U.S. Geological Survey, were writing reports about him. Even though no derogatory information concerning his loyalty to the United States was ever unearthed, a full field investigation was implemented in 1952. The first nugget that turned up was Abbey's second marriage, to Rita Deanin of Passaic, New Jersey, and the quickie divorce from his first wife, Jean.

The agent accompanied his finding with a cautionary note: "Although Bureau rules and regulations in the investigation of these cases do not appear to cover this particular situation, the Bureau is requested to advise whether or not any special handling of a matter in this special category should be followed."

From FBI headquarters in Washington, the word came to the Albuquerque field office to proceed: "Bureau authority is not needed prior to initiating a security investigation of a student or a non-academic employee."

The FBI did manage to get something right. Upon his return from Scotland, Abbey did marry Rita Deanin, a fine artist who was also very beautiful, in December of 1952. It was a union that would end bitterly twelve years later, leaving her with custody of two children, Joshua and Aaron, and unpleasant memories of her life and times with Ed Abbey.

All the while, agents kept turning up old facts, such as Abbey's being fired from the university magazine over the fake Alcott quote, and went on to interrogate faculty and some of Abbey's former fellow students. One agent filed this explosive report: "Professors consider subject as a pacifist. . . . He is a person of rashness and immaturity, irritating coming from a man of his intelligence and capabilities."

Another unidentified source told the FBI that he was a great challenge to describe. And the agent wrote down this incendiary tip: on the one hand, Abbey was "an exceptionally brilliant individual who graduated with honors. On the other, he was an individualist in his thinking in all respects, and as a student, showed evidence of being a potential writer."

The agents also learned another fact that raised their national security hackles: Abbey had attended a meeting of the California-based Fellowship for Reconciliation, a group of pacifists who opposed the draft in peacetime. Anonymous informants told the FBI that Abbey was against war in any form.

His new marriage to Rita was scarcely two months old before the FBI located an informant who predicted that marriage would fail, too, because Abbey's individualism was such that it might cause a "rupture in their marital relations. Subject and his wife do not get along well, he being the one who desires to follow his creative writing and she being one who desires a home and association with others."

The FBI, not at all discouraged by its inability to find any seditious dirt on their "subject," kept up the hunt into how he spent his time. As agents dug, one informant came to Abbey's defense. He was writing a book, the person argued, and if the investigation were to intensify, or become known, Abbey could lose his part-time job with the local water company.

"I know that job is his only means of support," the informant said. "The boy would be rather hard pressed to find another job where he could work enough to put himself through this period of writing. He has signed a contract with Dodd and Mead [for *Jonathan Troy*], and right now it is rather vital to him that he has some peace of mind in order to continue his writing."

The FBI ignored that plea, and also brushed aside comments from other students and faculty who said they had no idea why J. Edgar Hoover was so interested in Abbey; he was no Communist. He loved his country and was certainly no threat to national security.

Every once in a while, however, Abbey would write a letter to the student paper, *The Daily Lobo,* attracting the attention of federal agents and spurring them on. One such letter was published in 1952.

In this day of the Cold War, which every day shows signs of becoming warmer, the individual who finds himself opposed to war is apt to feel very much out of step with his fellow citizens.

As an isolated individual, he feels desperately inadequate either to check the tide or to make significant contributions which might serve to remove the occasion of wars. He feels, nevertheless, the essential wrongness of war, and is searching for an alternative.

Although written by Abbey, the letter was also signed by fifteen others and announced that a group was forming to discuss the "implications and possibilities of no wars." Although it was only a letter, FBI agents suspected sedition.

Soon thereafter a campus informant fed the agents more dirt: "Abbey's persistence in pursuing his own somewhat pointless course seems to me to suggest a stubborn ego, a taste for shocking the reader, a lack of maturity." Another source revealed that Abbey was "an intellectual type person and read many periodicals on philosophy. He is a believer in racial equality, opposed to strong government . . ."

During that year, an agent in Pittsburgh picked up several other disturbing (to him) details about Abbey: that he was reserved, had a suspiciously scholarly disposition, and was a good rifle shot. Indeed, Abbey had shot with several rifle clubs in and around Pennsylvania, and had to change from one club to another because of quarrels with club members.

Soon after his second marriage, Abbey took a wild gamble and enrolled as a philosophy student at Yale University, thinking he might enhance his reputation and earn a Ph.D. It was a truly eccentric experience because it only lasted a total of two weeks. Not only did Abbey dislike his professors and his classmates, he did not understand symbolic logic—and evidently did not try very hard to do so. Why did he want a doctorate, he was asked years later by author Lawrence Clark Powell. "Status, I suppose," Abbey replied. "Status and false ambition."

The following spring an informant tipped an agent that Abbey was trying to secure summer work as a fire lookout in the Carson National Forest near Taos, New Mexico. The informant, who claimed to be a friend of Abbey's, declared that "there's an honest doubt in my mind as to Mr. Abbey's temperamental fitness for the position he is seeking." Despite that Judas's assertion, Abbey got the job and began a seasonal career that would support his writing until it could support him. As he was to describe that career in his essay, "My Life As A P.I.G.":

> For seventeen seasons, off and on, I worked as ranger, as a fire lookout, as a garbage collector for the Park Service, occasionally for the Forest Service. Since most of these jobs involved, to some extent, what is called "protection" (law enforcement) as well as "interpretation," I too have played the role, or more exactly played at the role of Smokey the Cop. I wore a uniform and a badge. I carried a .38 in the glove compartment of a government pickup. I sometimes harassed people, especially hippies. And shot two dogs and a number of beer cans. In self-defense.
>
> An odd part to play, you might think, for an anarchist, a dedicated scofflaw.
>
> Perhaps not. I've never known a serious policeman who had respect for the law.
>
> —*Abbey's Road*

In future years, agents would follow him to Arches National Monument in Moab, Utah, where he compiled the notes that later became *Desert Solitaire;* to Hoboken, New Jersey, where he spent a winter as a welfare caseworker; to Sunset Crater National Monument near Flagstaff in 1963; to the Nevada

State Welfare Department in 1965, where he drove a school bus; and to Canyonlands National Park in Utah in the summers of 1965 and 1966.

For the moment, however, the FBI was busy probing into the months Abbey had spent on his Fulbright in Scotland. In response to a request from FBI headquarters, the American Embassy in London reported that Abbey had taken courses in moral philosophy and metaphysics: "He was not a very active student, and no one formed any particular impressions of him at all . . . he was not well known to anyone at the University."

Days later, another cable from London reported that Abbey went out of his way to avoid social functions, and held strong prejudices, "but his outlook was always very pro-American. He never left the impression that he had any radical views whatsoever." In retrospect, the FBI probably knew more about Abbey's travels than anyone but his parents.

Abbey loved irony, but there was one he didn't get to appreciate until the late eighties: though characters in his books talked about and performed acts that were decidedly felonious, such as dynamiting Glen Canyon Dam on the Colorado River (first suggested in *Desert Solitaire* and later developed as the main plot in *The Monkey Wrench Gang*) it's evident to anyone reviewing Abbey's FBI file that Hoover's agents never read a word their "subject" wrote. What if they had? What actions would the government have taken against him?

Consider, for instance, the plot of *Jonathan Troy*, in which Abbey creates his first anarchist, an egotistical nineteen-year-old who alienates everyone and gets into a bar fight that ends in the death of Nat Troy, his father. Nat is killed by a policeman when he pulls a pistol on some drunks who are trying to force him to kiss the American flag. Afterward, Jonathan hangs out with a group of men who are called "communist bastards" by the townspeople.

Though the novel was not a critical success—*The New York Times* called it "a symphony of disgust"—it did feature some striking prose about the damage coal mining was causing in the hills of Appalachia, where Troy had spent his early years.

> The monster was quiet now, empty, the brain abandoned for the day, but beyond the railroad and on the other side of the slow sulfurous creek the coke-ovens were alive, flaming and smoking, and a small mine-car crept across their tops over the narrow rails. Smoke came through the windows of the car and with it the smell of burning coal and hydrogen gasses.
>
> Jonathan rolled up the windows. They drove past the long lines of the coke-ovens and past hills of burning slag—great boney piles of waste from the mines, of yellow rock and red ash, with flames creeping like blue spirits from pits and craters in the smoldering mass.

In a preview of his later themes, Abbey depicted machines and technology as monsters from another world, monstrosities bent on destroying the very soul of the living land.

To be sure, *Troy,* in which Abbey developed the theme of anarchy, can be assailed critically from many angles. But the most trenchant criticism was delivered by Abbey himself.

He delivered it through the person of a teacher he called Feathersmith who castigated Troy's own first novel, *The Lyric Cry,* because it lacked "consistency of characterization, narrative continuity, scrupulous clarity in presentation, credible psychological motivation, integrity of purpose, authenticity of dialogue and description, and the orderly development of structure."

Here, Abbey was poking fun at one of his favorite targets—himself. Rather than list all the praises he had received over the years, Abbey fancied recording all the insults and threats; they somehow stirred the heart of the mountain rebel.

As for other book critics, while they complained about the novel's incoherence, some noted his perception of the West as a place of sanity, freedom, and escape. And some singled out his writing style in certain passages for being marked, as one put it, by "elegance, close detail, complex syntax, verbal force, symbolic power and vivid imagery. . . . Its style startles and arrests the reader; its grace and power of perception foreshadow greatness to come."

Most notable about his creation of *Troy* is that, as a young man, he recognized the dichotomy between what he regarded as a decadent civilization in the East and the promising freshness of the remaining Western wilderness. He told his readers that escaping from one to the other would not resolve the conflict. He found this to be true in his own life, yearning as he did for the deserts when he was visiting his parents, and dreaming of the hills of home when he was stuck on some remote fire lookout tower in the high desert.

Abbey sought the best of both worlds, and he succeeded by recognizing that paradox was to be embraced. It was necessary bedrock for himself and his writing, and throughout his life, he valued it.

Two years later, *The Brave Cowboy*, also sold to Dodd and Mead, arrived in bookstores, and this time, Abbey's tale of a young cowboy driven from the open range by barbed wire and government meddling drew considerable notice. Enter Jack Burns, a stubborn anarchist, adrift in the twentieth century with the illegal habit of cutting that freedom-restricting barbed wire whenever he happens upon it. For Burns, this is a routine and an honorable act of protest against the intrusion of powerful ranching interests and the U.S. government's program of leasing public land for livestock grazing at low prices, a program subsidized by all taxpayers. The plot turns on Burns's efforts to rescue a friend who has been jailed for refusing to be drafted.

Some book critics saw this as a perversion of the historical past; another said it was just another pulp Western.

Clearly, the cowboy's story is markedly different from the cowboy tales of Luke Short, Zane Grey, and Owen Wister. It's a pulp Western turned inside out: Abbey has Burns go to jail to save his friend after he intentionally creates a barroom brawl rather than relying on the old cowboy hero cliche of pulling down jail walls with a team of horses. Once inside prison walls, he discovers that his friend, Paul Bondi, refuses to break out, complaining to Burns that he is tempting him with "romantic, outlandish, impossible, nineteenth century notions. Frankly, Jack, I'm a little shocked."

Hardly a stock plot, this. The cowboy doesn't ride into town, shoot the guys in black hats, then ride off into the sunset. Burns decides to break jail without his best friend and gallop off to the smoky distant mountains. But his escape is a futile one. On his trail are swarms of police and an air force helicopter.

For a time Burns eludes the gathering swarms of lawmen, even shooting down a military helicopter with his trusty old Winchester. "You'd think we were chasing a ghost," rasps the sheriff, "an invisible cowboy with an invisible horse."

Burns is not destined to escape to freedom. He simply does not fit in; the mores of the Old West are gone and there is no room for him in the New West. Crossing a highway outside of Duke City, Burns is run down by a truck full of modern plumbing products; the last we see of this antihero, he's bleeding on a Navajo rug provided by a sympathetic passing motorist.

Does he die? The reader can't be sure. In any case, the symbolism is clear and vivid: what an overbearing bureaucracy is unable to accomplish, mindless modern technology, in the form of a modern truck loaded with modern toilets, does. The New West is bent on destroying the values of the Old West as represented in the person of John W. Burns. Abbey tells us that there is no place in modern civilization for an anarchistic, old-time cowboy who places freedom above all.

Whether or not Burns died in that book, Abbey just couldn't let Burns die for good. He shows up again in *The Monkey Wrench Gang*, then in *Good News*, and in Abbey's final novel, *Hayduke Lives*.

Symbolic of justice, Burns assumes many of the characteristics of the Lone Ranger. He moves in and out of the shadows, but by the time he reappears in *Hayduke Lives*, thirty-two years after *The Brave Cowboy*, he is haggard and one-eyed, but well-armed and still resisting Big Government and Big Business. He remains Abbey's symbol of America and justice, the frontier embodiment of the founders' dream, though battered and weary of battling injustice.

> [T]he Masked Man sat upon his saddle in the middle of his sagging horse. His gloved hands rested on the pommel, holding reins and a lead rope. His huge hilarious Hollywood cowboy-hat, once pure white and stiff as cardboard, now gray with filth and sweat and salt, floppy and frayed around the brim, rested on his small head.
>
> He wore the tight pullover shirt, no buttons, with lace-up collar, and the pants and the boots and the two big ivory-handled shooting irons in the tooled and silver-mounted holsters.
>
> —*Hayduke Lives*

With *The Brave Cowboy*, twenty-nine-year-old Abbey succeeded in placing the Old West in a modern setting. In Abbey's New West, stealing a horse or getting drunk is no longer a good cause for jailing. Far more challenging issues prompt citizens to break the law—belief, principle, and morality.

In Jack Burns, Abbey created a character who steadfastly refuses to go along with the requirements of a government he doesn't trust, whose bureaucracies are deaf and unaccountable to the people. Neither the rustler nor the hustler of a grade B Western, Burns's friend Bondi is jailed for his philosophical and moral convictions, even refusing Burns's offer to break him out because the moral thing to do is serve out his term, even if, in so doing, he suffers injustice.

There is futility in Burns's actions, critics pointed out; too much of it for some of their tastes. After all, this was 1956, when hope filled the air in America. But most central to the book's integrity, contended John McKee, writing in the *New Mexico Humanities Review,* "is that the voice one hears most is not that of any of the characters, but that of the author." While that was a fair assessment, McKee also found the book worth reading for the fact that Abbey "makes you see and hear and taste and feel. He comes as close to writing actuality as the language allows."

In reviewing Abbey's precocious "old tale in a new time," McKee and other critics took favorable note of the descriptions of Duke City, "waiting, stirring faintly but in silence—vague wisps of smoke and dust, glint of reflected light from moving objects, a motion of shadows . . . an undifferentiated patch of blue and grey shadow . . . edges ill-defined . . . extremities invisible."

From a distance, Jack Burns sees a world plagued by "pale phantoms, vexed by vagrant spirits, a mysterious realm . . . this valley of ghosts and smoke and unacknowledged sorrows."

Although the book is now recognized as among the finest novels about the modern West, many people only knew of *The Brave Cowboy* if they happened to have noted the screen credits of a movie based on it titled *Lonely Are the Brave,* in which the role of Burns is played by Kirk Douglas. Years later, Douglas called it his favorite film role, saying that he was moved by Abbey's theme: if one tries to be an individual, society will crush him.

The film came to Douglas in a serendipitous way, at one of those Hollywood cocktail parties he usually avoided. A man named Joe Berry, who wasn't even in the film industry, asked Douglas whether he had heard of Edward Abbey and his book about a doomed cowboy. Douglas hadn't, but he went out and bought a copy. "One look at the cover," Douglas was to recall, "and I almost never opened it: a cowboy with a gun in his hand, his bandaged head oozing blood. It had nothing to do with the story."

Once Douglas read the book, he knew he had to make the film. But it wasn't that simple. In previous times when Douglas loved a book and wanted to make it into a film, the studios denigrated the idea. To Douglas's dismay, the idea of turning Abbey's story into a film was also greeted antagonistically by studio potentates.

Douglas didn't give up. He remembered a clause in his contract allowing him to make a "disapproved" picture if it did not exceed a budget of three million dollars. That was it. The Abbey project would be a "disapproved" picture.

Douglas then got into a fracas with Universal Studios over the title. His choice was *The Last Cowboy,* whereas the studio wanted, *Forked Trail, Trail of Murder, Pursuit!, Ride the Man Down, Give Me a Gun,* or *The Granite Cage.* The studio finally settled on *Lonely Are the Brave,* though Douglas says to this day, he doesn't know what it means.

Abbey didn't like the title either, preferring the book's title, but was magnanimous enough to say that Dalton Trumbo's script, which went from his typewriter to location shooting with no revisions, was an improvement over his book. To Abbey, the film rights were worth $7,500, a bit part as a cop, and a couple days of pay as a location scout in and around Albuquerque, New Mexico. Nonetheless, he got to see his name on the silver screen.

For Douglas, filming the story of Jack Burns was physically exhausting, but he loved it. When it was completed, he pleaded with Universal not to release it like a cheap little Western. They did, and without press screenings, first-run theaters, or publicity.

For two weeks the film was a smash hit at the box office, breaking records in London and receiving fine reviews in *Time* and *Newsweek*. Abruptly, and inexplicably, the studio pulled the film. "The egos of the studio heads," Douglas recalled later, "wouldn't let them admit they had made a mistake, and capitalize on the publicity. They just dropped the picture flat."

Douglas never forgot Abbey's book, his own role in the film, or the way the studio fumbled what might have been an Academy Award candidate. When Abbey's obituary appeared in the *Los Angeles Times* in 1989, Douglas wrote a letter to the editor, taking him to task for failing to mention, as part of Abbey's literary legacy, *The Brave Cowboy*.

He wrote that he was "sad" about Abbey's death, and that he still received letters from fans calling *Lonely Are the Brave* their favorite film, and Douglas's portrayal of Jack Burns his best performance.

In *The Brave Cowboy*, Burns stands for anarchy. In the mid-1950s, while most Americans were still divided into Republicans and Democrats, arguing about the Cold War and either applauding or despising Senator McCarthy's witchhunts, Abbey was choosing a much different road. For him, Socialism, Communism, and Democratic Capitalism (the Welfare State) were all guilty of the same failing: accommodating themselves to and actively encouraging growth of the Nation-State.

And, when international rivalry intensifies nationalism, the State becomes, Abbey asserted, "the paramount institution of modern civilization, and exerts an increasing degree of control over the lives of all who live beneath its domination."

Abbey's primary contention was clear enough: as the State accelerates its power over the individual, the common man, everyman, begins to experience a change of role, from that of public citizen to "that of functionary in a gigantic and fantastically-complex social machine . . . a machine that is malfunctioning and dying."

He would describe this years later in his final novel, *Hayduke Lives.*

> . . . shark-nosed automobiles streamed in endless caravan through the gentle acid rain, spraying one another with a film of insoluble filth, a vicious servility oozing by in grease. Bonnie's heart sank when she considered the horror of the lives that most men led, trapped for nine, ten hours a day in slave gangs of traffic, the uniformed peonage—suit and tie and digital wristwatch—of the office galleys . . .
>
> . . .the nerve-wracking drudgery of the on-going, never-ceasing destruction and reconstruction, backhoes, front-end loaders, jackhammers, wrecking balls, freight trucks, nailguns, concrete culverts, asbestos insulation, I-beams, hardware, software, application forms, medical claim forms, auto insurance forms, income tax forms, garbage, mud, dust, sludge, whole monoclines of paper and anticlines of carbon and synclines of silent despair. The world of jobs.
>
> Koyaanisqatsi!

Koyaanisqatsi: turmoil, despair, life out of balance. It is an indelible experience to roam through Abbey's thesis, for this young prophet anticipated whole movements in American society that didn't become evident until the 1960s and '70s—most of them dramatizing life out of balance, and careening away from the hopes and dreams of Madison and Jefferson.

By the seventies, what had started as tremors shattered the crust of national complacency—the Vietnam War, the student revolts and race riots, the energy and environmental emergencies, and systematic lying by the executive branch and corporations to voters and consumers.

The thread that tied them all together was precisely the conundrum Abbey tackled in his thesis on anarchy: when the State and Big Business trounce the rights of individual citizens, how can their remedies be addressed? And by whom?

Abbey argued that the State dominates regardless of ideology, asserting that by the 1950s, the United States and the Soviet Union, despite the obvious differences in political philosophies, were showing distinct similarities: large, unresponsive bureaucracies.

Abbey refused to accept the conventional view that the process of "growth and convergence" could be explained in any satisfactory way. Certainly not in terms of Capitalism versus Socialism, or Democracy versus Communism. The theoretical key that could unlock the paradox was anarchy, he decided, and he set about to learn the movement's history and figure out its contemporary relevance.

It was obvious to the young student that anarchy had a very bad press, being associated traditionally with violence and illegality. "The word itself," he wrote, "is sufficient to evoke visions of riot, revolution, and bombings" even among citizens who might otherwise be empathetic.

In his thesis, the writing of which partially overlapped his first two novels, he poses two questions: To what extent is the association between anarchism and violence justified? If such a link exists, what justifies the use of violence? Abbey chose to define violence as the illegal or extralegal use of force, such as an act of terrorism, an assassination, or an organized insurrection to gain a political end.

This definition does not include occasional actions by criminals, or the "systematic and legalistic" use of violence launched by governments to protect their financial and strategic interests, such as petroleum reserves.

He used the term "morality of violence" to explore these questions: How can violence be justified, and under what circumstances; when is it right and when is it wrong? When is it good and when is it bad?

William Godwin was the theorist Abbey first assessed, an Englishman who pioneered a social theory so libertarian as to be anarchistic. In 1793, Godwin published a tract titled "Enquiry Concerning Political Justice," in which he advocated redistributing the power of the English State to parish communities, and eventually abolishing the State by peaceful methods.

What Abbey noted in particular about Godwin was that he was the first to establish a "terminological distinction," in Abbey's translation, that would become the standard for all anarchists (and the basis for much of Abbey's writings): "Human society is necessary, just and beneficial, but institutionalized government—the State—is a parasitic organ which feeds on society and also interferes, usually on behalf of the rich and powerful, in society's internal affairs."

In Godwin's scheme, violence was unnecessary because no social innovation, no matter how trivial, could be successful unless the majority of the citizens were not only willing and eager, but wise enough to accept such a change. "And if they are wise enough," wrote Abbey, "then violence is rendered not only pernicious but superfluous."

Godwin, however, was no pacifist. He believed in self-defense, and Abbey would weave that into his own works. If an Englishman's home is his castle, Abbey reasoned, then an American's home is his favorite forest, river, fishing stream, mountain, desert canyon, swamp, woods, or lake. "We have the right to resist and we have the obligation; not to defend that which we love would be dishonorable," Abbey asserted.

In his thesis, he also delved into the works of anarchist Pierre-Joseph Proudhon (1809–1865), known for his axiom "Property is theft" and for his belief that strong, centralized governments everywhere should be denounced.

Abbey utilized this idea in his third novel, *Fire on the Mountain.* It's the story of a New Mexico man, John Vogelin, whose ranch is being confiscated by the U.S. government for use as a missile range.

"You got any sense you better deal with these people while they're in a friendly mood. If you make them condemn the land, you might not get half of what they're offering now."

"I don't care about that. I don't want their dirty Government money. All I want is for them to let me alone, to let me work my ranch in peace, to let me die here and pass it on to my heir."

An equally effective passage expressing this idea is found in the later novel, *Good News.*

"What's your name man?" says the Chief softly. The prisoner swallows. "I got no name," he mutters. He bares his teeth in what is meant to be a grin. "My name is man. Hang me for it." "What is your name?"

The grin becomes wider. "My name is libertad. Viva libertad. My name is tierra o muerte. Hang me."

In place of a powerful, centralized State, Proudhon encouraged a loosely federated society of small independent farmers and craftsmen who would be entwined together in a system of mutual agreements and "free" contracts. Later in his life, Proudhon struggled to meld his anarchism with the inescapable reality of advancing industrialism. He never was able to shake his dream of the small working farmer, proprietor, and artisan.

Neither was Ed Abbey.

> We write . . . to defend the diversity and freedom of humankind from those forces in our modern techno-industrial culture that would reduce us all, if we let them, to the status of things, objects, raw material, personnel; to the rank of subjects.
>
> —*ABBEY'S ROAD*

What intrigued Abbey was that Proudhon agreed with Godwin's distrust of violence as a progressive political strategy, yet he peppered his language with violent notions. Proudhon the ironical anarchist comes alive in Abbey's writings in the form of acts of symbolic violence.

Abbey found kindred spirits in other sources, too, and recorded his feelings about the urbanization of the Southwest by favoring a line of Shakespeare's Marc Antony: "Pardon me, thou bleeding piece of earth, that I am meek and gentle with these butchers."

Abbey gleaned from Proudhon, if he hadn't suspected it already, that any bold social change would be seriously compromised if it came through a violent political revolution. In his heart of hearts, Abbey, like the nonviolent anarchists he studied, hoped for a program of general education that would lead peacefully and gradually, in time, to the suppression of the various liberty-draining agencies of the State—the Department of Defense, the FBI, the CIA, the Department of Energy.

Abbey, like Proudhon, viewed the society in which he lived as sick and divided; sick because the material interests of the modern world were divorcing individuals from their spiritual interests, which was leading to a moral imbalance and, ultimately, to violence. The solution to ending the schism and to restoring social peace was to reunite the material interest of equality with the spiritual one of liberty—under the reign of justice. Abbey concluded that the merging of the two *is* justice.

Through his studies, Abbey illuminated an historical fact that has been almost lost in our time; anarchy had been a benevolent movement for some two thousand years before 1917, when the nihilistic terrorism of the Bolshevik Revolution became synonymous with anarchy.

It was Karl Marx, a German, and later, Michael Bakunin, a Russian, who had distorted anarchy's true meaning, and now few people were able to recall its original thrust. Abbey decided it was Michael Bakunin (1814–1876) who was most responsible for the distortion. By fusing the anti-State libertarianism of Proudhon and Godwin with the socialism of Marx and his own theories, and by publicizing it through speeches and writing, Bakunin broadened anarchy's appeal from a handful of intellectuals to multitudes of unhappy factory workers, one-time craftsmen and farmers who had abandoned land and livestock for machines at the beginning of the Industrial Revolution.

Without "a terrible and bloody struggle," Bakunin believed, the defenders of the establishment (Church, State, and Capitalism) would never surrender their powers and privileges. And Bakunin was not one to make small plans. All institutions had to be destroyed, including armies and police, because all institutions were bound together in a series of informal ties.

While Bakunin was an apostle of violence when it was directed at the State, he was rigidly opposed to capital punishment, a paradox that fascinated Abbey and perhaps was one of the sources supporting his own reliance on irony, paradox, and contradiction.

In his writings, for example, Abbey thundered against ranchers and developers for wreaking havoc on the land, but at the same time, fervently believed they had the right to carry guns. He was a feisty opponent of any kind of gun control, which left some of his liberal friends uneasy, if not downright queasy; his environmental friends confused; and pro-gun people puzzled and nervous at their ally's position, since they disagreed with the rest of his positions on domestic and foreign policy.

Abbey's reasoning was that of the true anarchist:

If guns are outlawed, only the government will have guns. Only the police, the secret police, the military, the hired servants of our rulers. Only the government—and a few outlaws. I intend to be among the outlaws.

—"The Right to Arms," *Abbey's Road*

Although Abbey often quoted Bakunin in his writings, one senses a certain aversion that welled up in him about Bakunin's attitude toward violence. Perhaps the young scholar suspected Bakunin was less committed to the restoration of justice and morality than he was to violence—violence for violence's sake.

This sense is reflected in much of Abbey's writings, including his last novel, *Hayduke Lives*, in which George Washington Hayduke is warned by Doc Sarvis to harken to the code of ecowarrior: "Rule Number One is: Nobody gets hurt. Nobody. Not even yourself."

When reading Abbey's writings, it is wise to divine what lies between the lines, because he's not advocating the actual use of violence to destroy the industrial state, just numerous symbolic acts to shrink the power of the large institutions. He believed that the threat of violence is far more effective than actual violence. "Ed didn't believe in the system. It is that simple," says his friend Charles Bowden, "but he loved his country."

In the Southwest, Abbey described the system he warred against as "our own unique aristocracy, of a kind never before seen in the history of the world; this is an aristocracy of car dealers, land speculators, tract-slum builders, and Book of Mormon financiers.

"To oversee its aristocracy of overgrazers, clear-cutters, strip-miners, widespread operations, this aristocracy employs a corps of flunky journalists, who manage the regional TV stations and newspapers, and a regiment of Quisling politicians.

"This process is called 'growth.' Our Mafia aristocracy is indifferent to the fate of our children and grandchildren, for short-term profit is all that matters. To reverse this would require something like a political revolution in the Southwest, indeed, national politics."

Another anarchist that intrigued Abbey was Peter Kropotkin (1842–1921), a Russian aristocrat whose chief ambition was to provide anarchism with a scientific justification. As Abbey discovered, Kropotkin's writings zeroed in on one theme: The chief function of the State is to preside over the welfare of the various classes and rule through education and gentle persuasion.

Yet in his lifetime, when Russia erupted into a maelstrom of murder, terrorism, and assassination against the reigning czar, Kropotkin looked the other way. "He had a strange code of honor in that he was opposed to violence, yet he sympathized with it," Abbey observed in his thesis.

What emerges from Abbey's master's thesis is his affinity for those philosophers who felt a strong hatred for the morality of the modern middle class that was emerging in the nineteenth century—especially the commercial morality. Their feeling was the same one that nourished his own romantic vision as a philosophical anarchist, birthed in Allegheny mountains, and now flourishing in New Mexico.

As Abbey did in his own lifetime, the early anarchists confronted a world ever more controlled by the gods of merchandising and technology, and characterized by increasing subordination of individuals to vast national organizations.

Abbey saw these pressures growing exponentially in the twentieth century, threatening to create "a world in which there is less and less room for personal adventure, risk, daring, the pursuit of danger and glory."

Though it was already under siege by developers during his college years, the Southwest still offered plenty of room for personal adventure. And when he was alone in wild places, he was free to dream of a world in balance, unencumbered by pressures of money, family, and writing deadlines. There, he could be nourished by the deep spirit of nature.

Once, while riding on a bus to a drop-off point for a 115-mile hike through Arizona's Cabeza Prieta, Abbey encountered an old man bound from Houston, Texas, to Oakland, California. Looking out the window at the immense desert, the old man turned to Abbey and said, "Ain't nothing much out there."

> I was looking too. Somewhere about thirty, forty miles to the north, beyond the foreground of cactus, creosote bush and sand lay the route I planned to follow back.
>
> "Ain't nothing out there," I said. I wanted to reinforce his opinion. "Nothing but nothing."
>
> He nodded, smiling.
>
> In the double seat in front of us was a woman and her four children. A little girl with her hair braided in cornrows, with an elaborate set of strings and beads attached—like Cleopatra—looked back at us smiling at my ridiculous beard. She said, "Where you goin?" I said, "Home."

In researching his thesis, Abbey tried to find an intellectually safe harbor—as safe as his natural desert. He found it, concluding there was no lockstep relationship between anarchism and violence; it is possible, he wrote, to be "both an anarchist and a pacifist as the examples of Tolstoy and Gandhi illustrate."

Regrettably, Abbey concluded, few nineteenth-century anarchists were willing either to face the full implications of their enthusiasm for violence, or to contemplate the prospect that violence can do more harm than good, even if the cause is great. Though he valued their writings, he felt none had made anything other than a very "dubious" case for the use of violence.

In his thesis he asserted, "The anarchists devoted the chief effort of their lives to persuade their fellow men that the 'critical situation' had engulfed them and that political violence was therefore justified. But in this effort, for many and various reasons, they failed. And in so far as they failed in this, they also failed to justify violence."

The thesis was well received, but he could not resist satirizing the process in *The Fool's Progress*. The following is from Henry Holyoak Lightcap's final meeting with his master's thesis committee at the University of New Mexico:

Professor Ashcraft, existential phenomenologist, lit his pipe. The sweet odor of Old Sobranie began to pollute the air. Tell me, Lightcap, he said, how is your master's thesis coming along? What thesis was that, Henry thought. Quite well, sir, he said brightly, I've got a complete outline prepared and the introductory chapter.

When can we see it?

As soon as I get it typed up. Another week or two.

Typed up? Is it written down?

Henry hesitated. I cannot tell a lie. Yes I can. Oh sure I can. Of course, sir, he said. About forty pages with notes, (Cindy LeClair, 325-4484, Julie Mayberry, 326-5061, Candy Barton, 322-2191).

Herr Doktor Associate Professor Schoenfeld pondered Lightcap through the thick lenses of his academician's safety goggles——needed protection in a career devoted to the arc welding of ideas about ideas into ironclad structures of top-heavy, double-walled, unstable proportions. Mr. Lightcap, he said, tell us please eggzackly vat iss subject of thesis.

Henry rattled off the first phrase to pop into his brain: The Function of Erotic Love in the Analysis of Contingent Preconditionals in Heidegger's Sein and Zeit. No hesitation. A quick elusion.

Lightcap failed to win his master's degree, after being told by one professor that his future lay not in the groves of academe as a philosophy professor, but as a sanitation engineer, or better yet, as a shoe repairer. Unlike his character Henry Lightcap, Abbey of course did receive his master's degree in Philosophy, and true to his emerging anarchist spirit, refused to attend the graduation ceremony.

After graduation, Abbey knew he wanted to be a writer. But he really didn't know what that entailed. Although he'd had two novels published, he didn't see how he was going to make a living with his typewriter.

Neither did Lightcap in *The Fool's Progress*, who ruminates:

I sense a fork in the road. To the right, the right way, a bright shining highway led upward past the M.A. to the Ph.D., the tenured leisurely life of overpaid, underworked professorhood, a respectable life. Anyone who is paid much for doing little is regarded with great admiration.

To the left, a dingy path littered with beer cans and used toilet paper, led downward in darkness to a life of shame, part-time seasonal work and unemployment compensation, domestic strife, jug wine, uncertainty and shady deals, naive realism, stud poker, furtive philanderings, skeptical nominalism, pickup trucks, gross 19th century odd ball materialism.

In life, he created Abbey's road, a blend of Lightcap's two alternatives. He was hard at work on two new books, *Fire on the Mountain* and *Desert Solitaire*. There were already glimpses of the writer he was to become, and studying the anarchists had provided a powerful background. "It is said that the good old days are gone," he wrote in his diary around the time *Jonathan Troy* was published. "It is said that American anarchism was wiped out. That's true, but the ghost of it lingers on, haunting our souls, weakening our nerve with a sickly nostalgia."

He did much creative work during the many quiet hours spent on fire lookout towers throughout the Southwest. Lonely lighthouses of the forest, the U.S. government at one time maintained more than five thousand, many of them romantic places where men and women confronted raw undiluted nature, and themselves. It was a life that lured many other writers, including Jack Kerouac and Gary Snyder.

Shortly after receiving his graduate degree he took his first seasonal job with the National Park Service at Arches National Monument, then a remote outpost with few visitors, where he poured himself into honing his private journals. These became the basis for *Desert Solitaire*, published eleven years later, the work that would put him on the literary map to stay.

For Abbey, it was the beginning of a lifestyle, and a legend, that took him to astonishingly beautiful places such as Glacier National Park, Organ Pipe National Monument, the Coronado National Forest, and the North Rim of the Grand Canyon.

In those years, Abbey continued to find women irresistible. Yet he bridled against the yoke of monogamy and often couldn't wait to escape a relationship that was growing too intimate. It was another pattern, besides his anarchism, that he followed for most of his life. There were exceptions, and his marriage to Judy Pepper in August 1965, with whom he had a daughter named Susie, was one. Judy's death from leukemia five years later left him stricken with grief—and with a small child to care for.

Out of that tragedy he would produce a novel, *Black Sun,* the tale of a ranger who loves and then loses the love of a gorgeous woman. It was always his favorite, because it was really about his loss of Judy.

Like the *Black Sun* character Will Gatlin, Abbey wanted solitude and space. Yet there were times when he wished for visitors, so he would often write to young women he had met, asking them to come to visit him. Here is a letter he wrote one woman in Mesa, Arizona, many years ago:

Dear Anne:

I hope I didn't seem unfriendly the day you were here. I had a bad cold—but mainly I was constrained by the intense desire to touch you, to embrace you, kiss you. You looked (and you are) very beautiful. But obviously it was not the right day.

Please do come again, spend a weekend with me. I'll be alone here all through September . . . write to me. Send me a phone number where I can reach you. The melons were delicious. Bring more next time.

Affectionately, Ed. A.

Perhaps Abbey's favorite spot was Arches National Monument. It was there that Terry Gustafson, who had considered himself a close friend, discovered one day that visitors were not always welcome. Gustafson arrived unannounced to find Abbey stark naked, walking around the outside of the fire lookout tower, pad and pencil in hand.

Seeing Gustafson, Abbey yelled at him: "Go away! You're not welcome here. I already have company." Just then, a lovely young woman, also naked, walked out to see what the noise was all about. Spotting Gustafson, she scampered for cover, and Gustafson departed. "Ed was sarcastic and bitter that day," Gustafson recollects. "I never saw him again, though we did correspond before he died."

Southwest artist Cynthia Bennett remembers Abbey when he presided over the fire tower at the North Rim of the Grand Canyon: "His heart was always breaking over some woman. He was the most romantic man. Yet he was patronizing toward women, not contemptuous exactly, but bored. He found them tedious. When he wasn't with women, he always seemed to be surrounded by zealous young men who hung on his every word. There were some great parties. But I always had the sense that he really preferred being by himself."

Bennett was one of the women who once climbed the steep iron steps to visit Abbey in that remote outpost. "I'm terrified of heights, and the whole apparatus was swaying in the wind," she remembers. "When I reached the top, there he was, and I fainted dead away. He may have thought I was so stunned by his male handsomeness. But that wasn't it. I was pregnant."

To her surprise, she awakened in Abbey's lap. He was soothing her brow with his hand. "I'll never forget seeing the coffee can next to the chair. He said he used it to pee in."

Unquestionably, Abbey did some of his best writing in those towers, now mostly gone and experts in airplanes and helicopters now do the job. The FBI was still watching him at Arches in 1956 and 1957; during a stint at the Beaverhead Ranger Station in New Mexico's Gila Forest in 1958; and at the Casa Grande National Monument in 1958.

He was now writing his third novel, *Fire on the Mountain*. Federal agents still had not unearthed any damning evidence against him, and were mystified about why he liked to be alone. That he was writing novels never occurred to them.

They sure did not read *Fire on the Mountain*, in which Abbey launched another anarchistic hero, rancher John Vogelin, into the literary waters. Dismissed by many critics as either too simple or too much like the author's own voice throughout, the tale nonetheless attracted a modest following.

Few readers could forget the Vikingesque death scene in which the leathery grandfather, John Vogelin, having lost his ranch, dies of a broken heart. He is then cremated by his friend Lee Mackie and his twelve-year-old grandson Billy Vogelin Starr, who narrates the book.

> We faced the cabin, staring at the flames, and waited. Waited until the whole interior of the cabin became a seething inferno moaning like the wind, and bits and pieces and sections of the roof began to fall in. Grandfather on his bunk disappeared within the fire, wrapped from head to foot in flame, and cell by cell, atom by atom, he rejoined the elements of earth and sky.
>
> "The old man would approve of this, Billy. He'd approve of this...." Far above on the Mountainside, posed on his lookout point, the lion screamed.

In this novel, Abbey's romancer's vision, like Vogelin's cabin, really caught fire, transfiguring a simple tale of a man and his land from the literal to the metaphoric, and as one critic put it, to the mythic. When Billy asks him why the mountain on the ranch is called Thieves Mountain, Vogelin tells him, "It belongs to the Government. The Government stole it from the Indians. And the Indians stole it from the eagles, from the lion."

Here, Abbey fully develops the theme that would dominate his later work: in a rapidly urbanizing America, it is humans who are in the greatest jeopardy, not the environment; the planet will heal itself through fire and flood and vulcanism as it always has.

This concept separates Abbey from most contemporary environmentalists, who proclaim that their aim is to save the planet. For his part, Abbey's concern was for human nature, which becomes increasingly endangered when the land and its wild creatures are devastated by greed and senseless, so-called progress.

Even if man ceases to exist, Abbey was certain, the earth will replenish itself. It always has, and thirty civilizations have already come and gone.

Rancher Vogelin, like Abbey himself, would have preferred to live in a different time. When Billy asks his grandfather what he wants for his epitaph, the old man replies: "Here lies John Vogelin, born forty years too late, died forty years too soon." Billy asks him what that means, and Vogelin replies that in "forty years civilization will collapse and everything will be back to normal. I wish I could live to see it."

Reminiscent of Jack Burns in *The Brave Cowboy*, Vogelin is a proud, independent individual who battles against enormous odds. Many critics sniped that the two characters were disappointingly one-dimensional, failing to observe that the young writer was guiding the reader back and forth between the present and the past, showing the relationships between freedom and constraint, between the individual and society, between permanence and change.

Unlike *The Brave Cowboy*, *Fire* concludes on an upbeat note. Billy Vogelin, like Steinbeck's grandson character in *The Leader of the People*, will never have to suffer the difficulties and hardships of real ranch life, and he is blessed with firsthand knowledge of what the Old West was really like.

Abbey, in sharp contrast to Burns and Vogelin, was firmly established on a course that would transcend what a literary critic termed, "the suicidal strategy of defiance." Now in his early thirties, and ready to reveal his inner fears, Abbey was gearing up to map a plan of counterattack for his hapless readers.

All he lacked was a modus operandi, and it fell into his lap the day in 1963 when the federal government closed the penstocks on Glen Canyon below Lee's Ferry on the Colorado River.

In *Desert Solitaire,* published six years after *Fire on the Mountain,* Abbey creates a scene at the grand opening of that infamous dam in which the president of the United States plays a major role. It was the precursor to *The Monkey Wrench Gang.*

"The button which the President pushes," Abbey wrote, "will ignite the loveliest explosion ever seen by man, reducing the great Dam to a heap of rubble in the path of the river."

The FBI missed that passage, too.

Onward the desert anarchist roared—into life and fame, though never as much fortune as he had hoped. And it really was not until the last chapter of his life that Abbey found lasting love with Clarke Cartwright, a chestnut-haired, Texas-born beauty many years his junior.

In 1973, after Judy's death, he was married for the fourth time, to Rene Downing of Tucson. But, as was the case with his second wife, artist Rita Deanin, Abbey's frequent absences and often erratic behavior brought the union with Rene to an end after four years.

"Tell him to stop being so much of a shit," Rene told Abbey's friend Allan Harrington early on in the marriage.

But with Clarke it was different. She gave him two more children, Rebecca and Benjamin—and also some welcome peace of mind. "They make me the happiest I've ever been," he told a friend a year before his death. "After all these years, I've found the right place with the right woman."

Though he may have been happy during the 1980s, his fans were not at all pleased that their hero broke the anti-violence pledge he had made in the 1950s and on which he based his master's thesis. In *Hayduke Lives,* the sequel to *The Monkey Wrench Gang,* he introduces gratuitous violence for the first time.

It occurs when George Washington Hayduke, having said his farewells to the gang, tries to escape from the authorities by ship in the Gulf of California. Ultimately he makes it, but not before he shoots some national guardsmen and not before the pursuing colonel kills himself with a chrome-plated, long-range pistol.

Why did Abbey compromise his pacifist principles and resort to senseless violence, fictional though it was, in the winter of 1989? The truth is that it was not a matter of philosophical contradictions, but of rushing to finish the book. His original plan was to end it with a trial. But plans are subject to change.

Late one night, six weeks before he died, Abbey called a friend in Tucson to ask him exactly how an Uzi machine gun worked. The friend asked why, and Abbey replied, "There have been some changes."

Abbey knew that he was dying, and needed a quick ending. If he proceeded with the other ending to his book—a long trial— he figured, he might die before he penned the final paragraphs—and wouldn't get paid.

The desert anarchist had run out of time.

The Monkey Wrench Gang, Glen Canyon Dam, and the U.S. Government

The most beautiful, intricate, and important of all, the very living heart of the Canyonlands was Glen Canyon, at present submerged beneath the foul waters of Lake Powell.

—ED ABBEY

Hell, there was no way Barry Goldwater or I in 1955 could have said we were against Glen Canyon Dam. All hell would have broken loose politically, and we would have been regarded as traitors in our own state of Arizona.

—STEWART UDALL, FORMER SECRETARY OF THE INTERIOR

Existence. Time. Power. Abbey revered these universals of nature while adventuring both in the mysterious canyons of the Colorado Plateau and on the mighty river old-timers used to call the Big Red that flows through it, now dammed in twenty-one places.

In few other places on the globe is the earth's magnitude so brazenly revealed; startling buttes, mesas, plateaus, and outcroppings of rock formed beyond the imaginations of people living today. A beautiful, primordial, spooky region, the legacy of powerful, unknown forces that created the canyons, lifted them, shattered them, wore them down, and washed them away eons ago.

Abbey's respect for that region was deeply ingrained, not only feeding him with endless source material, but turning him into a literary watchdog, always on the alert for malevolent human forces intent on defiling the canyon and desert country.

If there was one transforming event in Abbey's life in the Southwest, rivaling the decimation of the Big Woods of his youth, it was the construction of Glen Canyon Dam. In the name of progress, the colossal cement hydroelectric dam built by the federal government on the Colorado River, sixty miles north of the Grand Canyon, destroyed one of the most remarkable wonders of the world.

To Abbey it was nothing less than a great—and unnecessary—holocaust that insulted his soul and also moved the anarchist within him to action. Beyond doubt, the huge dam was the most egregious example of bureaucratic power at its worst: the U.S. government had inundated a desert canyon of incomparable value to generate low-cost electric power for Los Angeles, Las Vegas, and Phoenix. And because there were no environmental laws of any consequence in those days, the general public was left in the dark during the crucial decision making.

Compounding the tragedy was a poignant irony: the high-minded Sierra Club, not some evil developer, was responsible for suggesting the site to the federal government in exchange for one it wanted to protect on a tributary of the Colorado River. It was an appropriate decision, club leaders insisted at the time, because despite its beauty and archaeological importance, Glen Canyon was so remote, few people even knew about it.

The deal was cut behind closed doors in Washington, D.C., and inside black limousines (and even dusty garages) in Salt Lake City and Phoenix. Countless political chips were called in. Billions of dollars were on the table in the form of windfall profits for private power companies that would now be able to buy federal power for a penny a kilowatt hour and sell it to the public for ten times that.

Shortly before Abbey died, his feelings about the loss of Glen Canyon received an endorsement from one of the dam's godfathers. Former Arizona Senator Barry Goldwater publicly declared that he regretted his earlier and enthusiastic advocacy. "I think of that river as it was when I was a boy. And that is the way I would like to see it again."

Abbey had not waited nearly three decades to recognize the monstrous truth. Although he was seasonally employed by the U.S. Department of the Interior, he immediately charged that the dam was not just a sacrilege against nature, it was also a massive financial blunder. For voicing those opinions in the early 1960s, he was dubbed a radical environmentalist and was roundly condemned for his prayerful pleas that the dam should be removed—peacefully or otherwise.

To Abbey, one of the last people to float through Glen Canyon before it was dammed, the $400 million federal "pork barrel" reclamation project was the moral equivalent of filling St. Patrick's Cathedral with nuclear waste.

"It is no longer a place of natural life," he wrote after the dam halted the ancient Colorado River in its tracks in 1962 to create Lake Powell and a 1,800-mile shoreline. "It is no longer Glen Canyon. . . . It is the difference between life and death."

Before the dam, Glen Canyon was a place of exhilarating and mysterious beauty. In its many side canyons, thrushes, warblers, and mockingbirds sang in groves of cottonwood and thickets of redbud, tamarisk, and willow. Along its steep walls, cavelike natural shrines shielded hawks, swallows, and owls intent on raising and protecting their young.

Deeper into the gulches and gorges, where Abbey had wandered before their inundation, flowering plants in small clefts hung from high on inner walls, as if some master gardener had planted and tenderly nurtured them. Below, along the river, waterfalls spilled into plunge pools; badgers, coyotes, wolves, mule deer, and other mammals browsed near abundant supplies of food and water, certain that safe shelter was nearby.

To native peoples, who thought it superior to the Grand Canyon, it had been a sacred place for thousands of years, long before some astonished Spanish conquistadores first gazed into its depths in the eighteenth century. Later, it earned a place in American history. Major John Wesley Powell, in 1869, boated the length of the Colorado River.

When word came that the Eisenhower (later the Kennedy) administration had plans for a dam, archaeologists and anthropologists descended into Glen, anxious for one last glimpse of the prehistoric cultures there. This was the last chance to recover artifacts, soon to be flooded over forever by the actions of so-called conservative politicians in the name of taxpayer-subsidized, low-cost electricity.

Few artifacts evaded the dynamiting dam-builders, compared to what had been there; much was lost in the rush to flood the canyon, including priceless pottery created by the Anasazi centuries before.

During Abbey's wanderings throughout the Southwest after his college years, he sometimes wondered whether the canyon country, for all its desolate beauty, had a heart. His soul-searching ended during a ten-day, 150-mile float trip through Glen Canyon when he was thirty-two years old. Finally, he found the heart of the landscape he loved on "the golden, flowing Colorado River."

For a civilization to annihilate the wildness of such a river so casually, he reasoned, was tantamount to destroying a part of the Southwest's very soul, its identity as a place of humankind's earliest origins. Any civilization that could act so senselessly, he concluded, was no civilization at all; the only response was self-defense, namely, dismantling the instruments terrorizing nature through sabotage—whether allegorical, metaphorical, rhetorical, or real sabotage.

After all, wasn't that what the Boston Tea Party was about?

Ironically, it was because the U.S. government eventually devastated Abbey's Eden that he wrote satirically about the efforts of a band of ecoraiders to demolish that dreaded dam in *The Monkey Wrench Gang* and in its sequel, *Hayduke Lives*. And it was because of those two novels with their theme of environmental hooliganism that he was elevated from the rank of regional author to that of international recognition.

Trumpeted *Newsweek:* "Abbey may have invented a new fictional genre [with *The Monkey Wrench Gang*], the ecological caper." "The most unlikely guerrilla army in the annals of contemporary literature," United Press International observed. "In pleasantly verbose style, Abbey masterfully weds the traditions of the romantic quest and the suspense novel . . . the major strength in the book is the startling contrast between the nature of the loose fraternity of the gang and that of the coldly and deadly efficient corporations," said the *Detroit Free Press*.

Drawing on the lives of real people, Abbey created a wealthy Albuquerque physician named Doc Sarvis who burned billboards for a hobby; a sexy, philosophizing exile from the Bronx named Bonnie Abbzug; and George Washington Hayduke, a deranged ex–Green Beret whose love for dynamite and beer was equaled only by his hatred of helicopters. Abbey teamed them up with an outcast, polygamous Mormon riverboat guide named Seldom Seen Smith.

Next, he mobilized this gang of fun-loving anarchists against power companies, logging conglomerates, and Glen Canyon Dam. The gang was unified by a single theme, allegiance to the earth, and the war cry: "Keep it like it was." Their goal: the murder of machines.

While Abbey intended *The Monkey Wrench Gang*, published in 1975, thirteen years after the dam was completed, to be an entertaining black comedy, the book was based on fact. Peabody Coal Company was rapaciously stripping coal from the holy lands of the Hopi. Power consortia were planning dozens of air polluting electric power plants in the plateaus near the Grand Canyon. Towering transmission lines resembling supernatural beasts were marching across the desert, and Glen Canyon had been gutted. The novel was real enough, one critic wrote, to "make the Board of Directors of Standard Oil start tithing to the Sierra Club."

Many who read of the exploits of Abbey's gang of ecoraiders are not sure to this day where his reportage left off and his satiric fiction took over. Perhaps Abbey didn't know or didn't care. It was only a novel, he said.

Early on, there was gossip in Hollywood about a film. Talk about an opening scene! An armada of bureaucrats, carrying oversized gilded scissors, parade to the middle of a new bridge extending across the Colorado River. As they prepare to cut the ribbons in what seems to be a routine ceremony, suddenly, fireworks and rockets explode all around them.

The crowd cheered, thinking this was the high point of the ceremonies. But it was not. Suddenly the center of the bridge rose up, as if punched from beneath, and broke in two along a jagged zigzag line.

Through this absurd fissure, crooked as lightning, a sheet of red flame screamed skyward, followed at once by the sound of a great cough, a thunderous shuddering high-explosive cough that shook the monolithic sandstone of the canyon walls.

The bridge parted like a flower, its separate divisions no longer joined by any physical bond. Fragments and sections began to fold, sag, sink . . . relaxing into the abyss.

Loose objects—gilded scissors, a monkey wrench, a couple of empty Cadillacs—slid down the appalling gradient of the depressed roadway and launched themselves, turning slowly, into space.

They took a long time going down and when they finally smashed on the rock and river far below, the sound of the impact, arriving much later, was barely heard even by the most attentive. The bridge was gone . . . and the dam was next.

After showing initial interest, some even paying Abbey option money for his story, film giants such as Universal, and potential producers such as Robert Redford and Dennis Hopper, decided that the plot was too violent. Implicitly, they agreed with the Tucson newspaper that castigated the novel as "Eco-pornography."

In the meantime, mainstream environmental groups held their noses, hoping the offending odor of radicalism would pass. But the saga of an idealistic band of ecoraiders, "warped but warped in the right way," wrote Abbey, was making him into a heroic, controversial figure.

A few months before he died, Abbey told an interviewer that he had written *The Monkey Wrench Gang* out of an "indulgence of spleen and anger from a position of safety behind my typewriter. But that was a tertiary motive. Mainly I wanted to entertain and amuse."

While he may have succeeded with most of his readers, he definitely failed with Jim Harrison, the novelist who declared in

The New York Times that America was probably the only country in the world where so violent a revolutionary novel as *The Monkey Wrench Gang* could be published with impunity. (Abbey wrote "pretty dumb review" across the top of the newspaper clipping.) He wrote no such notation across a review in the late *National Observer*, which found the novel to be an often sad, sometimes vulgar "fairy tale . . . part adventure, part melodrama, part tragedy."

In constructing this novel, Abbey veered from his earlier plot paths in *The Brave Cowboy* and *Fire on the Mountain*. The heroes of those novels, being out of place in the modern world, were vanquished. By contrast, Abbey here gives us Hayduke, "young George, all fire and passion, a good healthy psychopath." He is a surrogate Western hero, a cross between Tom Horn (a famed lawman and gunfighter) and the Lone Ranger. Badly shaken emotionally by combat in Vietnam, Hayduke is ready to take matters into his own hands—outside the law.

Hayduke strikes back. They all strike back, set on immobilizing the machines and technological structures invading the canyon homeland. Even if their efforts are doomed to failure, it doesn't matter. Abbey's avowed purpose, aside from having fun, was to utilize Hayduke and the others to explode readers' innocent and often oblivious regard for the dam, the mines, and the power lines in what they used to consider virgin West, and to underscore the fact that none of it was necessary; simple energy conservation practices could have done the job.

Abbey's meaning was that somebody had to do it, somebody had to bring criminals to justice.

"Okay. Here's one for you. A real conundrum. What is the difference between the Lone Ranger and God?" Bonnie thought about it as they rattled through the woods. She rolled a little cigarette and thought and thought and thought. At last she said, "What a stupid conundrum." Hayduke said, "There really is a Lone Ranger."

In evaluating Abbey's works, it becomes clear that *The Monkey Wrench Gang* comes the closest to reaching that place of Abbey's most steadfast convictions: a romantically idealized world in which the Industrial Revolution has been aborted, and society has reached a steady-state equilibrium where man and the land can exist in harmony.

Abbey experienced the desecration of many natural places he loved. As a writer, he drew attention to the real probability that if the populace failed to speak out, if they refused to involve themselves in the world around them—a world in which no sacrifice was unthinkable on behalf of growth and convenience—mad machines would devour all the untamed, beautiful places and steal their own souls in the process.

In aftermath of this novel, literary sleuths tried to determine whether the gang members were based on real people. Indeed, it has become something of a small industry as people continue to come forward claiming that Abbey used them as models. With the exception of Seldom Seen Smith, whose real-life inspiration was Ken Sleight, a Utah-based river guide, the characters were composites. Bonnie Abzug, Doc Sarvis, and Hayduke (borrowed from a thirteenth-century European revolutionary named Heiduc) were definitely drawn from many characteristics in Abbey's circle of friends; and even though the dam still stands, many of the gang's exploits were based on real incidents—or attempted incidents.

Undisputed is the fact that most of the characters' words sound suspiciously like Abbey's, offering another example of his disinclination to escape from himself.

Listen to Doc Sarvis, whose name Abbey borrowed from a physician friend in the Carolinas:

> [A]ll that ball-breaking labor and all that backbreaking insult to land and sky and human heart; for what? All that, for what?
>
> Why, to light the lamps of Phoenix suburbs not yet built, to run the air conditioners of San Diego and Los Angeles, to illuminate shopping center parking lots at two in the morning, to power aluminum plants, magnesium plants, vinyl chloride factories and copper smelters, to charge the neon tubing that makes the meaning (all the meaning there is) of Las Vegas, Albuquerque, Tucson, Salt Lake City, the amalgamated metropoli of southern California, to keep alive that phosphorescent putrefying glory (all the glory there is left) called Down Town, Night Times, Wonderville, U.S.A.

Abbey's plaint in this novel is both sad and defiant, more Orwellian than Thoreauvian. Mournfully, he acknowledges the final battle is at hand over the vestiges of pristine land left in the Southwest, then he layers the tale with bizarre episodes of train wrecking, bridge busting, and dam blowing.

What's the reader to think? Was Abbey actually advocating sabotage? Did he really want to blow up one of the largest sources of low-cost electric power in the Southwest? "No," he once told a group of students, "but if someone else wanted to do it, I'd be there holding a flashlight."

A madcap tale of "symbolic aggression," as critic Donn Rawlings called it, Abbey's novel can be seen as analogous to the attempt by the Yippies in the early 1970s to levitate the Pentagon by the force of their collective wills. Or, it can be understood as considerably more than that; for Abbey strove to illuminate a central fact of his own existence—the land is a primary source for our dreams, and thus must always be preserved.

Other critics saw it as a fairy tale, ignoring Abbey's clue in the beginning of the book in dedicating it to Ned Ludd, legendary leader of an early nineteenth-century British labor movement— and no spinner of fairy tales. Ludd, a normally peaceful fabric weaver by trade, provoked his countrymen to destroy machines and equipment in the early days of the Industrial Revolution.

Having become convinced that the introduction of unrestrained capitalism as represented by mechanized looms would be a disaster for working people, Ludd called for a new order of ethics based on the premise that industrial growth had to be regulated according to ethical priorities; the pursuit of profit must be subordinated to human needs.

For their version of monkey wrenching, Ludd and his group were first fired on by soldiers in 1812 after busting up some textile looms, then convicted in a mass trial a year later. It is believed that their leader, "King" Ludd, was among those hanged.

Although such a fate never befell Abbey (certain reviewers may have wished it), he shared Ludd's dream. When Abbey saw his dream being dashed in his beloved Southwest, he vented his outrage through his typewriter.

Although he called Ludd his mentor, Abbey was also indebted to "The Fox," a citizen outlaw operating around Chicago in the early 1970s. He drove law enforcement officers witless by plugging factory smokestacks and, in one truly bizarre act, diverting a stream of poisonous industrial waste into the offices of a company's chairman.

When asked by a reporter whether his tactics were immoral or illegal, the character the local press dubbed the "ecological Lone Ranger" replied: "No more so than if I stopped a man from beating a dog or strangling a woman."

That environmental outlaw was never apprehended or unmasked. Neither were the "Billboard Bandits" in Michigan, another gang that was trying to halt mindless growth by demolishing hundreds of roadside signs with chainsaws. And neither were the "Boll Weevils," a band of Minnesota farmers who took down electrical power lines that were advancing across their prairies—and their farms.

By no means was Abbey the first American author to select ecological sabotage as a worthy theme. Henry David Thoreau, writing in *A Week on the Concord and Merrimack Rivers*, published in 1849, worried about a dam being constructed on the Concord River that would interrupt shad spawning runs.

Expressing sorrow for the shad because their ancient rhythms were doomed, Thoreau asked: "Who hears the fishes when they cry?" He then shocked his readers by advocating the use of violence against the dam: "I for one am with thee, and who knows what may avail a crowbar against Billerica dam."

Exchanging explosives for crowbars, Abbey's ecoguerrillas are Thoreau's direct offspring. Henry himself would have cheered in 1981 when a band of ecowarriors led by Dave Foreman, sometime Abbey disciple, dropped a massive black tarp down the front of the 720-foot-high Glen Canyon Dam, emblazoned with a huge crack. "Free the shackled rivers," Foreman bellowed. "The finest fantasy of ecowarriors in the West is the destruction of Glen Canyon Dam and the liberation of the Colorado River!"

Although American history records countless acts of civil disobedience, Abbey was credited with inventing the practice of monkey wrenching. In reality, says one of his closest friends and an active monkey wrencher who prefers anonymity, "Ed was reporting what he saw around him. Truth be told, monkey wrenching is not even controversial in many areas of the Southwest. People just don't talk about it because it is part of living there. The story of the gang succeeded in crystallizing feelings about a place that is being destroyed, the last good place. Abbey's words merely gave people a way, a sanction."

In this complex novel, Abbey's extensive use of satire and irony also escaped the eye of many a critic. Few recognized Abbey's romantic quest, namely, to raise a simple outlaw tale to the level of myth and legend.

Abbey's gang, like the peace-loving Western lawmen of the nineteenth century, resort to force in order to stop violence, not of rustlers and bank robbers but of dam builders.

In the world of *The Monkey Wrench Gang,* anarchy rules; the gang's ends always justify the means because the giant machines they try to disable have forces at their disposal far greater than theirs. Abbey offers hope that the combination of human intelligence and wit, together with a common sense of purpose, will be enough to stop the giant machines. "I don't want to keep people out, just the machines," Abbey told a reporter.

In this tale, the gang gets help from a stranger wearing a black mask that is draped outlaw-style over his nose, mouth, and chin. Above the mask his dark right eye shines; the other socket is empty, a casualty of war or a barroom fight.

The masked man watches Hayduke draining the crankcase of a bulldozer, and says in a deep voice, "I can see you do a good job. Thorough. I like that . . . not like them half-assed dudes I seen up on the Powder River. Or them kids down around Tucson. Or them nuts that derailed . . ."

This masked man is not just the Lone Ranger, enduring symbol of justice. He is also Jack Burns, resurrected from *Jonathan Troy* and *The Brave Cowboy,* to supervise from the shadows—to direct a network of monkey wrenchers battling the forces of environmental havoc, from the coalfields of Montana to the forests of Oregon. Have heart, Abbey assures his readers, there's a phantom outlaw out there ready to lend a hand to save the earth—and human nature along with it.

After the book had been out for a while, Fred Hills, then Abbey's editor at McGraw-Hill Book Company, wrote to him to say that he couldn't understand why *The Monkey Wrench Gang* had not soared to the top of the best-seller list.

"Can it be," he wrote to Abbey, "that you are not a member of the mutual admiration, hoopla-trading game among writers and professional 'quoters' around the New York cocktail circuit? Maybe you should don your Bill Blass, Pierre Cardin fag rags, cultivate the proper list, and do warm-up exercises with a martini glass. Jesus, I don't really know, Ed, but TMWG is not only a superb piece of fiction. It should also be a damn commercial book. I can't explain it."

In the long run, Hills was proven right. News of the novel did begin to hum through the underground of counterculture magazines, student publications, and word of mouth. By the time of Abbey's death, more than half a million copies had been sold. Several million people have read the novel, which has never gone out of print.

It may still make the screen, but movie or no, the book that put the Glen Canyon Dam controversy—and Abbey—on the map refuses to die. Indeed, discord about the dam in the years since his death has only accelerated, and it is now a serious national political issue.

When Glen Canyon Dam was approved and constructed during the Eisenhower and Kennedy administrations, it was never anticipated, as former Interior Secretary Stewart Udall says, that "cheap electric power production and maximizing revenues would become the main justification for the dam. You can't make the argument that in order for people in Phoenix, Los Angeles, or Las Vegas to have a little cheaper electricity bill, the Grand Canyon has to be desecrated. It won't wash."

But it did until 1991. Until then the Bureau of Reclamation, the part of the U.S. Department of the Interior that runs the power plant and maintains the generators, operated the dam's huge hydroelectric turbines as though there was no tomorrow.

Before their reckless ways were halted by the courts, bureaucrats fired orders into a computer in Montrose, Colorado, that turned the flows of the once-mighty Colorado River on and off like the spray nozzle of a huge hose. This was done so that the Western Area Power Administration (WAPA), part of the U.S. Department of Energy, which manages the electric system and the power lines, could market the cheapest power in the United States.

What even Abbey never anticipated—nor Udall nor Goldwater—was that the river below the dam in the Grand Canyon would be forced to vacillate crazily, from more than 30,000 cubic feet per second to 1,000 cubic feet per second, at times causing the river to rise and fall as much as thirteen feet in a single day.

These fluctuations—to meet peaking power demands from power customers—have not only threatened people who happened to be in the bottom of the canyon, but have damaged flora and fauna and wiped out beaches and some of the Grand Canyon's archaeological heritage.

Seen as a "cash register" dam by the Ford, Carter, Reagan, and Bush administrations, the income from power sales is supposed to repay billions of dollars in loans that Uncle Sam made to farmers and others through the years for numerous water reclamation projects throughout the West.

The price of producing that cheap power has been very dear. According to David Wegner, manager of the Glen Canyon Environmental Studies Group for the U.S. Department of the Interior, the Grand Canyon is on the verge of being decimated by Glen Canyon Dam. "When someone's sick, say with a disease like AIDS, their immune system suffers. When they have a cold they are that much closer to visibly dying from it. Healthy ecosystems and healthy people can get colds and survive because they have a lot of resiliency in their immune systems," Wegner says. "Today, the environmental immune system is so weak below Glen Canyon Dam, that in times of flood, the river could get sicker, and it may never be able to recover biologically."

This shocking discovery has brought hordes of experts to study the patient, and they all have come up with the same diagnosis: A man-made illness in the form of erosion is spreading in the Canyon, and it is doing more than destroying age-old archaeological sites.

According to Wegner's task force, wild unnatural fluctuations in water releases have torn out large sections of beaches; more than half the beaches in the Grand Canyon are gone. By any standard, the loss of beaches is a post-dam phenomenon. For in the days before the dam, countless tons of sediment flowed naturally down the river, swirling around and, as if a wizard was at work, sculpting new beaches.

By 1992, the old sculptor was running out of clay. In fact, scientists have reported that trapped behind the dam is 99.5 percent of all the sediment that once refreshed the river and repaired habitat. Unless the dam ceases to operate for peaking power, sediment cannot flow downstream again. As a consequence, this silt is slowly filling up Lake Powell, the lake dubbed "the blue death" by Abbey.

And he was called a radical when he opposed Glen Canyon Dam.

When riverbanks go, all biological life within them vanishes as well—vegetation and aquatic insects on which birds and other wildlife depend. And when the mercurial water flows come without warning, thousands of nesting birds are literally washed away, and disintegration of the food chain accelerates apace.

Downstream, the native Hualapai people have also been watching the mighty river's changes. "We contend that nature is our culture," says wildlife expert Clay Bravo. Because of unnatural flows, his people have seen indigenous species of plants obliterated, cultural artifacts and skeletons washed away, and bighorn sheep habitat damaged—all sacred elements of their culture, and the losses are irrevocable.

The dam's flows have now been restricted due to the efforts of The Grand Canyon Trust, a powerful national citizen group based in Flagstaff, and the U.S. Congress. But the flooding of Glen Canyon and the resulting assault on the Grand Canyon are permanent scars on the region, not to mention the effect on the psyches of Canyon lovers, many of whom were inspired by the exploits of *The Monkey Wrench Gang*.

Nowadays, longtime aficionados of the Arizona and Utah canyon country sometimes wonder whether Abbey's ghost haunts the region, climbing around fluted sandstone spires and hoodoo mesas, always making notes, always curious to learn more about the extraordinary Colorado River and the ubiquitous salmon-pink tableland first studied by explorer John Wesley Powell in the 1870s.

No doubt his ghost would stop in its tracks upon reaching the giant lake named in Powell's honor, recall what created it, and reflect upon the fate of such transcendental places as Music Temple, the Crossing of the Fathers, the Cathedral of the Desert, and the swift and smooth-flowing red-brown river itself.

Standing there perplexed, Abbey's specter might be joined by two others, that of Everett Ruess, the youthful poet and artist who was lost somewhere in the area in 1933, and that of John Wesley Powell himself.

And Abbey might tell them that the river is not the Colorado they knew and loved. He would say that he tried to stop it, that he remembered their words. But the real Colorado died when the U.S. government closed the gates at Glen Canyon Dam.

He could also tell them that, while at first only he and a few others raised their voices, now more have joined the chorus, and now many of the dam's original supporters acknowledge the grotesqueness of the project.

"Glen Canyon Dam is a sad joke," says a veteran employee of the U.S. Department of the Interior. "Two years of Colorado River flow was lost in the sandstone; a really beautiful canyon was flooded—not to mention the inundation of Rainbow Bridge—and Lake Powell is silted up. The purpose of the dam was never stated publicly, namely, to prevent Boulder Dam downstream, a major source of California's electric power, from being clogged up by silt. Abbey was right."

At the outset, Abbey protested that damming Glen Canyon was an outlaw act, but now that the truth has emerged, he is turning out to have been more prescient than even he could have known.

Justified to taxpayers as a water regulation and conservation dam, part of the Colorado River Storage Project of 1956 (midway between the upper and lower basin states of Wyoming, Colorado, New Mexico and Utah, Arizona, Nevada, and California), congressional enabling legislation specifically limited the dam's hydroelectric potential.

Ignoring the law, dam operators did exactly the opposite of what it intended.

It is possible to glimpse the green ribbon of river one mile below the dam. The prospect of seeing the Colorado, long ago called simply "the Grand," lures millions of visitors from around the world to wander along the trails, worn through the centuries by Indians, mules, hunters, and river rafters. And it is a rare occasion when the canyon fails to deliver its bewitching allure.

But what visitors cannot see from that height is that something has gone terribly wrong further down the deep and distant river. Indeed, scientists now visit, not to enjoy the river, but for more macabre reasons. They come from Russia and Italy to observe David Wegner's activities; to discover for themselves what has happened to the canyon, asking whether it can be healed and how the U.S. government could have presided over such travesty.

Those questions continue to roil the political waters, because they lead to one of the most fundamental of national questions, one that Abbey often posed in his writings: Should Americans allow technology to drive their lives, or would it be wiser to exercise restraint and dare to leave the earth alone?

The choice is clear: Will the Colorado become a sterile river in which no life will grow? Or will habitat be restored, birds still sing, and vultures still soar in the skies above the Grand Canyon? Will it be left alone long enough for its wounds to heal?

Toward the end of his life, Ed Abbey stopped worrying about the dam, telling a citizen group in Flagstaff not long before he died that within the lifetime "of our children, Glen Canyon and the living river, heart of the Canyonlands, will be restored to us."

He foresaw the day when methods of generating alternative power, such as solar, would be developed, and the United States would establish a more sustainable way of life energized by renewable resources. As that transition occurs, Abbey predicted, demand for electrical power will fall, the Glen Canyon Dam power plant will be shut down, and the U.S. government will drain the massive reservoir. In one of his biblical moods, he then predicted something more apocalyptic: the shock of seeing "a drear and hideous scene: immense mud flats and whole plateaus of sodden garbage strewn with dead trees, sunken boats, the skeletons of long-forgotten water-skiers. But to those who would find the prospect too appalling, I say give nature a little time."

And then the Old Testament force within him rose to high dudgeon: a great flood will roar down from the Rocky Mountains, cleansing and healing man's grotesque mess. And soon life will return: cottonwoods, redbud, box elder. With the return of the plants, wildlife will wander back, too—lizards, birds, mammals.

And perhaps in a generation, when the resurrection is complete, Abbey told his rapt audience that "The wilderness will again belong to God, the people, and the wild things that call it home."

Because of Abbey's madcap but deadly serious novel, people of all ages can never again look the same way at massive freeway systems where desert and farmland used to be, at blankets of smog over their cities, at once-lush forests now clear-cut into lunar landscapes—or at huge dams on once-free rivers.

While millions of Americans stood by passively, Abbey questioned such projects' very existence. Looking the other way wasn't good enough for Abbey's gang of monkey wrenchers. They had to fight back; not to do so would be dishonorable.

After all, somebody had to do it.

After his death, a delicious example of the irony Abbey relished began to surface in academic journals. Now Abbey's fictional gang of radical saboteurs, who challenged the need for huge dams like Glen Canyon, are receiving fresh reinforcements in the form of real-life, ultra-conservative economists who charge that the project stands as one of the greatest boondoggles in history.

Some are even suggesting that the dam be removed—peacefully, of course.

THE WRITINGS AS A WHOLE

Edward Abbey never won a National Book Award, nor was he ever offered a blue-ribbon chair in English literature at an ivy-covered university. And he never received a grant from the National Endowment for the Arts. What's more, his chances of getting a good table at Elaine's in Manhattan, or a posh summer beach house on Long Island, were as likely as a desert snow-storm in August.

But that was fine with him. His books were what was important.

As for what critics said of them, Abbey professed never to pay much heed, saying to friends that he didn't give a hoot what reviewers east of the Mississippi wrote about his novels and essays. What counted was that a serious writer could get by quite nicely, thank you, in the face of eastern establishment indifference or hostility—if the writer had something to say and could say it well.

Here we encounter pure Abbey. He knew good reviews did matter; not only did they sell books, but bad reviews hurt and often sent him into fits of rhetorical outrage.

"Regarding reviews and reviewers," he once grumbled, "I have yet to read a review of any of my own books which I could not have written much better myself." On other occasions he complained of being ignored: "Each of my books, each defenseless child, has been met with sublime, monumental, crashing silence—a freezing silence. . . . When not ignored, [they] are greeted with . . . a coolness verging on outright frigidity, particularly by the doctrinaire buzz saws of chicken-shit liberalism."

Bombast! Equally outrageous was his complaint that his works were never reviewed by *Time*, *Newsweek*, or *The New Yorker*. In reality, all of his works were reviewed far and wide, except for his first novel, *Jonathan Troy*.

While he encouraged the image of the rough and tough desert rat, his feelings were easily bruised by what obtuse reviewers wrote. At times he felt he had become a kind of literary leper because he lived on the wrong side of the Hudson River.

"Why can't I be reviewed by my peers sometime?" he lamented in a letter to Edward Hoagland, the essayist who was then teaching at Bennington College in Vermont. "By you, or Mathiessen, or McPhee. Did I go to the wrong school? Live in the wrong town? Hoboken won't do?"

Bombast! He often was reviewed by his peers. Author Bill McKibben *(The End of Nature)*, for example, crafted a lengthy and, he thought, glowing review of Abbey's essays for the high-toned *New York Review of Books*. "I all but called him Thoreau's successor as the American philosopher of nature," McKibben recounts.

Abbey's reaction, therefore, came as something of a jolt to McKibben. In a letter a few weeks after the review came out, Abbey accused him of not having read his books before reviewing them.

In the eyes of the publishing world, close friends recall, Abbey wanted very much to be seen as legitimate, but he felt his provincial background was working against him, which sometimes plunged him into bouts of insecurity.

Abbey in his M.P. uniform, 1945.

*As a college student
in New Mexico, 19.*

*On a California
beach in 1958.*

On horseback, 1970s.

In an Indian ruin in the Back of Beyond.

Taking a siesta on desert floors with horses in attendance, 1970s.

With one of his favorite cigars.

Terrence Moore

With parents, Paul Revere and Mildred, 1970s.

Wearing a Monkey Wrench T-shirt, 1982.

Chip Hedgecock

Lecturing under M
Graham sign, 198.

With beat-up camper truck.

With television set he
shot, à la Henry
Holyoak Lightfoot,
mid-1980s.

Terrence M

Brother Johnny Abbey, sister Nancy, friend, and mother Mildred, 1986.

Teaching at the University of Arizona, mid-1980s.

With friends on river trip on the Salmon River in Idaho, 1985.

At Home in Pennsylvania, 1985.

With wife Clarke, daughter Rebecca, and son Benjamin, shortly before his death in 1989.

At the same time, he wasn't at all sure he wanted to be accepted by the Eastern literary establishment. He had little respect for that kind of success, especially if it meant pandering to the East Coast literati—"the castrati literati," as he called them.

It was his hope that critics would recognize that most of his writings harken back to the enduring premise of Western literature that, far from the confines of civilization, individuals can silence the droning of their consciousness and face the primal reality of their own existence.

Too often critics focused more narrowly on the numerous contradictions that seasoned Abbey's writings. Feeling that they had missed the point, Abbey would counter that, as he learned while earning his master's degree in philosophy, contradictions are the building blocks of life, that the only bedrock solid enough to stand on is paradox.

In *Desert Solitaire*, Abbey bluntly—and mischievously—warned people to get out of the way: "Serious critics, serious librarians, serious associate professors of English will, if they read this book, dislike it intensely; at least I hope so."

Most reviewers attempted to pigeonhole him into a category that would remain fixed from book to book. Many bookstores wrestle with the same problem today, uncertain whether to display his books under nature, fiction, nonfiction, philosophy, or autobiography.

Such indecision is easy to understand, because Abbey refused to regard himself as simply an environmental writer or a nature writer, sobriquets other writers might welcome.

A few weeks before his death, he protested, "I never wanted to be anything but a writer, period. An author. A creator of fictions and essays. I take all of life, all of society, for my proper realm of discourse, as any honest reader can discover."

As for being an environmental writer, he added, he first read the word "ecology" in an H. G. Wells story, and still wasn't sure what it meant. Despite these protestations, when author Larry McMurtry tagged him as "The Thoreau of the West" in the *Washington Post,* it stuck.

Abbey's prickliness nothwithstanding, book critics were not at all misguided to read his works against the backdrop of the nation's environmental awakening, usually noting that Abbey was one of the first postwar writers to sound forth the message that concern for the environment—and quality of life—deserved to be the overarching issue of the day.

As he himself explained it in the introduction to a marvelous collection of essays, *The Desert Reader:*

> If, as some believe, the evolution of humankind is the means by which the earth has become conscious of itself, then it may follow that the conservationist awakening is the late-flowering conscience of that world mind . . . through humanity the earth finds its voice.

Plainly, Abbey's ambition transcended environmental writing. "I consider myself a savage, vicious, embittered, utterly irresponsible critic of our society," he once told Tucson writer Peter Wild, "and for years, in my writing, I have been cultivating the art of the arrogant sneer, the venomous put-down, the elegant hatchet job. I want to be feared. I want to be hated." And there were people who took that seriously.

Regardless of what others wrote about his work, he was always writing his autobiography, a "slumgullion stew" of fact and fiction that was sifted through his imagination but saturated in the blood of his youth—his German-Scotch-Irish, God-fearing, Old Conservative background.

Years after his death, Abbey continues to be referred to as an environmental or nature writer, even though his works have given many a sleepless night to the very environmentalists who tried to review his books.

More than a few of them suddenly realized that, instead of being an ally, Abbey was a real menace to their cause because of his radical writings and bad image. Ironically, that was precisely the same conclusion reached by battalions of land developers, politicians, and chamber of commerce caliphs who charged he was anti-growth; and by liberals who abhorred the fact that he belonged to the National Rifle Association.

A memorable instance of the discomfort Abbey caused appeared in *The Nation* of May 1, 1982. A lawyer and frequent reviewer named Dennis Drabelle reviewed Abbey's book of essays *Down the River*, and lambasted it for its elitism, arrogance, xenophobia, and iconoclasm—for openers. Of Abbey, he wrote that his "immense popularity among environmentalists is puzzling; many of his attitudes give aid and comfort to the enemy."

After self-righteous, humorless appraisals like that, fellow authors, including Wendell Berry, jumped to Abbey's defense. In Berry's view, the Drabelles of the world were guilty of misunderstanding their subject, of arrogantly assuming that Abbey would write what they thought he should write—or be what they wanted him to be. Just as large business groups sometimes do with journalists who write sympathetic stories about their cause, environmentalists figured Abbey would consistently act as their mouthpiece. After all, didn't he write about nature?

"They further assume," Berry contended, "that if he does not so perform, they have a proprietary right to complain. They would like, in effect, to brand him an outcast and an enemy of their movement and to enforce their judgment against him by warning people away from his books."

Abbey never concealed what he was up to, and he stated it clearly in his essay "A Writer's Credo," first published in *One Life at a Time, Please.*

> Why write? How justify this mad itch for scribbling? Speaking for myself, I write to entertain my friends and to exasperate my enemies. I write to record the truth of our time as best as I can see it. To investigate the comedy and the tragedy of human relationships. To oppose, resist and sabotage the contemporary drift toward a global technocratic police state whatever its ideological coloration. I write to oppose injustice, to defy power, and to speak for the voiceless.

As his close friends knew well but, in his opinion, few book critics seemed to grasp, Abbey did not look upon his life of writing in the Western deserts as a career. It was a passion, fueled in equal parts by anger and love. "How feel one without the other? Each implies the other," he once wrote.

Abbey decided early that it was frivolous to spend time, as other contemporary writers did, raging about sexual misadventures in the suburbs, in cloakrooms at P.T.A. meetings, or behind the bushes at country club barbecues. That was both too easy and irrelevant to his mission. That is why he preferred Gore Vidal, B. Traven, George Orwell, and Cormac McCarthy.

The moral duty of a writer, Abbey avowed, was to be a "critic of his own country, his own government, his own culture." And the greater the freedom a writer possessed, the greater the moral responsibility the writer had to be a sharp critic.

In the event that writers felt uncomfortable with this quid pro quo, they would be wise, Abbey advised, to drop their facade and take up another profession, such as nuclear physics, perhaps. "Whereof one fears to speak," he wrote, "to speak thereof one must be silent. Far better silence than the written word used to shore up the wrong, the false, the ugly, the evil."

Deep in his viscera, Abbey knew that writing did matter, and over the long haul it mattered a great deal. If that was not the case, if the writer refused to appoint him- or herself a moral champion, then in the words of Alexander Solzhenitsyn, "the word's work is of no more importance than the barking of village dogs at night."

For all the uneven (if not downright antagonistic) reviews Abbey thought his works received, many of them came with this caveat: "Read him anyway," one reviewer prodded. "Read him for the unadulterated pleasure of reading an American original, a funny, angry, unlovable original."

Works of Fiction and Nonfiction

It was the publication of *Desert Solitaire* in 1968, a semi-autobiographical book featuring two main characters—Abbey and a nameless narrator—that launched his star into the firmament, with *The New York Times* proclaiming it "a passionately felt, deeply poetic book."

Based on extensive notes he made during two seasons spent as a ranger at Arches National Monument in Utah in 1956 and 1957, as he turned thirty, the final draft was completed both in a bar in Hoboken, New Jersey, and at a ranger's fire lookout tower in the Petrified Forest. He mailed it book rate to his agent, Don Congdon, from Death Valley, California.

Although this book was responsible for transforming this iconoclastic literary Quixote into a kind of environmental icon, it was never Abbey's favorite. Many years later, Abbey was poking around the Haunted House bookstore on the outskirts of

Tucson with fellow writer Allan Harrington, when a woman they didn't know began following Abbey around. Finally she got his attention. "Of all your books, *Desert Solitaire* is my favorite," she enthused.

Abbey grimaced and turned away, muttering to Harrington, "Good God. Did she really read all my other books? It's not my favorite."

Solitaire was a case of lucky timing, appearing amid the environmental movement emerging across the United States. Movement novitiates were eager for inspiration and anti-establishment eloquence, and in need of point men to lead the struggle.

Catching this wind shift, *The New Yorker* described *Solitaire* as "an explosion of healthy rage at the gaucheries of the lumpen tourist." Poet Barry Lopez, writing in *Not Man Apart*, asserted that Abbey "has laid the paradox of human nature on the bedrock of the desert and asked for some answers because he is a realist. Many of us as yet have not even perceived that there is a question."

Shortly after this book was published, a *Newsweek* editor named John Mitchell happened to pay a visit to a New York City writer named Charles Little. He brought with him a pile of books known in the publishing world as "review copies"—free copies of new books sent to magazines to review.

"Want any of these before I throw them out?" Mitchell asked. "I'll take this one," Little replied, wishing to be polite, but knowing nothing about the book he selected. It looked like a slim tome on the natural history of deserts, a subject that he had always wanted to delve into more deeply. It was *Desert Solitaire*.

The next day, Little called Mitchell: "Abbey's no ranger. He's a writer. And this is a pip of a book." There was a pause on the other end of the line.

"Give it back," Mitchell said.

"I will loan it back," Little said. "Forget give."

Little never lent his book to anyone else. Instead, he repaired to Washington, D.C., bringing along his tattered copy, for an editing job with the staid old Conservation Foundation, then being chaired by the venerable Russell Train.

Abbey's poetic ruminations soon became some of the grist for national policy in that foundation's 1972 report "National Parks for the Future," some of which was later implemented.

It was in *Desert Solitaire* that Abbey first elucidated the threat of "industrial tourism" in the national parks. Abbey regarded motorized tourists as saboteurs of sacred lands, on one hand, and as victims of their own auto dependency on the other—in refusing to get out of their cars, they did not get to enjoy the land, to crawl on the sandstone with the scorpions and the snakes and the animals.

According to the gospel of Abbey, the three remedies required were simple and straightforward:

- No more cars in national parks; let the people walk or ride horses, mules, wild pigs—anything. "We have agreed not to drive our automobiles into cathedrals, concert halls, art museums . . . and other sanctums of our culture," he wrote. "We should treat the national parks with the same deference."
- No more new roads in national parks. Abbey told his readers that once autos are prohibited, the second step should be easy; paved roads would be reserved for bikes, and dirt trails would be turned into trails for hikers. "The next generation would be grateful to us," Abbey declared.
- Put the park rangers back to work—"lazy scheming loafers," he called them. He felt they frittered away too many years selling tickets at toll booths and filling out forms to appease the bureaucracy's mania for statistics.

"They'll [rangers] be needed on the trail," Abbey proclaimed.
"Once we outlaw the motors and stop the road-building and
force the multitudes back on their feet, the people will need
leaders. . . . The only foreseeable alternative is the gradual
destruction of our national park system."

Was he joshing, readers wondered? Was he putting the world
on? Didn't he know that fighting that kind of progress was a losing cause, that the inexorable forces of population growth and
motorization were too formidable for mere individuals to fight?

"Somebody has to do it," was his reply to friends. "Let being be."

Reviewers greeted *Desert Solitaire* with a fair amount of
praise, crediting Abbey with being a kind of ecological Ezekiel,
raging against the attack on the planet by the forces of mindless
growth. And they applauded him for articulating the paradoxical
dilemma confronting the national parks, one that burns even
hotter today as motor traffic in crown jewels like the Grand
Canyon and Yellowstone is now deemed out of control by U.S.
government officials.

Studies confirming the fears Abbey expressed in *Solitaire*
started appearing in the eighties in academic journals and books
from specialized publishers. Without exception, they concluded
that even as the U.S. government attempts to preserve natural
beauty in all the national parks, industrial tourism is slowly erad-
icating the very quality tourists come to behold.

Solitaire was published during a tumultuous time in America,
a time remembered now for the Kennedy assassinations, urban
riots, the murder of Dr. Martin Luther King, and the Vietnam
catastrophe—all contributing to a surge in violence in the country. This led to serious questioning about whether there might be
a fundamental flaw in the American persona, which D. H.
Lawrence had described forty years earlier as "the essential
American soul, hard, isolate, stoical, a killer."

It was a decade in which feelings of hope degenerated into a kind of national masochism, and Abbey's rantings fanned the flames of outrage. His tirades against developers, dam builders, politicians, and even his own seasonal employer the National Park Service (in whose side he was always a thorn) caught the mood. In some circles, he was enshrined as a new ecological Merlin the Magician.

Overall, *Desert Solitaire* is a spicy, complex work, containing enough contradictions to provide a lifetime of challenge for any psychologist. As for reviewers, only a handful sensed the underlying rhythms of brutality, violent deeds, and morbid tales.

Abbey, the purported nature lover, slays a rabbit with a rock. He caves in anthills with his walking stick and pushes old tires into his beloved Grand Canyon. Concurrently, he lashes out at the violence being done to nature by others, choosing to open this book with some poetry by Pablo Neruda: "Give me silence, water, hope. Give me struggle, iron, volcanoes."

Award-winning author Barry Lopez sensed paradox everywhere. As he wrote in a review for *Not Man Apart*, "There's a strange twist to the man. He is violent and he is also a prisoner of the cultural perception he condemns in others . . . but to say Abbey is a violent man is to get nowhere."

Still, some readers were jarred by the episode in which Abbey kills a rabbit, accusing him of facile rationalizing and hypocrisy.

For a moment I am shocked by my deed; I stare at the quiet rabbit, his glazed eyes, his blood drying in the dust. Something vital is lacking. But shock is succeeded by a mild elation.

Leaving my victim to vultures and maggots, who will appreciate him more than I could; the flesh is probably infected with tularemia . . . I continued my walk with a new, augmented cheerfulness which is hard to understand but unmistakable.

What the rabbit has lost in energy and spirit seems added, by processes too subtle to fathom, to my own soul. I try but I cannot feel my sense of guilt. I examine my soul, white as snow. Check my hands; not a trace of blood. No longer do I feel so isolated from the sparse and furtive life around me, a stranger from another world. I have entered into this one.

We are kindred all of us, killer and victim, predator and prey, me and the sly coyote, the soaring buzzard, the elegant gopher snake, the trembling cottontail, the foul worms that feed on our entrails, all of them. Long live diversity; long live the earth.

Years before the biological concept of deep ecology entered the mainstream, there was Abbey, declaring where he stood: All creatures have equal rights, so if diversity is to be preserved, the anthropocentric, or man-centered, order of things must shift to a more biocentric view.

As he put it in *Desert Solitaire*, "I have personal convictions to uphold. Ideals, you might say. I prefer not to kill animals. I'd rather kill a man than a snake."

A case can be made that, besides showing the connections between humans and animals, he was tapping into his own paradoxical behavior to illuminate the contradictory aspects of all of human nature. He had in mind those politicians, engineers, generals, and developers who express their love of the land while simultaneously taking all the necessary steps to hurt it.

In *Desert Solitaire*, there was much more at play in Abbey's mind than environmental damage. Though he wrote of his love for the lonely and bleak desert, it could drive him crazy with loneliness. So he returned, at the book's conclusion, to the very dying, decaying cities he abhorred and left the sacred land behind.

I want to hear once more the crackle of clamshells on the floor of the bar in the Clam Broth House in Hoboken. I long for a view of the jolly, rosy faces on 42nd street and the cheerful throngs on the sidewalks of Atlantic Avenue. Enough of Land's End, Dead Horse Point, Tukuhnikivats and other high resolves; I want to see somebody jump out of a window or a roof.

I grow weary of nobody's company but my own; let me hear the wit and wisdom of the subway crowds again, the cabdrivers' shrewd aphorisms, the genial chuckle of a Jersey City cop, the happy laughter of Greater New York's one million illegitimate children.

This is the same author who would later describe New York City and its "Vampire" State Building in his essay "Manhattan Twilight" *(The Journey Home)* as a living hell: "When I was there, I thought New York was dying. Maybe it really is. I know I was dying to get out. But if it's dying, then it's going to be a prolonged, strange, infinitely complex process, a death of terror and grandeur. Imagine a carcinoma 300 miles long, a mile thick, embracing 50 million souls."

Here is the quintessential paradox of Abbey's work: he escapes to the desert, far from degenerate cities, but he cannot allow himself to escape permanently. He cannot stay away from "the rat race (Rattus Urbanus)," as he termed it, for long.

Despite all the fair-to-good reviews it received, *Solitaire* soon went out of print in hardcover. By 1971, having achieved an underground reputation, it was reissued as a paperback; before long, more than 500,000 copies were in print.

Desert Solitaire was important for Abbey's career, not necessarily because of its powerful environmental theme, but because his writing talents were displayed in essay form for the first time: the ever-present voice of a strong narrator without the less-strong fictional contrivances of his earlier books.

It was his most sustained work to date. Critic Garth McCann likely made the best point when he observed that *Desert Solitaire* focused on the complex and paradoxical presence of Abbey: "The overpowering figure of Abbey, with all his quirks, vanities, regrets and dreams. On a higher level, Abbey comes to represent all mankind, as he seeks to discover the essence of existence in our time."

For many reasons, the book has endured. In the summer of 1991, a band of young people, fresh off the Colorado River, were lounging around a laundromat in Moab, Utah, waiting for their drenched clothes to dry; all of them were reading weather-beaten copies of *Desert Solitaire,* more than two decades after it first appeared. Indeed, years after his death, in places all across the West, and now in Germany and Japan where translations have been published, Abbey's words in *Desert Solitaire* still offer solace and encouragement to the latent rebel-dreamer in the hearts of new readers.

Three years after *Desert Solitaire,* the novel *Black Sun,* always Abbey's favorite book, was published. Set in the same desert country as *Desert Solitaire,* that netherworld zone where urban civilization and wilderness infringe on each other, this novel asks: In the solitude of the desert, in a natural world being made unnatural by man's insatiable quest for cheap resources, is there such a thing as love?

A wood nymph named Sandy comes to ranger Will Gatlin's fire lookout tower. They share a steamy idyll until she abruptly vanishes. Soon afterwards, her robotic air force cadet boyfriend arrives to beat Gatlin up. He does, then leaves the lonely ranger to wander the far canyons in search of her. He never finds her. She is lost forever.

At the end of this poignant book, the ranger is alone again, wondering whether the woman was really only a dream after all:

"Oh my love, I see thee everywhere," Gatlin laments. "In the wild eyes of the doe. In the dove's song. In the secret places of the forest. Sun gleaming on grass." More so than his previous works, *Black Sun* is both introspective and rich in imagery. Here, Abbey writes in stream-of-consciousness style that works to accentuate the pain and loss Gatlin feels.

> What is it that slides invisible among my thoughts? What transparent thread weaves my days together? Always at the corner of my eye, just beyond the focus of my vision, something moves, disappears when I turn toward it . . .

In *Black Sun* there is none of the anger or sarcasm found in *Desert Solitaire*. It was more introspective than anything he had crafted to date, having been written shortly after the tragic death of his wife, Judy Pepper, in a New York hospital. Her death left him shattered and haunted for years, sending him into bouts of depression and loneliness.

Another inspiration for the novel, if that was not sufficient, was the mysterious disappearance of a young woman at Organ Pipe Cactus National Monument near Ajo, Arizona, where Abbey had rangered.

Her body, like Sandy's, was never found.

For the most part, critics didn't care for this tale of a man's ascent to heaven, and his descent into hell. *The New Yorker* pronounced it "sentimental," while others, like his sometime friend Edward Hoagland, merely dismissed it as "wilderness writing" in *The New York Times Book Review*, asserting that it couldn't be read as a novel, a romance, or even a statement.

By way of contrast, Tom Lyon, writing in *Western American Literature*, saw Abbey's ironic vision at play: "There is more than one voice in Edward Abbey; the multiple consciousness living with today's death of things, yet open to the forward territory, knowing the important foolishness of dreaming the old good dreams here on the downhill side . . . the source of both Abbey's highly regarded humor and his deeper power. . . . *Black Sun* is . . . much more profound than it looks."

From another vantage point, Ann Ronald, a serious student of Abbey's work from her perch on the faculty at the University of Nevada, believes that *Black Sun* signaled an important milestone in Abbey's writings: for the first time, he brought a structure, a vision, to the story, a design that controlled it from the opening page to the last.

Abbey felt that was fair.

With emotions ranging from despair to ecstasy, *Black Sun* chronicles Gatlin's search for self amid the senselessness of the times using a literary form that, Professor Ronald points out, has deep romantic roots beginning probably with Beowulf: isolation, contact, ecstasy, descent into hell, and return to earth.

One critic went as far as to compare Gatlin to Ishmael in Melville's *Moby Dick*, the sole survivor in Captain Ahab's lunatic search for the white whale. *Black Sun* is no *Moby Dick*, but it's a story that remains with the reader long after the first read. Abbey concludes this novel as he began it, with Gatlin staring "out the window, into the forest," having failed to find love, feeling alienated from society, and powerless. Stoicism, albeit wry, looms as Gatlin's last redoubt when the realization dawns that happiness in life is "possible," but sorrow is more likely.

This exchange between Will Gatlin and his friend Art Ballantine highlights Gatlin's alienation:

"What in God's name do you think you are doing here? What do you really want to do anyway?"

"Really want to do," Gatlin repeats softly, still gazing out over the forest, toward the desert. A pause. "Stare at the sun," he says.

"What?"

"Stare it down."

Ballantine sighs. "Will, you're crazy."

"Stare it out," says Gatlin smiling. "Stand on this tower and stare at the sun until it goes . . . black."

By the time *Black Sun* was published, Cactus Ed was already toiling away on *The Monkey Wrench Gang.* That was followed by *Good News,* which takes place in Phoenix in the early years of the twenty-first century.

Several book critics dubbed *Good News* the first recorded science fiction Western. In the book, despite hopes of many individuals that humans and nature might finally achieve harmony in an economic system, civilization has disintegrated. A paramilitary organization rules the populace, headed by an insane authoritarian visionary called simply, The Chief.

Ruins. Ruins. All in ruins. Coyotes slink among the blackened walls, hunting rats. Anthills rise, Soleri-like, from the arid fountains of the covered mall. Young paloverde trees, acid green, and globemallow, and sunflowers, and tumbleweed, and the bright fuzzy cactus known as teddy bear cholla (cuddly and deadly) grow from cracks in the asphalt of the endless parking lots.

The Chief is a satanic mélange of Adolf Hitler, Darth Vader, and Richard Nixon. Ruling over the remnants of modern civilization with his own army, he seeks to create "an island of decency in a sea of disorder." Though Abbey never tells us what caused the catastrophe, the implication is that the U.S. industrial system collapsed under its own weight. This triggers a replay of the oldest war of all: conflict between the city and the country, industry and the farm.

Desperate for supplies, the Chief's army pillages the countryside for food——and whatever else they can steal. The only resistance the Chief and his marauders encounter comes from Jack Burns, an older "brave cowboy," and his Hopi Indian friend Sam, who is a medicine man skilled at all kinds of magic, and who is helping Jack search for the son he hasn't seen in years.

The Indian points toward the smoldering city, the scatter of fires and lights spread across ten miles of the horizon. "How do you think we're going to find him? In that dying mess? All those frightened people? You don't even know what he looks like now."

"I know his name." Burns chews slowly and grudgingly, with little appetite, on the unsalted meat. "I'll know him when I see him."

Mysteriously, Burns dies in the search, stabbed by a medieval lance in this nightmare scenario of the future. Just as mysteriously, the remains of this ghostly anarchist are never found.

"Colonel, the men couldn't find the body."

The colonel looks cross. "That's absurd."

"Yes sir."

"Did they really look? Couldn't they find our tracks?"

"Yes sir, they followed the tracks and they found where the old man was. Found the lance. Dried blood all over the place. But no body."

"Absurd. What about the horse?"

"The horse was gone too."

"Ridiculous."

"Yes sir. Maybe coyotes dragged the body away."

"That's really absurd."

"I know sir. But no body."
"Absurd."
"Yes sir."
"Absurd."
"You're right, Colonel."

Few reviewers gathered that this book was not what it appeared to be, a fashionable environmental diatribe. On the contrary, Abbey meant it to be a parody of his own works to date, friends say, in the context of his first attempt at an artistic vision of a failed century. The result, seemingly preposterous then, is not necessarily such far-fetched fantasy today.

Abbey had a glorious time with this novel by tossing in double entendres, multiple ironies, and incongruities. He threw the classic Western cowboy storyline to the winds, but not before turning it upside down first.

Evidently unaware of Abbey's love of irony, many critics gave him a rough time with this prophetic novel. "A banal melodrama with one-dimensional characters," pronounced the *Cleveland Plain Dealer.* "It leaves much to be desired in terms of flavor and substance," wrote Alan Chuese in the *Los Angeles Times.*

Looking back, this work is a particularly fine example of Abbey's themes being ahead of their time. Since *Good News* was published, many details of the novel's fictional sweep have become reality in Phoenix.

Brownish-yellow clouds of air pollution, Los Angeles–style, now hang over the Valley of the Sun on far too many days, causing senior citizens who moved from Manhattan, Chicago, and California to Phoenix for health reasons, to wonder why they did. Towering high-rise buildings loom above what were once ancient Indian ceremonial grounds, pesticides are found in the drinking water, and teenage gangs roam the streets.

In the early 1990s, politicians and citizens began to face up to the most ominous problem of all—insufficient water for Phoenix to maintain its water-greedy lifestyle into the twenty-first century. Either drastic conservation actions need to be taken, or the price of water to all users will increase dramatically.

Abbey foresaw, years before the vast majority of politicians, that the Colorado River—principal water source for both California and Arizona—was being oversubscribed many times over by farmers, municipalities, Indian tribes, and yes, the federal government. Furthermore, aquifers, the life-giving support systems of the Arizona desert, are being pumped out twice as fast as they are being replenished.

Now, for the first time, academics and a few politicians are openly suggesting that unless residents of Tucson and Phoenix accept the stringent limits that desert living implicitly imposes, they will experience more silt and salts in their water, right up until the time their water-dependent lifestyle implodes. And then the people will disperse, leaving archaeologists in the future to unravel the mystery of what transpired—just as they now wonder what happened to Babylon, Persepolis, and Gomorrah.

Apart from the researches of Major John Wesley Powell and the writings of Edward Abbey, there is little evidence in the entire history of Southwestern Anglo settlements that anyone ever seriously wondered if the Colorado River might not have enough water to make Arizona and her neighboring states bloom forever like an Emerald Island amid the desert.

By creating this tragicomic, futuristic parody in *Good News*, Abbey tried to draw people's attention to the grim destiny that faces not only Phoenix, but also his hometown of Tucson.

"The job of all authors is to challenge us," Abbey once remarked, "to change our ways."

Abbey believed that the lesson of the desert is the need for limits for humans who dare to live there, limits that cannot be transcended or transgressed through science, technology, or chamber of commerce hype.

Abbey never wrote a formal autobiography. The closest he came to one is *The Fool's Progress,* the story of Henry Holyoak Lightcap.

> I'm alright. It's the world that is dysfunctioning.
> —HENRY HOLYOAK LIGHTCAP IN
> A LETTER TO HIS BROTHER

Soon after *The Monkey Wrench Gang* was published, rumors began to circulate in some literary circles that Ed Abbey was finally working on a major work of fiction, "the fat masterpiece," as he put it in a letter to a friend in the late 1970s.

After ten years of doubt, self-torment, and deteriorating health, Abbey's creation was the disturbing and hilarious saga of Henry, a kind of modern Tom Jones who thought like Flaubert and saw the world like Ambrose Bierce.

As the tale opens, this self-proclaimed bigot and curmudgeon is seen careening toward the ninth inning of his life. Adamant in his refusal to come to terms with modern society and civilization, he heads home to his roots in Appalachia.

Many reviewers didn't know what to make of *The Fool's Progress.* "If you've ever looked in the rearview mirror of your trim Japanese import," wrote a reviewer for the *St. Louis Post-Dispatch,* "and seen a wild-eyed man barreling down on you in his big, battered American pickup, its hood held shut with wire, a toy bald eagle swinging by its feet from the antenna, a water bag hanging askew from the twisted grill, the gunrack filled to capacity—and if you ever felt a shiver of fear and fascination and wondered what the wild-eyed man was thinking—then read this book."

> I may be the only redneck intellectual in America who's not yet been analyzed, psychoanalyzed, rolfed TMized, Estered, sensory-deprived, reborn, spinologized and had my colon irrigated.
> —HENRY HOLYOAK LIGHTCAP

Seemingly a cry for help and a love song, this "honest novel," as Abbey dubbed it, opens with Henry's third wife departing forever for parts unknown, leaving a note on the refrigerator door in magnetic letters: GO TO HELL HENRY.

Having always despised the old icebox anyway, Henry shoots it full of holes with a .357 Magnum, gets roaring drunk, then sobering up, packs his guns, his dog Solstice, and himself into his 1962 Dodge Carryall and heads for "home," which is Stump Creek, West Virginia (really Home, Pennsylvania).

The trip is bizarre: Solstice is sick with a Tucson fungus, Henry has a crablike pinch of pain near his liver, and the truck drinks oil.

Into this picaresque odyssey we readers wade, following Henry, a failed philosophical anarchist and social poet who tells the truth even when it's ugly. We wander with him back across the Mississippi to the "myth-infested hills of ancient Appalachia," wondering why the book—485 pages—is so long when Henry's life seems certain to be so short. Only at the end do we learn that Henry is not making his illness up. Neither was Abbey when he wrote this book—the only question was how long he had.

"Henry is difficult to understand," wrote a reviewer in the *Indianapolis Star.* "Abbey allows the reader to build a repressed dislike for the main character, much like the feeling Lightcap appears to hold of himself."

As always, the reviews were uneven, but the harsh ones were more caustic than usual, such as the one by Edward Marston, publisher of the *High Country News,* in the *National Review:* "From a distance, Abbey may sound like an environmentalist, but only from a distance. Environmentalists generally pay at least lip service to the rights and values of Native Americans. Abbey lumps Indians with other 'minorities'—women, Hispanics, Jews, well-to-do WASPS—as enemies of both the land and its rightful inheritors: Appalachian hillbilly white trash. . . . *The Fool's Progress* shows that nativist hostility is as much a part of Edward Abbey as is his love of the Western landscape and the sky."

So irritated was one Abbey fan by this review that a few days after Abbey died, Marston received an angry call at his office in Colorado and was accused of contributing to Abbey's death, which occurred a month after the review was published.

"It was scary," Marston recalls. For his part, Abbey was so irritated by the review, written by a man he thought was his friend, that he canceled his subscription to his paper.

There are as many definitions of a classic book as there are literary critics. Samuel Johnson said they are works that are "just representations of general nature." Samuel Coleridge used the quality of "organic unity" in his definition, while T. S. Eliot defined classic as "any work which displays the comprehensiveness expected of age, learning, and wisdom."

In assessing *The Fool's Progress* for the *Bloomsbury Review,* John Murray, contributing editor and college writing teacher, argued that all those definitions of "a classic" were too limited. To be a classic, as he saw it, five characteristics are apropos: universality of character and action, excellence of craft, moral and unequivocal truth of theme, integrity of style, and depth of feeling.

Wrote Murray: "Not only does *The Fool's Progress* measure up well when judged by these standards, it also stands up well when put beside the pre-existing classics of the Western American novel, *The Prairie, The Octopus, The Call of the Wild, The Big Sky, The Grapes of Wrath, On the Road,* and others.

"It just may be that this book, like its stubborn protagonist, will endure. There is really no higher praise a reviewer can bestow upon a work."

Not every reviewer was as enthusiastic. In an effort to promote the book, the publisher distributed a press kit with numerous quotes labeling Abbey everything from "arrogant, incoherent, flippant, nasty and unconstructive" (Gretel Ehrlich) to a "racist and an eco-fascist" and a "reactionary slime" (Alexander Cockburn).

Clever marketing it was, because rather than turning people away, it attracted them to the book, which is really about love and Abbey's own lifelong battle against what he considered one of American society's greatest afflictions—conformity to "the norm."

"Too many people live half-lives," Abbey once told an interviewer. "They are malled in. They are chained in. They are oppressed, even in this, the richest country on earth."

Near the end of this saga, Abbey writes about Henry Lightcap and the books he has read: "He remembered best not the development of character or the unraveling of plot or the structure of an argument . . . but simply the quality of an author's mind."

Was Abbey trying to catch the eye of some reviewer who, instead of seeing this novel as an angry work, might take note of quality of the author's mind, its racist, sexist leanings notwithstanding?

Life is a bitch, his dark companion said—and then you die. Not so cried Henry! Life is a glorious shining and splendid adventure, and then you die.

Time Magazine's reviewer overlooked Abbey's clue, finding the book to be like "mournful country music that makes your blue eyes water. Call it Sick-Dog Blues. Abbey, who must have written this on a banjo, not a typewriter, is feeling sorry for his hero and probably himself, too."

Having received several death sentences from his doctors in the years preceding *The Fool's Progress*, the amazing thing is why he wasn't feeling even sorrier for himself, knowing for certain that his days were numbered.

A friend who accompanied Abbey on his 1986 journey back to Appalachia, upon which *The Fool's Progress* is based, recalls that Abbey frequently picked up pain medicine mailed ahead by someone—although not his wife, Clarke—quietly taking it for the painful pancreatitis condition that made him almost always feel "yucky." But he never complained.

Other reviewers failed to note the thematic undertone in this novel, a restatement of the motif that had first emerged almost three decades earlier in *The Brave Cowboy:* Despite America's vaunted intelligence, science, knowledge, rationalism, and common sense, her people continue to tolerate, even encourage the creation of overgrown institutions that become top-heavy, keel over, and crumble.

Many critics saw in Abbey an angry, crepe-hanging pessimist who crafted depressing characters like Lightcap just for the hell of it. However, behind his sometimes wicked grin, something else was lurking; call it hope, call it a romantic belief that enough people would recognize the wrong path was being taken, and stop what Abbey called "the runaway train."

That is the intrinsic difference between Abbey and the swelling legions of other observers who sensed that the United States was on the wrong path—most concluded there was no chance of stopping the train. "I believe in fighting back," he once told an interviewer. "Just for the sake of personal honor and conscience, if nothing else."

So did Lightcap, and as Abbey's private journals suggest, Lightcap was no ordinary fool. Abbey borrowed him from the archaic Tarot card deck, and The Fool personifies the universal principle associated with the state of consciousness experienced by people prior to birth and after death.

The portraiture of The Fool is said to be Dionysius, that primitive springtime God with Bacchus horns and grapes, who stands for the creative power that gives birth to new forms from a state of wonder and anticipation, never from fear.

Abbey insisted he knew nothing about the Tarot but there are ample reasons not to believe him. The Fool, after all, underscores Abbey's principle of courage: the state of no fear, of ecstasy, and peak experience on a journey during which he is always revealing his spirit in a state of awe and curiosity. Like Lightcap—and Abbey—The Fool of the Tarot left fear behind, and faced death bravely.

Some fans felt that, in creating the Lightcap character, Abbey vastly overdrew both racial and sexual stereotypes. In response to Abbey's request to review the draft manuscript, his friend Greg McNamee expressed his feelings bluntly in a letter to Abbey in December, 1987:

> I am concerned, and not as an Eastern Liberal either, with certain aspects of Lightcap's character, especially his racism. . . . It just doesn't work; his racist cracks are not especially funny or profound, and, worst of all, they detract from a quite sympathetic character, make him much less likeable . . . most of the racist cracks are simply wasted words, I'm afraid, that seem to serve no purpose whatever, they're dead weight on the page. . . .
>
> I am afraid they'll—and only they—will make reviewers hostile to a book that should be regarded as important in the body

of your work (and I believe *The Fool's Progress* goes up there with your best writing); I can't really see the point in doing that, even if you do have fun in angering the pundits by poking fun in "outrageous" ways.

Lightcap is likely to be read as Edward Abbey (anyone who has read your essays knows that this novel richly partakes of your own life) and I really don't think your readers want to think of you as someone given to racism. Do you want to be explained away like Ezra Pound, after all? I urge you . . . to rethink this, and to excise most, if not all, of the "little brown people" jokes and diatribes.

Abbey reflected upon McNamee's eleven-page letter and thanked him in one of his famous postcards, which he sent by the thousands, over the years to fans and friends. Praising his friendly critic for his insights, he proceeded to ignore most of them.

As McNamee recalls, "Ed was a provocateur in his writings, but in *Fool's,* we see beneath that in the character of Lightcap. Ed was a WASP and he really believed that a flood of immigration into the U.S. would cheapen our way of life. I disagreed with him here. He overdid the hyperbole, but Ed was Ed."

After the book was out, Abbey acknowledged some flaws. "I don't claim it's a great book. I think it has too many jokes," he told the *San Jose Mercury News* in November 1988. "I think it has too many jokes and too much sex. But I think it's an entertaining book. I'm proud of it."

The seeds for this novel were likely sown in the late 1950s, during a stint at Stanford University in the late Wallace Stegner's creative writing workshop. In those days, Abbey was still a self-styled beatnik whose drug of choice was jug wine, and his favorite author was the greatly undersung Kenneth Rexroth, considered in some academic circles to have been the father of the beatnik movement.

It was during Stegner's workshop that Abbey got the idea for a "sensational new kind of American novel." The theme was "sub-Bohemian life and the desperate search by young Americans for spiritual enlightenment, emotional fulfillment, and sexual liberation."

He planned to title it *Down the Road,* and got enough writing done so that 100 pages were completed when Jack Kerouac's *On the Road* was published. Discouraged for the moment, he saved the pages, and large swatches found their way into *The Fool's Progress,* his private papers reveal.

"I don't throw anything away," Abbey told a visitor six months before he died. Almost every aspect of Abbey's life is contained in *The Fool's Progress:* birth and death, loves and lost loves, prejudices and dreams. Funny, touching, outrageous, it is a tumultuous look at twentieth-century America and a man's soul, "if you don't mind full-bore sexism," wrote the reviewer for *The Boston Globe,* "and raging self-pity, shoot-from-the-hip purple prose and hot gonads on the half shell. Abbey doesn't."

Abbey certainly didn't—not for the purpose of his story.

In *The Fool's Progress,* Abbey draws word pictures of a paradise lost, the decomposing, damaged face of America, whose people are losing touch with the land, with the goals of the Founding Fathers, and are becoming either greed-addicted opportunists, or worse yet, subjects of same.

"At heart, Mr. Abbey is a sentimentalist," wrote Howard Coale in *The New York Times Book Review,* "who loves this country in a corny absolutely authentic way. Ironically, it is when he is sappy that Abbey is at his best. When he writes of the boy dreaming of 'the ghosts of Shawnee warriors' watching 'from the shadows of the red oaks,' he is stirring something real in himself, and the writing becomes more persuasive.

"These moments come every so often. They're quiet, simple scenes, and they're wonderful. Unfortunately they are drowned out to almost a murmur by the harpings of a slightly malevolent voice."

Lisa Miller, in the *Arizona Republic*, probably put it best: "This is no ho-hum novel. Readers will cherish it or burn it, but they're not going to leave it out in the rain."

On his last book tour, in 1988, Abbey was disappointed that his enemies didn't show up to heckle him. "I have expected a pie in the face everytime someone has walked up to me with a bag in hand," he told an interviewer in Seattle. "But so far I've encountered nothing but love. It's sickening, really decadent. But very nice."

The desert anarchist was mellowing now, even if just a little.

Hayduke Lives, Abbey's final novel, was published posthumously. It almost wasn't completed. Writing thousands of words a day in a secret cabin miles from his home on the outskirts of Tucson, Abbey found the energy and the inspiration to deliver a comic last will and testament, beginning with a warning: "Anyone who takes this book seriously will be shot. Anyone who does not take it seriously will be buried by a Mitsubishi bulldozer."

Here, Abbey brings *The Monkey Wrench Gang* together again, though now a little long in the tooth. Even George Washington Hayduke is back, the ex–Green Beret and environmental avenger who was last seen by his fans clinging to a cliff, under fire from both a posse and a helicopter for his efforts to free the Colorado River of Glen Canyon Dam.

It develops that Hayduke didn't die after all, but now "the authorities" have him under constant surveillance. To elude them, he's become a bag lady in Albuquerque, sneaking in and out of alleys and cheap cafes—waiting.

Meantime, the world's largest self-propelled strip mining machine, appropriately dubbed GOLIATH, is rumbling ominously toward the still-unravaged reaches in the Arizona-Utah borderlands to Lost Eden Canyon, hungry for uranium deposits.

Abbey is setting the stage, as he did in *Good News,* for another final battle for the desert, complete with The Lone Ranger (Jack Burns), glass eye and all, who waves them on from high atop ghostly mesas.

To Abbey followers, the players are familiar: The NPR (National Parking-Lot Service), the USFS (United States Forest Swine), the DOE (Department of Entropy), the state DG&F (Department of Game and Fishiness), and J. Dudley Love, investor in the $37 million GOLIATH. Love is a uranium mine owner and known pilager of Indian tombs throughout the Four Corners region (Utah, Colorado, New Mexico, and Arizona) whom Abbey modeled after a real Utah developer, who, incidentally, died of cancer not long after Abbey did.

"Smells like money to me," he tells a cheering audience of reporters and investors. "I like the smell of money, yessir. We don't need more so-called wilderness; only attracts more environmentalists. Like a dead horse draws blowflies. . . . I'm still here and I don't glow in the dark; radiation is good for you."

Enter *The Monkey Wrench Gang* and Earth First!, the fringe environmental group trying to stop the beast with a variety of demonstrations and acts of civil disobedience.

The ever-horny Doc Sarvis explains their actions: "They'll last until they become effective. Then the state moves in, railroads some of the leaders into prison, murders a few others for educational purposes, clubs and gasses and jails the followers and viola!—peace and order are restored."

Not many sacred cows escape Abbey's rhetorical birdshot, including environmental groups, women, and politicians. Generally, *Hayduke Lives* was reviewed widely but not well enough to please Abbey's ghost. "Pocked with holes," spat the reviewer for the *Fort Lauderdale Florida Sun-Sentinel,* "and contrivances and conceits. Hayduke is a disappointing attempt to recapture the energy and momentum of *The Monkey Wrench Gang.*"

The *Minneapolis Star and Tribune* advised readers to take Abbey's advice in general and "resist" reading it. "Let the book lie, and let Abbey rest on the laurels of his better work."

As for the *Tulsa Tribune,* reviewer Bob Bledsoe expressed doubt that Hayduke "would ever fire the spirits and imaginations of budding young ecologists," as previous adventures of the gang had done. Nonetheless, he tabbed the novel a "worthwhile trip down memory lane." The *Dallas Times-Herald* said it was no such thing, terming the novel "sour and tired . . . unhappily not the finest of farewells from a very original American writer." Echoing those sentiments, the *San Diego Tribune* reviewer carped, "R.I.P. Edward Abbey. We'll remember your palmier days."

"Shopworn," agreed Grace Lichtenstein, one-time Rocky Mountain Bureau Chief for *The New York Times.* "In 1975, action-oriented environmentalism was still new, even radical. Now, it's so mainstream (except in the state of Utah), even some Republicans embrace it . . . the result reads as though Abbey were firing an Uzi at an anthill."

From a man who professed to abhor violence and who advised others to abide by the code of the ecowarrior, the final pages of this book are puzzling. The old gang is being hunted by the federal police, but their main target is Hayduke, who is trying to flee the country for Australia, which he considers, as Abbey did, "the last country left."

A CIA agent pursues Hayduke to the Mexican beach where an escape boat is waiting, but lets him get away, and then kills himself. "It's a provocative ending," noted Ray Murphy in the *Rocky Mountain News,* "and a disturbing one given the source."

Publishers Weekly, which usually found much to admire in Abbey's books, took note, too, that in the course of the ecosabotage, a man gets killed, "contradicting what used to be the whole point of Abbey's writing: only machines died."

Beyond that, the novel has a slapdash quality, and there is the overwhelming sense that, at the end, he downplayed his greatest gifts, his lyricism and poetic odes to the wilderness. By his own standards, this final novel has an unfinished feeling to it.

Whatever the shortcomings of Abbey's fiction, most reviewers of the works discussed in this chapter acknowledged that Abbey was among a handful of eloquent, passionate authors in the twentieth century, devoting their lives to warning of the dangers of runaway industrialism and the value of wilderness to a free society.

As usual, Abbey told his readers what he was up to clearly enough in *Desert Solitaire*. "Love of wilderness," he wrote, "is an expression of loyalty to the earth, the earth which bore us and sustains us, the only home we will ever know, the only paradise we ever need—if only we had the eyes to see."

"I put the best part of me in my books," Abbey once told an interviewer. "The evil side I hope to keep secret." As Peter Wild, his colleague at the University of Arizona, has pointed out, this was an effective statement toward advancing Abbey's romantic image, but it was not entirely true.

With a few variations, Abbey's own life was the pith of all these books. "In the best romantic tradition," Wild has written, "Abbey the writer and Abbey the man are much the same person: craggy-faced and lean, cagey in private conversation. He is the image of the desert rat with a shady past projected by his novels."

In Abbey's early years, he had hoped to avoid the fate of other novelists based in the West, those whom Wallace Stegner likened to the old folks in the Beckett play, *Waiting for Godot,* who rise up out of the garbage cans intermittently to say something, only to have the lids crammed down on them, who are allowed to speak only in their own back alley or within the "echoing hollow of our own garbage cans."

As far as most of Abbey's devotees were concerned, bad reviews didn't mean a thing. Regardless of what *The New York Times* said or did not say about his books, fans devoured every word, and as of five years after his death, more of his books were being bought than when he was alive, including translations into French, German, and Japanese.

What Abbey's novels amount to as a whole, suggests Bob Lippman—Arizona lawyer, legendary river-runner, and Abbeyite—is that Abbey's voice, "howling strident from the wilderness, successfully linked the factioned civil rights, labor, peace, and environmental movements, by clearly illustrating that the domination of nature leads to the domination of human beings, both collectively and individually."

In the final analysis, influential book critics, with only a few exceptions, never regarded Abbey as a major American writer. But so what, close Abbey-watchers say, because more than any of his contemporary writers, he was able to put into words what his readers felt in their hearts about the struggle of individuals in a shrinking natural world. He was able to rekindle their idealism and romanticism in a nation being suffocated by greed, corruption, and collapsing institutions. And he made people laugh, as well as think, in his various guises as storyteller, lyricist, satirist, buffoon-drunk, philosopher-scholar, environmental advocate, and moralist.

Walt Whitman had shown Abbey the way early, and provided him with a satisfactory answer in "Leaves of Grass" to those who chided him for the contradiction and inconsistency in his novels—and in his life as a rebel: "Do I contradict myself? Very well, I contradict myself. I am large. I contain multitudes."

Works of Nonfiction

I too have been mistaken for a member of that squalid profession, journalism. . . . I am not and never will be a goddamned two-bit sycophantic journalist for Christ's sake.

—*ABBEY'S ROAD*

When all his protestations about never being a member of that "squalid profession" are measured against his determination to be remembered for writing fiction, even Abbey's closest admirers contend that he was mistaken. Where is most of his best work to be found? In his nonfiction essays—precisely the genre of quasi-literary travel writing and environmental, sociopolitical journalism he reviled.

One aficionado of Abbey's works who holds this opinion is Greg McNamee, the Tucson writer to whom Abbey went for draft comments on *The Fool's Progress:* "Ed's nonfiction is superior to his fiction. It will be what he'll be remembered for. This is not to say that *The Brave Cowboy* and *Fire on the Mountain* weren't good, or that *Black Sun* wasn't a perfectly realized novel. But the apocalyptic novels, *The Monkey Wrench Gang* and *Good News,* his best-known works of fiction, are really little more than comic books, and the writing isn't as sustained as in the essays."

Abbey was at his best when writing about himself, stirring up what he called "redneck slumgullion stew," a tasty, nutritious, and coherent whole. "And why not? Society too, human society, is like a stew—if you don't keep it stirred up you get lots of scum on top."

In Abbey's first book of essays, *The Journey Home,* and in the following essay collections *Abbey's Road, Down the River, Beyond the Wall,* and *One Life at a Time, Please,* Abbey's goal was audacious: to make sense of his personal experience, by searching for the "connections and contradictions," as he put it, between wildness and wilderness, between community and anarchy, and between civilization and human freedom itself.

Taken together, these essays do amount to a stew, part daydream and part nightmare, seasoned with shards of autobiography and outdoor experiences, cooked, as he put it, in "the ancient iron pot" of his imagination over a fire of juniper, mesquite, and passionflower, in order to serve up his main course: agitation.

Virtually all reviewers were more upbeat about his essays than his novels. "We need people like Edward Abbey," gushed Ted Morgan in *The New York Times Book Review* (the publication Abbey said a hundred times never wrote a decent review of his work). "He is a combination of Thoreau and Marion the Swamp Fox . . . he is a living American artifact, part maverick, part pastoral extremist, part semi-hermit, part latter-day Jeremiah Johnson. I like him best at his most ornery," Morgan concluded.

In *The Journey Home,* Abbey is all the things Morgan says he is—beyond doubt he is far more than an environmental writer. "Readers . . . who hear only the polemics of a wild-country advocate have closed their eyes and ears to half his intent and accomplishment," wrote Ann Ronald in *The New West of Edward Abbey.* "They have forgotten his romancer's vision."

Abbey tells us that the source of that vision comes from the particular way he saw the land and man's relationship to it: the slickrock country—the rivers, canyons, and desert—which must be seen, or better yet, confronted directly by the senses to be believed.

Despite the efforts of countless painters, writers, and scientists—native Americans and newcomers alike—the Colorado Plateau, Abbey wrote, remains beyond even their considerable reach: "When all we know about it is said and measured and tabulated, there remains something in the soul of the place, the spirit of the whole, that cannot fully be assimilated by the human imagination."

It is that "something" that is the surest path, for most people, toward understanding that Abbey's works transcend issues of pollution and rapacious public-land practices by government and corporate pirates.

In the essay "Come On In," Abbey opens the door and allows the reader to comprehend his passion. "For us," he writes, "the wilderness and human emptiness of this land is not a source of fear but the greatest of its attractions." Calling his red rock canyon world "a place for the free," he issues a clarion call for it to be defended so that humankind can "rediscover the nearly lost pleasures of adventure, adventure in the physical sense, but also mental, spiritual, moral, aesthetic and intellectual adventure."

For the unconvinced reader:

Here you may yet find the elemental freedom to breathe deep of unpoisoned air, to experiment with solitude and stillness, to gaze through a hundred miles of untrammeled atmosphere across red rock canyons, beyond blue mesas, toward the snow-covered peaks of the most distant mountains——to make the discovery of the self in its proud sufficiency which is not isolation but an irreplaceable part of the mystery of the whole.

To the casual reader, *The Journey Home* is a seemingly incongruous melange of twenty-three essays on subjects ranging from

Hoboken to Death Valley, from mountain lions to the strip mining of an Indian reservation. Yet they are all linked by a cardinal theme: Abbey's love for the West, and his rancor at those who would despoil it while telling the world how much they love the region.

In the piece titled "The Second Rape of the West," Abbey reports a conversation with a widow named Mrs. Cotton, who lived "in a land of almost painful beauty" on a ranch near the Montana-Wyoming border. No work of fiction surpasses the passion of her plea for a modicum of sanity in a modern world gone loony. Alone among her neighbors, Mrs. Cotton refused to sell her beloved prairie grasslands to an energy company determined to strip off a thousand years of precious topsoil. She intends to fight back. She refuses to move on because she lives in the "last best place."

For good measure, Abbey summons forth a quote from *You Can't Go Home Again,* the Thomas Wolfe classic: "Behold how rich and powerful I am . . . would you destroy this glorious incarnation of your own heroic self?"

Abbey, always the provocative nonconformist, roars into full view in these essays in *The Journey Home,* informing and entertaining with artful humor and narrative. For new Abbey readers, some of his patented resistance to the intrusions of the modern world may come as a shock; to old Abbey disciples, his ideas are refreshing:

- Always remove and destroy survey stakes, flagging, advertising signboards, mining claim markers, animal traps, poisoned bait, seismic exploration geophones, and other such artifacts of industrialism.
- Every Boy Scout troop deserves a forest to get lost, miserable, and starving in.

- We need wilderness because we are wild animals.
- The earth is not a mechanism, but an organism.

This is the essential Abbey as he describes the need for wilderness as a psychiatric refuge from mechanization, explaining that it's wildness that keeps people free in a region where a cowboy with a rifle and a horse can shoot down a military helicopter, and a man with a monkey wrench can disarm a bulldozer. And wilderness is also a place where rebels can plan counterattacks against the tyrannies of the modern world.

Unlike most of his novels, *The Journey Home* was well received. "This is another good book about his life in America," wrote Larry McMurtry in the *Washington Post*. "Abbey points out with characteristic bite what a stupid nation we are to so atavistically destroy our own origins . . . being repeatedly called a naturalist has obviously goaded him beyond endurance . . . he is not a naturalist . . . he is a writer who *feels* a lot, and thus manages to transcend most of his own notions of himself."

Earlier, Abbey had written to McMurtry, expressing hope that he would not always be seen by the literary world as a nature writer and saying that he saw himself in the ranks of B. Traven and Knut Hamsun.

McMurtry raised the ante, writing in the same review that Abbey's works "are about twice as good as anything Traven or Hamsun ever wrote . . . his prose and general demeanor are closer to that of Wilfred Thesigar, the great English traveler and travel writer, than to anyone else."

McMurtry declared, too, that in his love of the heterodox poetry of American place names, Abbey ranks with Walt Whitman, the literary renegade of an earlier generation. Like Whitman, "Abbey writes with a fine particularity."

In *The Journey Home,* several critics thought they perceived an undercurrent of pessimism in some of the essays. Abbey, in turn, felt that many reviewers were overlooking the faith and hope implicit therein. True, many Western towns, like Telluride, Colorado, have been raped, and greedy folk are trying to Californicate the great American desert.

But wait.

Wrote Abbey: "The machine may seem omnipotent, but it is not. Human bodies and human wit, active here, there, everywhere, united in purpose, independent in action, can still face that machine and stop it and take it apart and reassemble it—if we wish—on lines entirely new. There is after all a better way to live."

Abbey's romancer's vision in *The Journey Home,* was never more vivid. "This is Ezekiel with a sense of humor," observed Peter Wild in the *High Country News,* "Zorro with a high IQ."

Two years later E. P. Dutton brought out *Abbey's Road,* another assemblage of travel essays, polemics, sermons, and personal history. It amounts to Abbey's private odyssey—bawdy, hilarious, and irreverent—based on excursions to the Rio Grande River in Texas, Canyonlands National Park in Utah, the Great Barrier Reef of Australia (on assignment for *National Geographic*), and the Sierra Madre in Mexico.

There are tales here of his life as a ranger, his one and only experiment with LSD in Death Valley, and his encounter with wild javelinas, piglike desert animals, one Christmas Eve: "Have you ever stood alone under the full moon in the prickly cholla-mesquite desert on the night before Christmas," he asks the reader, "and found yourself surrounded by a herd of hungry, snuffling, anxiety-ridden javelinas? I have, and it's a problematic situation. Some of those little fifty-pound beasts can carry tusks and have been known to charge a full-grown man right up to the hairy trunk of a saguaro cactus."

As that confrontation played out, the beasts scrutinized Abbey. Upon smelling the odor of Jim Beam whiskey, they erupted in various directions, leaving the holiday celebrant to his solitary libations.

Scenes like that caused the gorge of an anonymous reviewer for *The New Republic* to rise: "If you want to read 200 pages of Edward Abbey's self-flattery, buy this book. If you're looking for a writer who captures some of the beauty and mystery of the natural world, though, I suggest Dillard's *Pilgrim at Tinker Creek*, which is a hundred times superior to this smug, graceless book."

For some who have been down a few of the same roads Abbey has, there is a sense that he sees more than they ever did. "Reading him," suggested John Leonard in *The New York Times*, "is often better than being there was . . . he's telling us that the wilderness is too good for us, that we should stay at home and read his books. Maybe he is right. I should stay home reading, and out of his way."

In our time, the use of rhetoric, especially by politicians and businesspeople, often works to conceal real feelings, rather than to express them. In contrast, it is Abbey's honesty in these essays—like it or not—that comes through, his willingness to raise questions that overpaid public relations men discourage their clients in government and business from answering: What is the point of America? Why are we here? What will it be like a century from now?

And considering the way America is headed, how much more time do we have? Even though the threat of A-bomb attack from across the seas has faded, Abbey muses, America seems more threatened now than ever by enemies from within, by the same people voters believed were their guardians, people who have now, too often, joined or created lawless companies and renegade federal agencies.

In the essay "The Sorrows of Travel," Abbey writes of gazing out at desert mountains.

> I want to embrace it, know it, all at once and all in all; but the harder I strive for such a consummation, the more elusive and mysterious that IT becomes, slipping like a dream through my arms. Can this desire be satisfied only in death? Something in our human consciousness seems to make us forever spectators of the world we live in.
>
> Maybe some of my crackpot, occultist friends are right; maybe we really are aliens here on earth, our spirits born on some other, simpler, more human planet. But why then were we sent here? What is our mission, comrades, and when do we get paid?
>
> A writer's epitaph: He fell in love with the planet earth, but the affair was never consummated.

Abbey's Road is a travel book in the same mode as D. H. Lawrence's travel stories, reflections about new places written in a less complicated, sometimes primitive, perverse way. Abbey is at his cantankerous best ridiculing both scientists—"How can we think of a man who spends years studying the behavior of hamsters in an electrified maze as anything but a harmless idiot?"—and tourists who think they are camping—"What has a Winnebago to do with camping?"

Unlike most modern writers, Abbey was even harder on himself: "I am forty-nine and a half years old (and will be for the next decade or two), beer-bellied, broken-nosed, over-weight, shakily put together, with a bad knee—lost the cartilage years ago."

Abbey's perceptions are maverick versions of reality as he perceived it to be. Toward the end of *Abbey's Road* he observes in

Whitmanesque fashion, that "the despair that haunts the background of our lives, sometimes obtruding itself into consciousness, can still be modulated, as I know from experience, into a roaring affirmation of self-existence. Even, at times, into a quiet and blessedly self-forgetful peace, a modest joy."

Abbey's introduction to this volume, titled "Confessions of a Literary Hobo," is of lasting value to would-be writers and to readers everywhere. Here Abbey wrestles with the question of why people bother to write in the first place.

Some reviewers thought he was being facetious when he said he did it only for the money and the other traditional inducements: motorcycles, fast cars, fast women, Gustav Mahler and Waylon Jennings on the quadraphonic sound system, good booze, fame and glory, alcoholism, and an early death.

Abbey was being playfully absurd, shielding his romantic idealism as if it were too fragile for scrutiny.

> But maybe there is something a little better. We write in order to share, for one thing—to share ideas, discoveries, emotions. Alone, we are close to nothing. In prolonged solitude, as I've discovered, we come very close to nothingness. Too close for comfort.
>
> Through the art of language, most inevitable of the arts—for what is more basic to our humanity than language?—we communicate to others what would be intolerable to bear alone. . . . We write to record the truth . . . to keep the record straight.

Three years later, E. P. Dutton brought out another book of essays, *Down the River,* comprising magazine articles and some previously unpublished work from 1978 through 1982. These essays, nineteen in all, were generally well-received, though the reviews were not as numerous as Abbey had hoped.

Kirkus Review concluded that this collection of what it termed "sage, idiosyncratic essays," reveals a man who "can write like an angel while lashing a forked tail at the technological/military/industrial Perpetual Growth and Power Machine!"

In the *Washington Post,* John Cole asserted that Abbey's writings have a "fine humility; the wires of ironic humor that he weaves through . . . this memorable book and his charming modesty prevent him from preaching. He doesn't tell us what we should or shouldn't do to 'save' our environment.

"He writes with zest and passion about his voyages down the rivers of the natural world, and that becomes that. Our response is not dictated, but left to us to decide."

Cole was one writer, Abbey was relieved to note, who *had* read his works. Another was John Mitchell, the former *Newsweek* senior editor who penned this for the *Chicago Sun-Times:* "Blue-plate-special Abbey fare—one part eco-polemic, two parts travelogue, a dash of wrinkled philosophy."

Typically, Abbey spares few targets, lashing "the forked tail" at the MX missile, Schlitz beer, silicon chips, King Arthur (the real good guy was Robin Hood), and paper profits. By his own admission, the essays "deal with unpleasant and ungrateful subjects, the damnation of another river, the militarization of the open range, the manufacture of nuclear weapons. . . . They were written from a sense of duty, as well as for the easy money. I prefer sweeter, funnier, happier themes."

And he writes here about rivers, choosing some lines from Sealth, the legendary Duwamish chief who is remembered today as Seattle: "The rivers are our brothers. They quench our thirst. The rivers carry our canoes and feed our children. . . . You must give to the rivers the kindness you would give your brothers."

Rivers were Abbey's brothers, too; he liked to say he did them the way Huck Finn and Jim did, and the way La Salle and

Marquette, the mountain men, Major Powell, and a few hundred others did. Abbey ran more white water than most people dream of, yet it saddened him never to have floated the Congo, the Kolyma, or the Mississippi.

His very first float—and sink—occurred when he was nine years old. That was when he and his brother Howard borrowed a boat from their father, actually a rectangular wooden box used for mixing cement, about four-foot-by-three and one-foot deep. They launched it on Crooked Crick near the family farm. "We clung to the gunwales," Ed recalled years later, "as our scow sank peacefully and immediately to the bottom of the creek, leaving us sitting in water up to our necks." It was good experience for future dunkings in the rivers of the West.

Fortunately for Chief Seattle, Abbey tells us in the preface, the great chief did not truly foresee what would come to those rivers: "How could he have imagined, for instance, that a time might arrive when the rivers would not even be fit to drink from? But certain consolations remain. Thoreau said, 'who hears the rippling of rivers will not utterly despair of anything.'"

Of all the pieces in *Down the River*, two alone are worth the entrance fee; the account of his trip down the Green River in Utah, reading a worn and greasy paperback of Thoreau's *Walden and Civil Disobedience*, and the tribute to a bizarre and unsung painter and friend by the name of John De Puy.

"Thoreau's mind has been haunting mine for most of my life," Abbey wrote. "It seems proper now to reread him. What better place than on this golden river called the Green? In the clear tranquillity of November."

Along the way, Abbey has conversations with Thoreau's ghost. And here we have some of Abbey's finest writing. "As for the pyramids," he quotes Thoreau, "there is nothing to wonder at in them so much for the fact that so many men could be found degraded enough to spend their lives constructing a tomb for some ambitious booby, whom it would have been wiser . . . to have drowned in the Nile. . . . "

Abbey advises us that the institutions dominating our lives—governmental, corporate, technological—"weigh on society as the pyramids of Egypt weighed on the backs of those who were conscripted to build them. The pyramids of power. Five thousand years later the people of Egypt still have not recovered . . . as if the pride and spirit had been crushed from them forever."

He has fun with Thoreau, calling him a put-on artist who loved to shock and exasperate, as if Abbey were not totally familiar with that role himself. He detects some embellishment in Thoreau's descriptions of his own life, namely, that Henry was not at all the hermit as legend has it, hardly even a recluse.

In fact, his celebrated cabin at Walden Pond—some of his neighbors called it a shanty—was only two miles from Concord Common, a half-hour walk from pond to post office. "Henry lived in it for only two years and two months. . . . We shall now discuss the sexual life of Henry David Thoreau," quipped Abbey, intimating that the latter was semi-mythical, too, if it existed at all.

Abbey tells us of his disapproval of Henry's "fastidious puritanism. For one who claims to crave nothing but reality, he frets too much about purity. Purity, purity, he preaches, in the most unctuous of his many sermons, a chapter of Walden called Higher Laws."

Abbey felt a bit sorry for Thoreau, too, referring to him frequently as "poor Henry," a great American oddball who raised beans not to eat but to sell, his only cash crop. Poor Henry David Thoreau.

His short (forty-five years), quiet, mentally passionate life apparently held little passion for the opposite sex, Abbey notes.

He had a sister-brother relationship with Ralph Waldo Emerson's wife, Lidian, and a series of rejections from several other women.

Abbey bemoans the fact that "poor Henry" evidently never got around to enjoying sex. "He lived and probably died a virgin, pure as shriven snow," Abbey frets, "except for those sensual reptiles coiling and uncoiling down in the root cellar of his being. Ah, purity!"

After a while, the paradoxical Abbey muses that modern men and women make too much of the sexual, yet, "It is the only realm of primordial adventure still left to most of us. Like apes in a zoo, we spend our energies on the one field of play remaining; human lives otherwise are pretty well caged in by the walls, bars, and locked gates of industrial culture."

Abstaining from sex, Abbey acknowledges, would have been fine for Thoreau had he pursued other experiences in his day. He could have toured the Western plains with George Catlin, the artist; but he led an unnecessarily constrained existence, Abbey informs us, and not only in the "generative region."

Abbey laments that his spiritual ancestor never saw the Grand Canyon, the Rocky Mountains, Alaska, the Upper Nile. Poor Henry. But what a writer, and Abbey loved that oddball who was much like himself, "A crusty character, an unpeeled man. A man with the bark on him."

In the cool, bright evenings by blazing river campfires, Thoreau's homilies often lulled Abbey to sleep: "The light which puts out our eyes is darkness to us. Only the day dawns to which we are awake. There is more day to dawn. The sun . . ."

Abbey responds with: "Yes, yes, Henry, we know. How true. Whatever it means. How late it is. Whatever the hour . . . Poor Henry. And then I hear that voice again, far off but clear: 'All Nature is my bride.'"

John Cole suggests that Abbey, like Thoreau, is really "there" in his writing, but he is also continually wary of encouraging too much intimacy: "Like one of the tall saguaro cactus that grows in the deserts of his home near Tucson, he protects himself with barbs that turn up as delightful surprises in the mainstream of his prose. His needles protect his soul. Like the saguaro, the inner Abbey stores bright truths that can quench our thirst for hope."

"Be of good cheer," Abbey writes toward the end. "The military-industrial state will soon collapse." After his death, with the collapse of Soviet Communism, plummeting defense budgets, millions of defense workers unemployed, and big corporations imploding, his predictions loom true.

Two years after *Down the River*, Henry Holt and Company published Abbey's fourth book of essays, *Beyond the Wall*. The collection is dedicated to his wife, Clarke Cartwright, and her family, with whom friends say her husband had the first powerful feelings of familial happiness during his adult years.

These ten essays, all previously published in magazines, deal with aspects of the desert that, to Abbey, make it akin to Eden at the dawn of creation, existing beyond the walls of cities, security fences, asphalted superhighways, beyond the worst examples of polluted air and water.

Abbey invites the reader to go there, and to walk gently and quietly.

May your trails be dim, lonesome, stony, narrow, winding and only slightly uphill. May the wind bring rain for the slickrock potholes fourteen miles on the other side of yonder blue ridge. May God's dog serenade your campfire, may the rattlesnake and the screech owl amuse your reverie, may Great Sun dazzle your eyes by day and the Great Bear watch over you by night.

——FROM THE PREFACE TO *BEYOND THE WALL*

These essays are also about the landscapes of the human mind, and Abbey's mind is ever-present on his sojourns through a wildlife refuge in southwestern Arizona, Old Pariah River in Utah, and the Colorado River's Glen Canyon Dam.

Here, too, is a journal of a trip down the Colorado, another to the Sea of Cortez, and more. "Marching on," he writes, "north, I follow this condemned jeep road as it meanders toward the mountains. Why do I do this sort of thing? I don't know . . . don't even care why. It's not logical—its pathological."

Reviewers treated this volume kindly, noting with regret Abbey's promise in the preface never to write again about the subject of wild places and the desert. "This book is my last to be 'writ in sand,'" he wrote.

"Don't count on it," quipped Paul Krza in the *National Review of Books*, "unless technology swallows him up first." But the *Washington Post* reviewer fell for the bait: "This may be the last great desert book by one of the nation's great writers on the arid wildernesses of the West."

Beyond the Wall found a kindred spirit in reviewer Harry Middleton of *The Philadelphia Inquirer.* He understood Abbey better than most when he suggested that among future genera-tions, "When it is asked how we came to know the desert, surely the most lasting and valuable images left us will be those of Abbey—words set on paper, durable as lines cut in stone."

Abbey also managed to sneak in the motif which dominates all his work: Unless people feel and live the desert and float the rivers; unless they walk alone or with a friend into the ancient, blood-thrilling, primeval, vast, and democratic vistas, they "will never understand the secret essence of the word freedom . . ."

The year before Abbey died, Henry Holt and Company pub-lished his final package of essays, *One Life at a Time, Please.* "If there's anyone still present whom I've failed to insult," Abbey snapped in the preface, "I apologize."

Nothing could soothe the tempers of conservatives, liberals, feminists, politicians, government agencies, and cattlemen after reading these essays, even if they had believed the author's apology.

Many ranchers in the West, even some who had liked his previous writings, this time saw nothing amusing in Abbey's words, which were reprinted in several publications before they turned up in this volume.

He depicted ranchers as a thoughtless lot who shoot eagles, bears, and cougars on sight; replace native grasses with cowshit and tumbleweed; string barbed wire all over God's creation; then grin at TV cameras and chatter about how much they love the American West.

Ranchers weren't Abbey's sole target. He saved some of his rhetorical artillery for cities, and for the apostles of growth at any cost.

On cities:

> Why not consider the possibility that a city, like a man or a woman or a tree or any other healthy living thing, should grow until it reaches maturity—and then stop; a human who never stopped growing would be a freak, a mutant, a monster, a sideshow geek eating live chickens for supper and toppling dead of diabetes and kidney failure into an early grave. . . . When a city finally stops growing, its citizens can finally begin to live. In peace. Security. With a modicum of domestic tranquillity.

On growth:

> For more growth we must give up the very qualities that make a high standard of civilized life still possible. . . . For more development we will transform what we prize into temporary

jobs . . . and fat bank accounts for the powerful minority of land-speculators, tract-slum builders, bankers, car dealers and shopping mall hustlers who stand to profit. . . . Growth for the sake of growth is the ideology of the cancer cell.

Reviewing *One Life at a Time, Please* for the *St. Petersburg Times*, Marion Loeb concluded that Abbey "has the particular responsibility to present unpopular truths. Else why do we need him. . . . His writing is honed and against the edge of something larger than ourselves in the natural world."

The *Chicago Tribune* also showed some insight into Abbey's technique: "This brave and blunt man, called by Thomas McGuane, 'the original fly in the ointment,' has an irritating habit of writing incomplete sentences that leave the reader grasping for a noun or verb. My guess is that he does it on purpose."

Although Abbey was physically unwell when most of these essays were written, suffering bleeding attacks at irregular intervals, remarkably they are not drenched in despair, but punctuated instead with flashes of iconoclastic humor—and hope.

"If you like to think and laugh out loud from time to time," wrote Charles Bowden in *City* magazine, a now-defunct Tucson publication, "buy this book. If you like to have everything you read confirm your own ideas, avoid it like the plague."

Writing in *Outside* magazine, Gregory Norman drew parallels between Abbey and a curmudgeon of yore: "Abbey offends people in a cheerful, enthusiastic way that reminds you of Mark Twain, who could tell a nation of pious Protestants that their God was petty and vengeful to the extreme. . . . Any man who can both love and hate with conviction is, by my definition, complete and happy. This, more than anything else, accounts for the peculiar, durable, and irresistible appeal of Ed Abbey. May he live forever."

Abbey may have preferred that America's natural places stay on the rough, untamed, and savage side, but that was not his hope for its citizens. If anything, he was trying to arouse their love, to offer hope that the end is not near—yet—and finally, to say that a balance must be struck between pre-civilized and post-civilized barbarity.

One of the most troubling, some say crushing, critiques of all Abbey's works was delivered by a man who was his friend and colleague on the faculty at the University of Arizona in the 1980s. And that was Peter Wild, with whom Abbey shared an office, and who was invited to Abbey's home for parties.

Writing in the *New Mexico Humanities Review,* Wild accused Abbey of being a childish middle-class maverick, a kind of of P. T. Barnum who made a living deceiving a public always eager to be deceived.

What infuriated Wild was Abbey's romanticism, the sentiment that has been burning at the center of the middle class since the birth of the Republic. "A list of its attributes," Wild wrote, "almost serves as a roll call of favorite Abbey topics: revolt against authority; celebration of the common man and misfits; the hero as rebel; nature as a refuge from the nastiness and responsibilities of civilization; the joys of escape and of the quest; adoration of women, that is unpossessed women; and lastly, elevation of ego above all other concerns . . . a mindless pride in lack of consistency, the inconsistency that Abbey delights in serving up to his readers.

"Childish? . . . We're talking about childishness! Precisely isn't that what the infant wants, to have everything! Americans cling desperately to an emotional immaturity prolonged into adulthood, fostered by the media and by Edward Abbey, Zane Grey with a rapier wit and the buzz words of the environmental fad.

"At best, we're a nation of emotional teenagers. And it is the teenage mind, albeit an intelligent one aided by substantial learning, that is the genie of Edward Abbey's oeuvre."

Wild was equally vexed by the sentimentality in Abbey's works, the way in which he idealizes the "Good Old Days," the way the world supposedly once was, agrarian and free, its wilderness the touchstone of freedom. Such a world, Wild suggested, never existed, except in dreams.

"Whatever virtues Abbey possesses, he has put the millstone of middle-class romanticism around his neck and plunged into his writing. As readers, howsoever moved, we might pause for a moment to consider just what it is in ourselves that makes us follow so readily after him."

Abbey was stung by that critique, and some of his friends rushed to his defense and avoided Wild socially. A short time later, however, Abbey passed Wild in the hall at the university, paused and tapped him on the shoulder. "It's okay, Peter," said Abbey. "It's okay."

And that was all Abbey ever said to him about that vicious review, which, incidentally, is not included in Abbey's papers at the University of Arizona special collections library.

Abbey gets the last word. As he once defined what he was about in "A Writer's Credo" in *One Life at a Time, Please:*

> The task of the honest writer—the writer as potential hero—is to seek out, write down, and publish forth those truths which are not self-evident, not universally agreed upon, not allowed to determine public feeling and official policy.

With all due respect to Peter Wild, who was judging Abbey by European standards, that doesn't sound very much like P. T. Barnum.

FAREWELL TO THE
MUDHEAD KACHINA

I'd like to say that coyotes passed the word along,
that leafless willows dreamed it up the roots of cottonwood
and sage along each muddy stream. I'd like to say the Colorado
told the Green, the Escalante, the San Juan, that grief
rose up each tributary to the melting snow.

  . . . .

I'd like to say the wished-for vultures carved
those long bones clean as limestone in the sight of sky.
If words are truth despite our eyes, then I'd say that. The father
of our grinning anger's gone; I never knew him better
than in song, the page turned in a thousand lights.

            —C. L. RAWLINS, "ELEGY: FOR EDWARD ABBEY"

To some he was a legendary character. To many others he was a
misanthropic, sexist, elitist, cranky, barbarian, creeping Fascist
hyena. Ed Abbey's tireless circling came to an end on March
14, 1989. Born under the sign of Aquarius, he uttered his last
words under the sign of Pisces: "I did what I could."

Death struck him after a siege of illness that would have caused most men to lay down their pens and depart voluntarily for The Great Gate through which one of his mentors, B. Traven, said everyone must pass.

Only days before, this disputatious lover of life and nature had finished his twentieth book, *A Voice Crying in the Wilderness*, in which he wrote: "If you feel that you're not ready to die, never fear; nature will give you complete and adequate assistance when the time comes."

Despite pain, discomfort and the certain knowledge that death was near, he was the essential Abbey, explaining that the Deserto in the title didn't have anything at all to do with dry climates but with " . . . the barren neon wilderness and asphalt jungle of the modern urbanized nightmare."

During the final hours, Jack Loeffler, his closest male friend and Santa Fe–based environmental activist, reportedly leaned close to the bearded, and by then nearly emaciated, man and said: "So long. Any ideas for an epitaph?"

"No comment," Abbey reportedly replied.

Years before, the two amigos made a pact that, if either of them ever had the misfortune to be sentenced to long hospital stays, tangled up and tied down with a bizarre array of tubes and hoses, one would liberate the other.

Loeffler kept his part of the bargain.

Marooned in a Tucson hospital for emergency treatment in March, Abbey decided he had had enough. With the help of friends, he disconnected himself from the wires and tubes, hoping that if the time had come to die, it would be in the desert, far from the wintry confines of modern hospitals.

Abbey had written of his own mortality: "To die alone, on a rock under the sun at the brink of the unknown, like a wolf, like a great bird, seems to me to be a very good fortune indeed. To die in the open, under the sky, far from the insolent interference of leech and priest, before this desert vastness opening like a window onto eternity, that surely was an overwhelming stroke of rare good luck."

That good luck was denied him. He was to die in his writing cabin on the outskirts of Tucson with Clarke, his beloved wife, his two small children, Ben and Becky, and a few friends close by.

The afternoon before he died, Clarke and several friends drove Abbey to a remote locale near Tucson where, when evening came, it might be clear enough for him to see two of his favorite stars, Spica and Regulus; there he lay by a fire, to wait for the last burst of blood, and his last breath.

To everyone's amazement, Cactus Ed awoke later that evening, feeling somewhat better. He was driven home and stretched out on a mattress in his writing cabin, where he said his farewells.

He was gone the next morning.

Abbey had written that when his turn came to lie down, die, and decay into the earth, there to nourish a "higher" form of life such as a clump of sage, a coyote, a prickly pear, or a pissed-on aspen tree, "I hope the blessed event takes place high on a canyon rim, with a final vision of red cliffs, magenta buttes, and purple mesas in my fading eyes."

In reality he had selected another resting place. According to his written instructions, he wished to be transported in the bed of a pickup truck into the desert, wrapped in a sleeping bag, and covered by rocks.

And so he was.

Friends laid him atop dry ice on Loeffler's flatbed truck and drove him to a desert spot where a rare bird sings and four types of cactus converge: saguaro, organ pipe, senita, and cardon.

"Death is every man's final critic. To die well you must live bravely," he wrote in *A Voice Crying in the Wilderness*. And so he did, and he was buried nobly, too—and illegally.

It is said that he rests there today under a pile of black rocks. The few sworn to secrecy about the place visit him now and then, among rabbitbrush and ocotillo, deer, antelope, and bighorn sheep. It is also said that buzzards circled as the grave was being dug, waiting for a new philosophizing, red-necked feathered companion.

In *The Fool's Progress*, Henry Lightcap speculates, "Life is a dog and then you die? No no, life is a joyous dance through daffodils beneath cerulean blue skies. And then? Then what? I forget what happens next."

News of his death spread like a firestorm in a tinder-dry forest in Abbey country, gusting through the places he had lived as a ranger and wrote about—the Colorado Plateau, Basin, and Range.

Terry Gustafson, who had rangered with Abbey, remembers hearing the news on the radio a day or two later while he was driving through northern Arizona on his way to New Mexico. Suddenly, he felt Abbey's presence next to him on the passenger seat. Years before they had had angry words, but suddenly Gustafson felt a wave of love and delight: "Ed communicated to me that he was excited to discover that he still existed, even though he'd died. I forgave him. He forgave me and then he was gone."

In Hong Kong when he heard the news, Ken Sanders, long-time friend and publisher, was busy printing the Western Wilderness Calendar, which had been inspired years before by Abbey's writings. "Ed wasn't fond of the technology that enabled me to learn of his death so quickly from so far away. . . . I read the fax over and over again, fax in one hand, calendar proofs in the other. Stunned, I cannot really comprehend the meaning of those words, cannot accept the implication, and am unable to understand their significance.

"Edward Abbey died today, and I'm here in Hong Kong, all alone, surrounded by six million people who are unaware of the passing of a legend. If the death of Buddy Holly was the day the music died, in like manner the death of Edward Abbey is the day the passion died."

"I was paralyzed for weeks," wrote Doug Peacock, reportedly the inspiration for the madcap George Washington Hayduke in *The Monkey Wrench Gang.* "Ed would have disapproved. He would have said, 'Douglas, why all this moping around. Go do something.'"

One reason people were caught short by his death, suggests Mike Lacey of *New Times* in Phoenix, "is because he died well. When his body began strangling on its own blood, the man finished off his last novel. He did not attempt to live forever by wiping out a lifetime of small deaths.

"He did not get into shape, join an aerobic class, eat sensibly or do cautionary commercials for Mothers Against Drunk Driving. He kept it to himself, passing quietly and at home."

Two months after Abbey's death, by the invitation of his widow, friends were asked to a sunrise memorial service atop a crumbling washed-out road overlooking Arches National Park near Moab, Utah. It was where Abbey had begun writing *Desert Solitaire.*

As the morning sun filtered through billowing gray clouds wafting in and around the surrounding red and black rocks, some five hundred friends, fellow writers, and family members gathered to say farewell against the background of flute music, guitars, and the incessant hissing of popping beer cans.

The first to pay homage was Ken Sleight, boatman extraordinaire and local rancher, otherwise known as Seldom Seen Smith from *The Monkey Wrench Gang*, an Abbey friend for two decades.

Choking with emotion, Sleight read from a letter he had written to his departed old pal: "I wish I could rise above this. Your sudden leaving on this great journey caught me unprepared as I'll not be able to see you for a while.

"Why did you have to leave us now, my dear friend Abbey, just when we need you the most? How can we manage without you? You came to this beautiful land suddenly, you made your mark, and you departed just as suddenly . . . I wish you were here."

Mourners then heard the resonant voice of poet and essayist Wendell Berry from Port Royal, Kentucky. He said he had a letter to read from author Wallace Stegner, who had known Abbey as a student in his creative writing course.

Addressed to "friends gathered for Ed Abbey's journey home," Stegner, now dead himself, confessed that he had not seen Abbey in years, not since Abbey had left Stanford in the late fifties. But he had never been far from the sound of his name, "never for a moment out of reach of the waves he caused and the influence he radiated. He squatted in a country that I had known and loved since my boyhood and made it singularly and importantly his own, as Frost made New England his own, as Ansel Adams and Muir made Yosemite.

"His books were burrs under the saddle blanket of complacency. His urgency was a lever under inertia. He had the zeal of a true believer and a stinger like a scorpion when defending the natural free unmanaged unmanhandled wilderness of his chosen country.

"He was a red hot moment in the conscience of the country and I suspect that the half-life of his instransigence will turn out to be comparable to that of uranium. We will miss him. The comfort is that when we need him, he will still be there."

Then Berry spoke for himself, acknowledging a debt to Abbey's work, which he said had been a source of happiness and comfort for more than twenty years.

"I have thought myself his friend for that long. It has been a written friendship, exchanges of books and notes, and on my part, much thought. A sort of law at our house is that I should not read an Abbey book after bedtime. For if I did I would be apt to laugh loud enough to wake people up.

"For many years I assumed that in our several wanderings we would meet face to face. It never happened. The other day I was talking to a friend about patriotism; patriotism, let us remember, is the love of one's country, not the love of air conditioning or the interstate highway system, not government or the flag or power or money or munitions.

"It is the love of country, and patriotism of that kind is in short supply. In our day, people who love their country, outnumbered as they are by our country's domestic enemies, are often in need of courage, of courage, moreover, that no one is capable of having alone. And to them, Abbey has been and will be a giver of courage.

"I'm glad to say that I never laid down a book of his that I did not feel more encouraged than when I picked it up. For that and for much else I give him my thanks and my great respect."

Then Berry read a poem he'd written for the occasion:

The old oak wears new leaves,
It stands for many lives,
Within its veil of green
A singer sings unseen
Again the living come

To light, and are at home.
And Edward Abbey's gone.
I pass a cairn of stone
Two arms-lengths long and wide
Piled on the steep hillside
By plowmen years ago.
Now oaks and hickories grow
Where the steel coulter passed.
Where human striving ceased
The Sabbath of the trees
Returns and stands and is.
The leaves shake in the wind.
I think of that dead friend
Here where he never came
Except by thought and name.
I praise the joyous rage
That justified his page.
He would have liked this place
Where sight receives the grace
Of bloom in a dark time.
Larkspur and columbine.
The flute song of the thrush
Sounds of the underbrush.

Next to speak was Dave Foreman, cofounder of Earth First!, for whom Abbey's writing and friendship had been a formidable experience.

"I loved him more than I can say. A number of years ago, after Earth First! was started I got a letter from an old Wobbly who related that John Muir had spoken to his graduating class. I was trying to imagine what that was like, thinking of what it would be like to carry that memory.

"Many of us know that. We knew Ed Abbey in person. I think for those of us who have a year left, ten years left, or fifty years, that will be a memory to carry and cherish just like the old Wobbly carried his of Muir. Those of us who saw Ed Abbey, who knew him, felt his handshake, shared a cigar or a beer with him, truly have been privileged. So rejoice for that. We have a memory that is unbeatable."

An American flag flapped in the desert breeze as Foreman went on with his eulogy. He said he was glad to see the flag: "Ed was not a counterculturist. He was an American. He knew where he came from. He knew that he was born out of the hillbilly bones of this country, what made him—what's made all of us—and by being part of this culture and not denying it, by accepting his place in it, by knowing from whence he came, is what made his criticism more incisive, more biting, more trenchant, more important.

"For when we try to deny who we are, when we hate everything about us and what produced us, I think we lose something there. We lose the connection of feelings of belonging. Abbey was a great man, a great American.

"He represented the best of the American dream . . . what this country could have become had it not turned its back on its ideals of two hundred years ago. We need to remember that we are Americans like Ed Abbey and that by accepting that, we become stronger in our criticisms of the prostitution America has become.

"Abbey received a great deal of criticism from people who didn't understand him, who did not know what he was talking about. I remember twenty years ago on the Zuni Reservation [in New Mexico] going to Shalako on a frozen December evening, and watching the mudhead kachinas."

In primal cultures, he related, there have always been forces like the mudhead kachinas, the tricksters who make fun during the most sacred ceremonies. He compared these kachinas to a group of nuns and priests making obscene gestures in St. Peter's Square while the Pope was doing the Easter sermon. That's important, Foreman told the mourners: "In every real society the planet has ever seen, we've had to laugh at our most sacred ideas, at our most honored personages.

"Ed Abbey was the mudhead kachina of the environmental movement, the mudhead kachina of the whole social change movement in this country. And it's to our everlasting shame as idealists that more of us didn't understand that Ed was a trickster, farting in polite company, pissing on overblown egos, making a caricature of himself and laughing at himself, laughing at all of us because we have to do that. Ed was the wise prophet from the desert who tried to keep us on track and [tell us] not to take ourselves too seriously."

On many occasions, Abbey said that one brave deed was worth a thousand books. "He was disparaging his own contribution," Foreman observed that day. "Every book of Ed Abbey's, every essay, every story has launched a thousand brave deeds."

How do you evaluate that kind of contribution, that kind of magic that he possessed, Foreman asked. "All we can do for that is to continue to be motivated, for each of us to go out and commit those brave deeds in honor of Ed; whether for wilderness proposals or a wrench in Cal Black's latest development, whether farting in polite company. Let's be inspired to do those brave deeds. That's the only legacy that we can return to Ed. Salud Ed!"

Another speaker was Terry Tempest Williams, the Utah-based author who compared Abbey to a coyote doing a dance upon the desert. "Edward Abbey didn't have to die to find paradise," she declared. "He understood and lived it in the here and now."

Then she recalled some of Abbey's words: "When I write the word 'paradise,' I mean not apple trees and only golden women but also scorpions and tarantulas and flies; rattlesnakes and gila monsters, sandstone volcanos and earthquakes, bacteria and bear, cactus, yucca, bladderweed, ocotillo and mesquite, flash-floods and quicksand, and yes, disease and death and the rotting of flesh."

Paradise is "the here and now" she told the mourners that day: "The actual tangible dogmatically real earth on which we stand. Yes, God bless America, the earth upon which we stand. Ed Abbey knew we had it all, right here right now. We need not look further. We need not go farther."

Recalling the last hike she had gone on with him, she said she still could hear his voice on ahead of her as they descended into a canyon, dropping from ledge to ledge: "What most humans really desire is something quite different from industrial gimmickry, that is, liberty, spontaneity, nakedness, mystery, wildness, and wilderness . . . what we need now are heroes and heroines, about a million of them. One brave deed is worth a thousand books. Sentiment without action is the ruin of the soul."

In closing she said what she would miss most were Ed Abbey's "gifts of listening, of asking the poignant question, the generosities. This strong tall man, both shy and fierce, reflective and combative, in love with his public and in revolt against them. This human being of complex paradox and passion who lured us out of complacency."

Douglas "Hayduke" Peacock, for his part, was not about to get too morbid: "This is not the end. It is not something you sign off on and just close the book on and walk away from. That's why I am here. I knew Abbey for twenty years, which is nothing; such a gift. Despite the wisdom that death is part of the great cycle of life, and Ed's going wasn't exactly a surprise, although difficult, it wasn't unlike what he would have wished for himself. But I have to admit to having been floored by the whole experience.

"Somewhere his spirit lives on. We've always had Abbey to walk point. That is a great hole. Without him walking point anymore, there will be more work for all of us. I recommit myself to that purpose."

Ann Zwinger, one of the nation's foremost nature writers, was the next speaker, a friend who knew Abbey's frustrations at being called solely a nature writer by many book critics. She explained that she understood the difference between nature writing and Abbey writing: "As a nature writer, I believe that if you can get people to be curious, they may begin to ask questions; answers will come and more questions, all leading to understanding, knowledge, caring. What and who you care about, you will not destroy. Obviously this philosophy is too slow moving to move mountains, and obviously Ed Abbey was out to move lots of mountains."

Zwinger recalled that their paths had crossed on river trips and at writers' conferences: "If I have an image of Ed Abbey, it's in a canyon on a rainy day. A boat flipped, and there was Ed holding my son's sleeping bag up to the wind. My last view of him was his craggy profile lit by campfire . . . and lots of people talking late around the fire.

"Abbey undertook to educate us all about the difference between the distance of earth and sky out here, between fossil and fable, between the human psyche and a landscape littered with the shards of immortality. I once wrote a book quoting Thoreau, with whom Abbey has been compared. No comparison, Ed. Thoreau went into the wilderness but came home to mother for dinner every night. Ed Abbey went into wilderness and he never came back."

The last speaker of the day was author Barry Lopez, with whom Abbey had kept up a steady correspondence after he reviewed *Desert Solitaire* back in 1968. "I came to speak of what he stood for so that the meaning of him might resonate and be called upon and not be among us mute like a portrait in a gallery or an artifact in a museum. I've been traveling in recent months, China, Africa. My job is to listen, and I thought of Abbey talking of 'the beast with the stone heart,' the drive to regiment, to standardize, to win, to produce, to possess.

"We can't see the price, the thirty thousand miles of drift net in the Pacific. We live, most of us, as though we could close a door on it. Ed Abbey had a capacity for outrage. He espoused Jeffersonian ideals. He liked calling a spade a spade. It's part of what made me a writer.

"Abbey called things by their names. He did not mince words. He didn't equivocate. He was death's trenchant witness, not its complacent voyeur.

"Abbey added to that dimension of social responsibility in literature without which a country's literature is bankrupt, or merely decorative. And he could laugh. The beast could not devour him because he would not let the beast possess him.

"Ed looked around the Southwest and said the news is heavy and it stinks. Ed left us two legacies: his words of love and anger, and his person, in all its seeming contradictions. When I remember this man, I think carefully on just a few things.

"To read *Desert Solitaire* was to hear a clarion call like *Silent Spring;* to know this man was to know that integrity was not just admirable but humanly possible. And now his work courts the dimension of John Muir, not merely an iconoclastic hero but as a galvanizer.

"The news will always be heavy, and Ed will always remind us to speak clearly, to assault the venality, duplicity, and cowardice of those charged with administering our fare, and he will remind each of us to do what we can to bring light, to envision a world larger than our own, and to throttle the beast. We heard what you said, Ed. Thank you. Travel well."

There was a party the night of the memorial service, hosted by Ken Sleight. Music, dancing, and rivers of strong drink flowed in celebration of Abbey's memory. Headed back to her own cabin, Ed's widow ran into Nancy Abbey, Ed's sister. "Well, Clarke," said Nancy, "have we heard about all we want to hear about Ed Abbey?"

Abbey likely would have smiled. "I'm no guru," he told an interviewer in the eighties. "I want to write a few more books and die. I've had the love of good women and friends and I've traveled half the world. I'd like to grow wise and venerable, but I haven't figured that out yet."

Toward dawn, an Abbeyite scrawled some words on a gnarled plank outside the Sleight spread:

ABBEY LIVES.

In a notebook fourteen years earlier, Abbey had written, "One should rehearse one's death from time to time so as to perform the part properly when the curtain of eternity does indeed finally rise."

The curtain rose on Abbey, but it didn't stem the flow of his words, still ringing, always ringing, in his mourners' ears as they left the memorial service that night and early the next day.

And some of those words were: "Enjoy yourselves. Keep your brain in your head and your head firmly attached to your body, the body active and alive, and I promise you this much . . . "

One hears it said often nowadays that a great silence has fallen on the canyon country. What then are those words, echoing off red rock canyon walls, whistling through the pines, ringing in classrooms, libraries, and dark and dingy saloons?

" . . . I promise you this one sweet victory over your enemies, over those desk-bound men with hearts in a safe deposit box and their eyes hypnotized by desk calculators, I promise you this: **You will outlive the bastards.**"

THE LEGACY OF A DESERT ANARCHIST

When Daniel Boone goes by, at night,
The phantom deer arise
And all lost, wild America
Is burning in their eyes.

—STEPHEN VINCENT BENÉT

As far as anyone knows, Edward Paul Abbey never studied botany, zoology, or ecology; the only Latin he acknowledged knowing was *in vino veritas.* Nevertheless, his readers, friends, and some critics argue that his works deserve high rank in the lofty pantheon of nature writers, together with Mary Austin, John Van Dyke, John Muir, Aldo Leopold, Henry Beston, Loren Eiseley, and Annie Dillard.

Laughing off that idea, Abbey would snort, "I am not a naturalist. I never was and never will be a naturalist. . . . The only birds I can recognize without hesitation are the turkey vulture, the fried chicken, and the rosy-bottomed skinny dipper."

His bluntest refutation appeared in *The Journey Home:* "I am not even sure what a naturalist is except that I'm not one. Like so many others in this century, I found myself a displaced person shortly after birth and have been looking for a place to take my stand. Now that I have found it, I must defend it. My home is the American West. All of it."

The West, that wild, lordly land of phantoms and new possibilities, the nucleus of the American Dream.

But which West?

Is it the Old West, the land of dreams conjured up by Hollywood film factories and writers of purple prose—the one-third of the nation stretching and sprawling between the borders of Canada and Mexico, and California and the central plains? That part of America, Ronald Reagan once said, is the quintessential "American sound—hopeful, big-hearted, idealistic, daring, decent, and fair. That's our heritage. . . . There is always a better tomorrow. There are no limits to growth."

By this view, according to Abbey, the West is a storied place in North America that "remains little more in the literary world, than an old joke," as he once assessed it, "a vast, grand but empty stage whereupon cavort, from time to time, the caricatures of myth and legend, noble cowboys and ecological Indians, sentimental gunfighters, and whores with vaginas of pure gold. Hollywood on location. Whores, bores, and melodrama. Who can overcome such a curse?"

For all his grumpy protestations, Abbey was indeed a nature writer. But beyond that, he was a social critic, an independent voice not tied to any ideological special interest, who left behind an important legacy: Prepare yourselves, he advised his readers, because the reality of the New West cannot be easily reconciled with the idea of the Old West so deeply ingrained in twentieth-century American culture.

Specifically, he asserted, the motif of the rugged individualist, as exemplified in films like *Shane* and novels like *The Virginian*, lacks basis in fact. Put simply, it is a lie.

Abbey's legacy is that he not only blasted gaping holes in the mythology of the Old West, paving the way for the current generation of revisionist historians, he also refused to ignore what was happening around him.

Early on, he identified clues that presaged a series of momentous societal changes before they were apparent to the rest of the populace. But when he put forth his views in the 1950s and '60s, he was accused of being on the lunatic fringe. After his death, the bulk of those views are now accepted as conventional wisdom.

His against-the-grain, contrarian view first emerged clearly in *The Brave Cowboy,* in 1956.

> I see liberty being strangled like a dog, everywhere I look. I see my own country overwhelmed by ugliness and mediocrity and overcrowding, the land smothered under airstrips and super-highways, the natural wealth of a million years squandered on atomic bombs and tin automobiles and television sets and ballpoint pens.

The old myths this desert Quixote tried to split asunder with his rhetorical weapons were formidable indeed, having been etched into the nation's consciousness more than a century earlier, beginning with Hector St. John Crèvecoeur and, later, James Fenimore Cooper.

It was Cooper's character, *The Deerslayer,* who created the perennial archetype of the selfless, stoic, fair-minded individualist who keeps his moral integrity intact, never kills except for food, and never confronts complex ethical dilemmas.

High though the windmills of myth were, Abbey never stopped flailing at them, and did manage to arouse the public consciousness to the point where many Americans now recognize that real life in the New West is falling far short of the dream of the Old West. No longer the promised land, it has become an exploitive and exploited, reactionary part of America that is now in serious danger of being injured irreparably by the same ruinous pressures Easterners like Abbey went West to escape.

What Abbey learned in his early historical investigations was that, beginning after the Civil War, the West had begun to be developed and abused, not by individuals but by large corporations and government agencies. And so had the Indians, Spanish, and Mexicans from whom the land was stolen—not to mention the bison, grizzly bear, mountain lion, and wolf populations.

"It was all prices to them," poet Archibald MacLeish has written of that post–Civil War period. "They never looked at it; why should they look at the land? They were Empire Builders: it was all in the bid and the asked and the ink on the books."

Nowadays, old Wild West myths continue to be perpetuated in glitzy advertisements and films via fleeting romantic images of Monument Valley, the Colorado River, the Grand Canyon, cowboys and Indians.

Never shown is the yellow, sickly air pollution in the Grand Canyon; overgrazed rangelands; and habitat damage to the Colorado River due to hydroelectric dams like Glen Canyon.

And rarely acknowledged are the thousands of bears and lions killed with taxpayers' money, the wreckage of chain logging in the national forests, toxic waste dumps, and the thousands of residents who were sickened and killed by the fallout from decades of nuclear bomb tests, a consequence of the Cold War that was not acknowledged by the U.S. government until 1994.

Through Abbey's words, readers perhaps not only learned of those offenses for the first time, but many developed a special fascination and appreciation for the desert and the remaining wilderness, for their beauty, fragility, and timelessness.

Abbey's writings underscored and dramatized the most enduring battle of our time; not the Cold War, but the irreconcilable clash between the political-technological juggernaut and every citizen's right to protect our wilderness heritage, in all its variety. The wilderness is priceless, because it is bound up in the spiritual destiny of all Americans.

For Abbey, reminding people of that heritage, and urging them to fight for it, was a task that transcended day-to-day environmental battles. "We have yielded up too much too easily," he wrote in *Beyond the Wall*. "It is time to start shoving cement and iron in the opposite direction."

Edward Twining, a professor at Denver University, has expressed his regret that many Eastern reviewers dismissed Abbey as an often-angry, snide, incomprehensible econut. They missed the fact, he believes, that beneath his surface irreverence, Abbey was dealing at a much deeper level with what were for him sacred objects, holy places, and consecrated people— all part of a numinous, sacred landscape, all sources of our freedom.

Abbey's playing field, the West, Twining has written, "is a real embodiment of alternative vision, the palpable symbol of spiritual beauty, the demonstration in nature that man's hopes and dreams are not without parallel in the forms of earth itself. . . . The Southwest, which exists only because of its uniquely clear and brilliant sky, is the most priceless natural heritage we have."

To draw attention to the industrial mayhem unfolding about him, Abbey chose to explain the invasion of the Southwest in science fiction terms in *The Journey Home:*

Something alien and strange has invaded the Southwest, a gigantic and inhuman power from, in effect, another world. You first notice the invaders as you approach the village of Cameron and the turnoff to the Grand Canyon.

They look like Martian monsters in this pastoral scene: skeleton towers of steel go to 90 to 120 feet tall, posted across the landscape in military file from horizon to horizon.

From the silence of the desert to the clamor of Glitter Gulch, the fool's treasure of one region is transported and transmuted into the nervous neon of another. Energy, they call it, energy for growth. And what is growth for? Ask any cancer cell.

Seventy years before Abbey was born, the Old West myths began to take root, having been planted by politicians, the so-called empire builders, "robber barons," and fiction writers. These myths formed the center of the American creation myth itself, the archetype of the self-sufficient, wild, individualist male following his whims and fancies, the loner riding the range far from the corrupt East, bucking on a bronco across a pristine playground where one could tell the good guys from bad 'uns just by the color of their hats.

In the works of Zane Grey and Owen Wister, in particular, the West was depicted as a secure world of the imagination, reinforcing fictional notions that lulled generations of Americans into a false sense that a safe haven existed beyond the Mississippi.

All the while the stage was being set for a myth-shatterer, a truth-teller, but he would not appear until the 1950s, a backwoodsman anarchist whose name would be Abbey.

As a precondition to understanding his legacy, one must journey back to the time when the myths were created, when the West was opening up to development, when poet Walt Whitman dubbed it the "newer garden of creation."

Hundreds of romantic images helped to shape the notion in the public mind of the "natural man," the innocent in full flight from the damp, crumbling sin-filled cities of Europe, and New York and Boston. Divinely guided to settle in the promised land, the natural man would reap its God-given harvest by farming in pastures and fishing in rivers of unimaginable plenty.

Never was this dream of paradise peddled more cleverly than by the railroad magnates. Between 1850 and 1871, the federal government gifted them with more than 200 million acres of land. That is one-tenth of all United States land, and an area larger than France, England, and Scotland combined.

All that was missing was business, so railroad marketing men blanketed Eastern cities with pamphlets promising health and good fortune beyond the Missouri and the Mississippi rivers.

Typical of the ballyhoo was the brazen press agent for the Rio Grande and Western Railroad who announced unequivocally that the Utah territory boasted a likeness to the very cradle of civilization. Accompanying the pitch was a land chart of Utah overlain with a map of Palestine. It was dubbed "The Promised Land."

To be sure, such flagrant deception was not the sole province of railroad executives; territorial governments played a role in the myth-making, too. During the peak of the Westward boom after the Civil War, Kansas territorial leaders boasted to Eastern farmers about Kansas's forty-four inches of annual rainfall. That number had absolutely no basis in fact, annual rainfall being far from it then, and never even approaching that much since.

As soon as the migration West began, there were rumors that rather than being an El Dorado, it was a harsh, arid place. Wrong! cried boosters for the railroads as they cooked up a new scientific theory: soil cultivation on a grand scale would affect the atmosphere to such an extent that the desert would be transformed into an oasis rich enough to accommodate a billion people.

Historians recall their slogan, "Rain Follows the Plow," as one of the cruelest lures of the nineteenth century, a classic deception that stands out even against the sordid backdrop of many others like it. Gulled by such pitches, pioneers by the hundreds of thousands went westward to enjoy the Jeffersonian dream that a farmer with 160 acres could raise a family and become rich off the land.

Many crossed the plains only to find a hostile world of hail and drought, followed by more drought and more hail, grasshopper plagues, and vast salt beds. "It was like expecting a fisherman to survive on a little square of ocean," writes Ian Frazier in *Great Plains.*

The real West, as Abbey discovered during his student days in New Mexico, was not the land of enchantment that press agents, politicians, and speculators had promised. The late Wallace Stegner describes how it really was in *Beyond the 100th Meridian:*

> When their fields dried up they had little choice but to sell out to large landowners. In almost no time, "the rugged individualist" of myth and folklore had become little more than an impoverished wage laborer toiling for large Eastern-based corporations, and foreign organizations such as the Scotland-based Prairie Land & Cattle Company which after the Civil War owned a strip 50 miles wide from the Arkansas River to New Mexico.
>
> Visions of wagon trains rolling West, firmly embedded in the nation's consciousness, turned out to be tragically flawed. The myth-makers had omitted the fact that during the 1870s and '80s, many of those wagons were headed back east, full of broken bodies and shattered dreams, some of them bedecked with the slogan: "In God We Trusted, In the West We Busted."

In the so-called "Promised Land," they had chopped and plowed and shoveled and stripped the land "until visions gave out . . . leaving behind them failed ranches and farms, the spreading wounds of erosion and overgrazing," as Peter Wild put it in his valuable book, *Pioneer Conservationists of Western America.*

This is not to suggest there weren't heroic efforts mounted in those days to strangle the myths in their cradles. And, in the nineteenth century, no one tried harder than Major John Wesley Powell.

After he and a team of amateur daredevils plunged down the Colorado River in 1869 in crude wooden boats, Powell, with the depth and breadth of a Charles Darwin, became the first Anglo to assess the role of man as a geologic force in the Southwest.

By the time his ten-year mission was completed, says Santa Fe–based environmental historian and former Secretary of the Interior, Stewart Udall, Powell had accumulated "a storehouse of land wisdom about the West. A friend once said he knew more of the live Indian than any other man, but knowledge of the Indians was only a piece of him: Thoreau himself would have admired his sensibilities."

Just under two hundred pages, Powell's *Report on the Lands of the Arid Region,* published in 1878, enraged those who wanted to believe, and who wanted others to believe, that the West was the promised land. His message: No potential agrarian paradise was the land west of the 98th meridian. It was arid, and the laissez-faire methods of settlement that had succeeded in the rainy East were a catastrophic failure west of the 100th meridian; without a plan for irrigation and a workable system of water rights, land in the West was virtually worthless.

This bold scientist, who had lost an arm at the battle of Shiloh, told the Congress exactly what it didn't want to hear: If the westward experiment was to flourish, man would have to work with nature, as the Indians had done for thousands of years, and as the Mormon settlers and Spanish colonizers had learned to do.

Despite its prescience, Powell's plan was ridiculed and ignored. Asserts Udall: Powell had committed the unpardonable sin of using "bear language in a bull market, and most of the Western leaders would have none of it. . . . He was an instinctive enemy of the myths and the myth-makers."

Fortunately for Powell's legacy, though unfortunately for the modern Southwest, although he failed as a reformer, as a prophet of the consequences of raids upon land and water resources, he had no peer. "In the whole range of American experience from Jamestown on, there is no book more prophetic," historian Bernard De Voto said of the Major's contributions

Edward Paul Abbey, who would eventually carry on Powell's tradition—creating evocative word pictures of values in conflict—would not be born for another four decades.

The "Big Raid" on the West gathered momentum. The towering myth of "superabundance" Powell sought to smash gained credibility, even in the face of the first tangible indications of land overgrazing, plunderous mining practices, general land abuse, and the senseless, wholesale slaughter of wild animals.

Gifford Pinchot, later to become an intimate of President Teddy Roosevelt, and the father of the U.S. Forest Service, was one of the first Americans after Powell to summon the courage to say publicly that in the great open spaces of the West, the domination of "concentrated wealth over mere human beings was something to make you shudder."

Despite the fables of infinite pastures of plenty, by the early 1880s, the frontier had vanished, and with it the very symbol of Western expansion—the bison, or buffalo. In a macabre display of anthropocentric butchery, the bison had been reduced from perhaps 100 million before the Civil War to a few scattered herds.

In the fall of 1885, a large hunting party encountered a herd of some 10,000 bison near a river in North Dakota. Within a month, the last herd was gone.

Come spring, Plains Indian hunters anxiously awaited the buffalo migration, which for thousands of years had been a predictable, annual event for them and their ancestors. When only a few stragglers arrived, they wept. The slaughter was finally complete, and so was 15,000 years of the Indian way of life on the Great Plains.

In my youthful days, I have seen large herds of buffalo on these prairies, and elk were found in every grove, but they are here no more. For hundreds of miles no white man lived, but now trading posts and settlers are found here and there throughout the country, and in a few years the smoke from their cabins will be seen to ascend from every grove . . .

. . . the red man must leave the land of his youth . . . the armies of the whites are without number, like the sands of the sea, and ruin will follow all tribes that go to war with them.

—SHABONEE, A PEACE CHIEF OF THE POTAWATOMI, 1832

The white man does not understand America. He is too removed from its formative processes. The roots of his tree of life have not yet grasped the rock and soil. The white man is still troubled with primitive fears. The man from Europe is still a foreigner and an alien. He still hates the man who questioned his path across the continent.

—LUTHER STANDING BEAR,
CHIEF OF THE OGLALA SIOUX (CIRCA 1878)

The buffalo-killing frenzy was fully endorsed by the U.S. Congress and the White House in the form of the Dawes Act of

1887, which mandated that all native Indian cultures were illegal. Arguing for its passage, one supporter said, "The Indian needs to be touched by the divine angel of discontent . . . to get the Indian out of the blanket and into trousers, trousers with a pocket that needs to be filled with dollars."

Historians have recorded the lamentable irony that just as scholars and historians, such as Frederick Jackson Turner, announced the closing of the American frontier, a consensus was building that the frontier and remaining wilderness were the primal sources of the American liberal and democratic tradition, and must not be plundered.

In Turner's frontier thesis, published in 1893 and remembered in history books for formally announcing the end of the frontier, he advanced the theme that America's most essential ingredient was its wild places. Indeed, those were the formative influence on the national character. He urged citizens to regard democracy with the same respect as a forest product, and with a powerful moral certitude, contending that "the very fact of the wilderness appealed to men as a fair, blank page on which to write a new chapter in the story of man's struggle for a higher type of society."

As Abbey did much later, Turner labored to convince people that wild country had real value aside from timber, gold, and silver. Therefore, its role should be recast from that of an unknown enemy to be conquered, to that of wellspring of psychic benefit. In retrospect, suggests University of California Professor Roderick Nash, author of *Wilderness and the American Mind* and *The Rights of Nature*, perhaps Turner's greatest contribution to the wilderness ideal was "linking it in the minds of his countrymen with sacred American virtues."

Among those quick to see more than passing import in Turner's writings was Theodore Roosevelt, the cowboy-cum-

Harvard gentleman, who had expressed his own alarums in a book called *The Winning of the West* in 1889. In that volume, the once and future "rough rider" and U.S. president argued for preserving wilderness on the grounds that immigrants to America, because of the hard conditions of life there, had become "new men in dress, in customs, and in mode of life."

Roosevelt, in ripping through the myths about the frontier, showed his own great concerns over future sources of national greatness and virility. For without a wilderness ethic, he asserted, the modern American was in serious danger of turning into an "overcivilized man, who has lost the great fighting, masterful virtues."

Although the historical record reveals that Roosevelt produced an abundance of ideas to fight the trend, his whole campaign was heavier on rhetoric than reform. In 1899, he called on citizens to recognize the finiteness of America's resources of land, timber, water, and air: "In the past we have admitted the right of the individual to injure the future of the Republic for his own present profit. In fact there has been a good deal of a demand for unrestricted individualism, for the right of the individual to injure the future of all of us for his own temporary and immediate profit. The time has come for change. . . . We have the moral duty of requiring and doing justice, to protect ourselves and our children against the wasteful development of our natural resources."

But what became of the dreams and plans that Roosevelt trumpeted with so much gusto? Some historians insist that he and his works heralded the start of the modern conservation movement. Other scholars take a contrary view.

The 1908 Conservation Conference at the White House expressed, says Nash, "an overwhelmingly utilitarian attitude toward nature. . . . They were only extending the conquering/

developing emphasis of the pioneers with emphasis on greater efficiency."

Many voices were drowned out in the din at the conference, including that of Aldo Leopold, the forester with a dream whose classic work, *The Sand County Almanac,* was to form much of the foundation for the surging environmental movement of the 1960s. Not long after that conference, Leopold broke with federal resource policy because of what he regarded as radical and rapacious timber harvesting practices.

Leopold's basic principle of the ecological conscience became one of the inspirations for Abbey's writings: "A thing is right when it tends to preserve the integrity, stability, and beauty of the biotic community. It is wrong when it tends otherwise."

For all the hullabaloo surrounding Teddy Roosevelt's years in the bully pulpit, the American notion of "progress" remained essentially unchanged. The natural environment would continue to be replaced with man-made creations, whether clear-cut forests and stripmines, or despoiled hills and valleys, or smokestacks and emissions that abruptly erased the azure blue from the sky in many Western regions. Until the 1980s, "cut and run" development practices would remain the order of the day.

So little was to change, in fact, that A. B. Guthrie, one of Abbey's favorite writers, could create the following in *The Big Sky,* published in 1950. Mountain men Dick Summers and Boone Caudill are troubled about what has happened, and Boone tries to place the changing West in focus:

> "It's all spoiled I reckon, Dick. The whole caboodle."
>
> "I don't guess we could help it," Summers answered, nodding. "There was beaver for us and free country and a big way of living and everything we done looks like we done it against ourselves and couldn't do different if we'd knowed.

"We went to get away and enjoy ourselves free and easy, but folks was bound to foller and beaver to get scarce, and Injuns to be killed or tamed, and all the time the country gettin' safer and better known. We ain't seen the end of it yet, Boone, not to what the mountain man does against hisself. Next thing is to hire out for guides and take partyies acrost and sp'ile the country more. . . . It's like we heired money and had to spend it, and now it Is nigh gone."

After Turner's verdict about the frontier, some Americans, such as conservationist John Muir, founder of the Sierra Club in 1892, were moving far beyond the obvious political battles over timber and coal. They argued for greater respect for "the rights of all the rest of creation." By 1915, Albert Schweitzer was discussing "reverence for life," the same year in which U.S. horticulturist Hyde Bailer began urging "ethical consideration for the whole earth."

There is little evidence that the nation's leaders either took those arguments seriously or suspected they were seeds that would later flower into the radical idea of environmental ethics, or deep ecology. This movement, whose central principle is that nature doesn't exist solely to serve man, and that all living things have rights, is a concept that is still on "the far frontier of moral theory," in the words of Rod Nash.

Another important aspect of Ed Abbey's legacy is that he infused these environmental ethics into fiction, many of his works being a reenactment of symbolic drama between man and nature.

Beside him was his source of fuel; a degenerate juniper tree, shriveled and twisted, cringing over its bed of lava rock and sand. An underprivileged juniper tree, living not on water and soil but on memory and hope. And almost alone.

—THE BRAVE COWBOY

Thoreau's influence on Abbey was also significant. Writing as the uncrowned leader of the New England School of Transcendentalism in the 1840s and '50s, Thoreau, with Emerson, postulated the existence of an "Oversoul," a divine moral force that flowed through and existed in every living thing, humans being just one niche in a diverse planetary ecosystem. "The earth I tread on," the Walden Bard wrote in a journal, "is not a dead inert mass; it is a body, has a spirit, is organic and fluid to the influence of its spirit . . . "

Emerging as an advocate of taking a broader view of the universe, Thoreau made himself quite unpopular among the local Massachusetts farmers by protesting when they cut down trees and ripped out underbrush. He wrote to a friend, "If some are prosecuted for abusing children, others deserve to be prosecuted for maltreating the face of nature committed to their care."

While Thoreau stopped short of demanding that all living things should be vested with legal rights, he believed firmly in their equality. In his writings, he regarded plants, skunks, fish—and even the planets and stars—as equal partners in the world around him. "The woods," he wrote during a Maine camping trip shortly before the Civil War, "are not tenantless, but choke-full of honest spirits as good as myself any day."

Two years later he expressed an idea that had never appeared before in American literature or in the discourse of public affairs: "What we call wildness, is a civilization other than our own."

Thoreau became the first modern American writer to challenge the destruction of nature on moral grounds, and to sound the alarm that national policy framed around the belief of inexhaustibility of resources was dangerous.

Abbey carried on Thoreau's crusade, but his fight went further, to assert that wilderness was indispensible to the health of the human psyche, and also that humans will never understand the essence of the word freedom unless they visit wild places.

In mulling about the techno-industrial state, the "red world" that was devouring the "green world," ravaging it mile by mile, canyon by canyon, river by river, Abbey concluded about capitalism: "Nothing so mean could be right. Greed is the ugliest of capital sins."

How to translate those feelings into words of awareness for his readers? It was Abbey's self-appointed task to translate the canyon country of the Southwest from emotions of love and anger into words, about the landscape, the light, the air, and the primordial inhabitants, scorpions, snakes, and critters.

> I feel myself sinking into the landscape, fixed into the landscape like a stone, like a tree, a small motionless shape of vague outline, desert-colored, and within the wings of imagination look down at myself through the eyes of the bird, watching a human figure that becomes smaller, smaller in the receding landscape as the bird rises into the evening—a man at a table near a twinkling campfire, surrounded by a rolling wasteland of stone and dune and sandstone monuments.
>
> —*DESERT SOLITAIRE*

In recent years the vast Colorado Plateau, equal in size to New England, New York, and Pennyslvania, where Abbey did most of his wandering, has come to epitomize a paradox festering in the national soul ever since the dawn of the Industrial Revolution: In the world of politics, wilderness protection is irreconcilably at odds with the imperative to develop wilderness at all costs, whether or not that leaves less for future generations.

Since over 70 percent of the Plateau is administered by the federal government, many Americans have been going about their daily lives, confident that someone, somehow, was protecting this astonishing bioregion, this "last best place," said the late

Wallace Stegner, with everything but their lives. And residents thought those protectors were the Bureau of Land Management, the Forest Service, the National Park Service, the Bureau of Indian Affairs, the U.S. Fish and Wildlife Service, state agencies, and a dozen stringent anti-pollution laws.

To their chagrin, many know now that they were sadly mistaken, and recognize that all along they should have been watching the watchers.

Less than a century ago, many hundreds of species of plants, seventy species of fish, and unknown numbers of other life forms were unique to the Colorado Plateau. "The Plateau's repository of biological diversity has been decimated," asserts Roger Clark of The Grand Canyon Trust, a nonprofit watchdog group in Flagstaff, Arizona, dedicated to more prudent management of public lands on the vast plateau. "Many of those species no longer exist," Clark declares.

Speaking for numerous inhabitants, as well as for countless foreign visitors shocked that America allows power plant air pollution there, Arizona land use planner Richard Hubbell was heard shouting near the Grand Canyon one day. Into a descending, dirty, yellow haze he bellowed: "Who gave anybody the right to take the blue out of my sky?"

No small part of Abbey's legacy is that today, more people are feeling freer to challenge the federal agencies and corporations for their failings. No one will ever know how many individuals have been moved to action by Edward Abbey's words, but there are many stories wafting on the winds of the Southwest.

Some of them are true. Here is one.

Up on northern Arizona's dusty Hopi Mesas a few years before Abbey's death, a young couple noticed a non-Indian water truck parked near one of the reservation's small reservoirs. For hours, they watched some non-Indians, from Phoenix, more than a hundred miles away, operating hydraulic pumps that were sucking up scarce Hopi water——illegally.

Furious at this outlaw operation, the couple reported it to the legal arm of the tribal council. True, it was an illegal act the Indian lawyers said, and they went to court to seek an injunction, but not before asking the operators of the water truck to cease and desist. Laughing off that request, the truckers kept on filling their eighteen-wheel water tanker with stolen Hopi water.

Then the couple heard the bad news: A judge told the Hopi lawyers that the case could not be heard for at least two months. That wasn't good enough for the couple, who had once heard Ed Abbey say at a gathering in Flagstaff: "We must strike back at the Empire, oppose, resist, subvert. It's a matter of honor."

Gathering a small group of Indians and non-Indians together after midnight, the couple crept toward the truck while the operators were sleeping in a motel nearby, and carried out their plan. Two of them deflated all eighteen of the truck's tires while other monkey wrenchers poured Karo syrup and sand into the engine crankcase and then disconnected all the important wiring. Before dawn, they walked silently away.

It took about six weeks for the trucking company to repair their huge vehicle so that they could pump water again. Then, two days after the pumping had resumed, the injunction came down and they were forced to abandon the operation. "Nobody was hurt," one of the monkey wrenchers said later. "When we saw that the justice system wasn't working, and the instruments of terrorism were operating outside the law, we felt we had no choice but to strike back. So we sabotaged that instrument— Abbey Lives."

Ever since he went West, Abbey had become incensed by outlaw activities like illegal corporate water trucks. They made him hunger for a different time: "If America could be, once again, a nation of self-reliant farmers, craftsmen, hunters, ranchers, and artists, then, the rich would have little power to dominate others.

"Neither to serve, nor to rule: That was the American dream."

Abbey knew that his dreams were probably doomed, that the Colorado Plateau would not be able to hold off or withstand the forces of development—more dams, hotels, cattle grazing, the final harvesting of old growth timber, theme parks, grizzly bear zoos, and superhighways. Yet imbued in his writings is the request that people fight for their future anyway. They must try to preserve and enjoy what is left, to survive the Leviathan's worst with beauty, freedom, and honor.

Are we masters or slaves of the industrial machine, Abbey asked? It's not that technology and industrialism are evil in themselves. The problem is to get them under control, down to human scale, and prevent them from ever again becoming the self-perpetuating, ever-expanding monsters that citizens have allowed them to become.

"What we need," he explained in *The Journey Home,* "is an optimum industrialism, neither too much or too little . . . but we cannot pick and choose this way, some technophiles [say] it's the entire package, plagues and all, or nothing . . . but it is not true. We can pick and choose, we can learn to select this and reject that. Discrimination is a basic function of human intelligence."

Another piece of the Abbey legacy is his conviction, which turns modern definitions of environmentalism upside down, that nature is certain to outlast mankind. Even though nature is the backdrop of his writings, and his love for rocks and rills, and buttes and red mesas is surpassingly strong, preservation of the human race, and all living things, was probably his greatest concern.

Few Americans have given as much thought to the value of Abbey's works as Roderick Nash. Other aspects of Abbey's legacy aside, Nash finds his literary efforts singular, for two reasons. First, Abbey helped to change conventional ideas about the desert. When the European vision confronted the arid land west of the 100th meridian, it was with a sense of shock. Mark Twain, for example, wrote of the barren, desolate, monotonous scenery. He didn't see scenery in the traditional sense, but some kind of purgatory lacking purling brooks and smiling meadows.

Nash asserts that Abbey called the attention of new generations of Americans to the fact that the desert was different, precious not for what can be seen, but for what is absent, the cleanness, the stripped-down quality: "I think his most impressive statement is from *The Journey Home* where he finds the arrow pointing to 'nothing.' Abbey liked the desert not because it contained or reflected God—as did the transcendentalists in their attitude toward nature—but because it was so hostile, and devoid of 'meaning.'

"I recall him saying that he once sought to find God in the desert, and so he fasted on the edge of the desert mesa for three days and finally had this glorious vision of God in the form of a baked chicken. So much for Emerson and Muir.

"So Ed reminded a generation that the desert was not an empty barren place, but was valuable, paradoxically, for being a wasteland. After *Desert Solitaire*, young Americans left the Sierras and headed for the slickrock canyon country, discovering beauty and wildness in new places."

Another part of Abbey's legacy, according to Nash, was his dedication to biocentrism, or what has come to be known as deep ecology: "Pervading most of his works, right from *The Brave Cowboy* to his last, *Hayduke Lives*, is the idea that nature does not exist for humans; not for their life support, not for their enjoyment. Nature is valuable in and of itself, all of it—rattlesnakes included. I think of the encounter Ed had with the snakes at the start of *Desert Solitaire.*"

> . . . facing the sun, drinking coffee. . . . I happen to look down and see almost between my bare feet, only a couple of inches to the rear of my heels, the very thing I had in mind. No mistaking that wedgelike head, that tip of horny segmented tail peeping out of the coils. He's under the doorstep and in the shade where the ground and air remain very cold.
>
> In his sluggish condition he's not likely to strike unless I rouse him by some careless move of my own. There's a revolver inside the trailer, a huge Webley .45, loaded, but it's out of reach.
>
> Even if I had it in my hands I'd hesitate to blast a fellow creature at close range . . . it would be like murder.

As Nash sees it, what is also memorable about Abbey's work is that he was writing about philosophy, "but not as a philosopher. He wrote as a lover, as a defender in terms the average person could understand. He brought environmental ethics down to earth, and he had a vision of human defense of the rights of nature long before 'environmental ethics' and 'deep ecology' were even coined."

For example, the idea behind *The Monkey Wrench Gang,* Nash believes, "was not to defend the West so that the gang of Hayduke, Seldom Seen, Doc, and Bonnie, could run rivers and go hiking. It was to defend it because that was the right thing to do; the moral thing, the ethical thing."

In that vein, Abbey's legacy can be measured by the contributions his writings have made to the tradition of Western American literature that Professor Max Westbrook has called

Western "sacrality, the sacred force [that] can be felt but never tangibly grasped, much less defined. It is simply the unnamable energy that is the source of man's intuitive and instinctual knowledge."

It is now accepted wisdom, but years ago Abbey argued that most social and economic assumptions governing Western civilization and American politics were becoming obsolete and unworkable, in many cases cruelly destructive. Underlying much of his work is the theme of foolish insanity, his targets being the blue-ribbon establishment, well-educated people who speak of beauty yet cause mayhem to be done to the land; ranchers, newspaper publishers, politicians, indeed nearly everyone with economic and political clout who have eyes they refuse to use.

Throughout Abbey's years in the Southwest, the region lent him the sun and moon, rivers, sparkling desert nights, and amethyst mountains. As generously, he gave back his love of the land, his passion for beauty, and his grief at its exploitation. And the pages of his books are branded with this love and passion.

Motivated by Samuel Johnson's challenge that it is the writer's duty to make the world better, Cactus Ed, no matter what he said in public, wrote to make a difference.

As he wrote in *A Voice Crying in the Wilderness*, "Distrusting all answers, [I write] to raise more questions. To give pleasure and promote esthetic bliss. To honor life and praise the divine beauty of the world. For the joy and exultation of writing itself. To tell my story."

All along he also was guided by George Orwell's words: "By retaining one's love of such things as trees, butterflies and toads, one makes a peaceful and decent future a little more probable."

How Abbey wanted to achieve that "peaceful and decent future" is what separates him from other writers: Fight back. "A man wrote a book, and lives were changed. That doesn't happen often," is the way David Quammen once put it in *Outside Magazine*.

Wherever one travels in the Southwest, the Abbey legend grows. Feeding the legend are many tales about people who have changed their lives because of Abbey's words, and still live with them in their daily lives.

There's the tale of a New Jersey schoolteacher who moved to Arizona in 1989. In a larger sense it is the story of everyone who has ever read *Desert Solitaire*. Her name is Joanna Kuruc, and her home had been New York City, outdoor experiences limited to walks through Manhattan's Central Park.

After arriving in Arizona, a boyfriend gave her a book about the desert. "Unfortunately," she recalls, "the author placed a lot of emphasis on the dangers of the desert. He wrote vivid descriptions of the variety of wildlife that were lurking behind every rock and under every log, particularly snakes and scorpions. He especially warned about being out at night, and related some frightening tales of folks who had camped out at night and woke up to find that rattlesnakes had crawled up into their sleeping bags. Having read all this, and not being familiar with the desert at all, I was too petrified to go hiking."

On the few occasions when someone did drag her along for a hike on the Mogollon Rim in northern Arizona, she was frightened to sit down anywhere on the trail for fear that a snake was surely waiting for her, preparing to strike.

After ten months of anxiety, she had convinced herself that she would never feel comfortable being outdoors as long as she lived in Arizona. And then it happened. A man she scarcely knew sent her a copy of *Desert Solitaire*, written by an author she'd never heard of before. "Edward Albee I'd heard of," she remembers. "But Abbey? Who? What? Never!"

But she was eager for new ideas, so one night, when the moon was high over the Verde Valley, she read the book and has never gotten over it: "After that, my feelings about the desert and the life it supports were transformed. Looking at the desert through Abbey's eyes, I saw things in a totally different light. I began to understand the oneness of nature, and to see the beauty of the desert and all its life forms.

"I was especially affected by the section where he goes hiking alone in Havasu Canyon and gets trapped on a ledge where he really believes that he is going to die. He manages, finally, to climb out of the little canyon, only to be caught in a terrible storm. He spends the night, wet and cold, aching, hungry, and wretched and then concludes that it had been one of the happiest days of his life."

That episode had a life-changing effect on Kuruc. She saw Abbey in the classic paradoxical situation of facing death, yet being awestruck by the beauty around him. Slowly, her self-confidence returned, and she began to think about going out alone into the wilds.

Under a clear bright night sky, she set out for a special butte called Bell Rock near Sedona, Arizona. She had always wanted to make this hike, but her fears had stopped her. As she recalls, "I climbed up Bell Rock by myself, finding my way by the light of the moon. I felt very at ease and safe being there alone. For four hours, I watched the moon and the stars, and listened to the night sounds.

"It was wonderful. I marveled at how I had come from being too terrified to sit on a rock during the day, to being stretched out in my sleeping bag in the middle of the night just one year later.

"Thank you, Ed Abbey, wherever you are."

And there is Arizona sculptor Thomas Jefferson Bollinger,

whose late father, a renowned history professor, handed him some Abbey writings when he was in his twenties. "I became an activist, a river runner, a sky diver," Bollinger recounts. "I learned something I might never have learned had I pursued the academic life: enjoy what's out there.

"Above all, in a time when truth was not fashionable at the highest levels of the nation, Abbey told the truth. We owe him a debt. He changed the way we saw things. His books will keep him alive for many generations."

And there is Carol Reush, who, in a moving letter to Clarke Cartwright Abbey after Abbey died, wrote, "Edward Abbey was a dangerous man. He ruined my life. Forgiving him is easy, but forgetting takes a long, long time."

Her problem with Abbey began during the 1974 fuel crisis in a local drugstore in southern Utah. Paging her way through a magazine and book rack, chockablock with diet cookbooks and astrology magazines, she came across a copy of *Desert Solitaire.*

"Little did I know," she recalled a month after Abbey's death, "what lay in store. Here was a holy book, a brand new testament that defined beyond my wildest imaginations, the scent, the aura, the anesthesia of the American Southwest.

"For fifteen years now, sleep does not come easy. The howl of the coyote, the holler of the hawk, the wail of the lonesome dove seeps into my dreams and alters the reality of all that seems reasonable and right.

"A red hot wind blows sand and silt into every chasm of the room and into the spaces between my teeth. Instead of slumber, I hallucinate. About pools of rainwater on mesas, sixty-three miles of dirt and gravel road, and a sheer drop-off a mile above a canyon that existed eons before the ancients discovered the sacredness of nature and the hoop of the world. He ruined my life."

Desert Solitaire had a similar effect on Lee Shively of Shreveport, Louisiana, who had never met Abbey but wrote after his death: "With each book I read by Ed, I began to grow in my understanding of the natural world, and I also began to appreciate the belief that nothing, no thing, is more important than this wonderful world on which we live.

"I also began to recognize the mass of bullshit we are fed by our governments, institutions, and especially the mass media and industrial complex. Ed Abbey became my friend, even when I found a point on which to disagree. He became the person I quoted most often. Ed Abbey started me to thinking about what is really important, and for that I will be eternally grateful to him."

Throughout his life, John Palmieri of North Hollywood, California, felt he had been alone. "I had come to what I believed to be a unique set of principles," he wrote in 1989, a few days after Abbey's death. "It was not until I discovered Ed's writing seven years ago that I realized I wasn't alone. He said what I wanted to say. And he did it with style, conviction, and passion. Can anyone love the desert Southwest without loving Ed?"

Other citizens have resorted to a more militant path. Take four unusual women living in Tucson, who, in their outrage over the senseless killing of mountain lions, bears, and other wild animals, have formed a group called Wildlife Damage Review.

One of the organizers is none other than Clarke Cartwright Abbey. Slightly annoyed with people's tendency to describe her only as Abbey's widow, she is emerging as a force in her own right. "It's a senseless slaughter," she asserts, pointing out how few taxpayers realize that nearly $50 million is spent annually killing thousands of wild animals, all because ranchers claim that their livestock is being cut down. Moreover, ranchers don't need proof to call in government exterminators.

Clarke Abbey and her three friends, Lisa Peacock, Marian Baker-Gierlach, and Nancy Zierenberg, have as their objective to strike back at a federal agency they see as unjust, cruel, and wasteful of taxpayers' money: Animal Damage Control (ADC), a little-known arm of the Department of Agriculture.

Using leg-hold traps, leg snares, M-44 poison cartridges, rifles, and a bizarre assortment of other weapons from the air and on the land, ADC's Arizona wildlife total for 1989 was: 9 black bears; 1,676 coyotes; 44 mountain lions; 177,277 blackbirds; and assorted skunks, badgers, and raccoons.

The Arizona Cattlegrowers' Association is furious with the Tucson group, insisting that the cattle industry is worth in excess of $300 million annually to Arizonans, and that unless federally subsidized predator control continues apace, ranchers will no longer be able to raise enough beef to feed the people.

In turn, ranching critics underscore the fact that most ranchers in Arizona, and the West, are leasing public land, and their water and grazing rights have historically been subsidized at a fraction of the market value of these commodities.

"The few cows and sheep that lions and bears do eat," observes Dan Dagget of Mountain Lions Unlimited in Flagstaff, "are already bought and paid for by the taxpayer."

Another Arizona citizen who is fighting back in Abbey fashion is Nadia Caillou of Sedona. She is raising a nearly full-blooded wolf named Dances, and she was brought up with lions at her family's home in the California mountains. "When people know the facts, they will speak out," she explains. "For coyotes and lions, cattle are not the food of choice, despite all the myths that have become part of the conventional wisdom. They prefer deer or mountain sheep, but they have been driven off the range by cattle.

"What ADC does is beyond predator control. It is vengeful eradication. Take coyotes! The ADC program transforms them from omnivores to carnivores. After their pups have been poisoned and strangled by ADC people, the females react by breeding faster, and the males turn angry and mean, and go after larger prey.

"Oh, the program is wonderful for a few big ranchers, but what of the rest of us? Are we headed into a world without wildlife, where all animals are domesticated? There are nonlethal alternatives, and they must come. To intervene in nature is to create boomerangs that will be flying back at us for decades. Abbey pointed the way."

Not everybody is happy that, inspired by Abbey, individuals are taking action. To them, Abbey's legacy is that he made them angry, and they are still angry. Not atypical is Guy Trotter, a retired navy officer in Utah. He despised Abbey when he was living, and now reserves those feelings for his legions of followers.

To put it mildly, Trotter regards Abbey's demands that conservationists strike back, even violently if necessary (as in *The Monkey Wrench Gang*), as promoting criminal acts. To Trotter, nobody has any business carrying on Abbey's ideas because he—and his ideas—were rationally vulnerable in several respects: constitutional, moral, and practical. "Abbey? A loose cannon on deck. I'm sick to death of trendy, irresponsible gurus of the pseudo-intellectual segment of our society who urge their naive sycophants to illegality. Wasn't there enough of that in the 1960s and '70s?

"Have we learned nothing from the Kent State tragedy? Has no one noticed it's never one of these tweedy demagogues who has his posterior peppered with birdshot at the scene of a protest he's inspired? Oh, no; their millieu is the academic lectern, it's the poor dumb slob who swallows their line of swill who winds up with his portrait on the post office bulletin board."

And then there was George Orians of Boulder, Colorado, teacher, philosopher, writer, and passionate admirer of Abbey's works who "carried it on." For him Abbey's legacy was not anger, but love.

Orians met Abbey at a meeting in Arizona in the 1980s, and in the years thereafter read and digested all the Abbey books he could find. "George felt that somehow in writing and talking about his feelings for his hero," his mother recalls, "he could alleviate pent-up emotions inside." One of George's lifelong friends, Dale Rezabek, remembers that George was struck by how Abbey showed little fear of death in his writings: "This helped George form his own philosophy against fear of death, at least in the abstract."

During the 1988–89 school year, George took a leave of absence from his teaching to complete a master's degree in Humanities at the University of Colorado. When news of Abbey's death reached him, he decided to dedicate his thesis to Abbey, and borrowed some of Abbey's frequent references to Dr. Johnson for the project.

In his thesis, "Artist as Advocate," Orians wrote that "Abbey left us a vision; one of desperation but also one of hope. He unabashedly addressed his perception of the truth, of his reality. He suggested solutions and plans of action. He voiced a challenge for the next generations to accept and defend.

"He advocated action, any action, to help fight for and save what is still left, what is still ultimately savable in our natural world."

George received a high mark for his thesis, even though it was three times the acceptable length. He was jubilant. Then, four months after Abbey's death, George himself was killed in a terrible United Airline crash in Sioux City, Iowa. His memorial service was held on the banks of the Colorado River, and several of his friends and relations came to speak about his love of life and his love of the wild places, and how he had imparted this love to hundreds of his students. After his ashes were scattered, the readings began, and they chose the words of Abbey.

> Where have the years gone? Why, into the usual vices of the romantic idealist: into sloth and melancholy, each feeding upon and reinforcing the other, into love and marriage, into the begetting of children, into the strenuous maneuvers of earning a living without living to earn, into travel and play and music and drink and talk and laughter, into saving the world—but saving the world was only a hobby. Into watching cloud formations float across our planetary skies. But mostly into sloth and melancholy and I don't regret a moment of it.
>
> —*THE BEST OF EDWARD ABBEY*,
> AUTHOR'S PREFACE

Many brave men and women are carrying it on in Abbey's wake: John Parsons saves rivers; David Wegner, Bob Lippman, Jim Ruch, Roger Clark, and Tom Jensen are working to save the Grand Canyon; and thousands of others are fighting to safeguard their country from their government.

And then there is Steve Thompson, rancher-architect from Camp Verde, Arizona, who nightly reads Abbey's books to his ten-year-old daughter, Savannah. Now all she wants to do is head for the wilderness, and be a ranger like Abbey.

At an early age, Thompson himself went through a transformation similar to Joanna Kuruc's. While growing up on an Arizona ranch, he recalls, "I always thought the mountains and the forests were sacred, and that the desert was a wasteland. Then I discovered Abbey's writings about twenty years ago. I started to realize that the desert is also a very sacred place. It is where the medicine and food is. And whenever I'm hiking across it, I think of Abbey and his ability to verbalize the most sacred feelings.

"Am I going to lose those feelings his words created in me? Not a chance. You can say that I belong to a special school that has no campus. We call it the Abbey School, and we don't need a campus."

Abbey's lasting epitaph may be that he is remembered as the intellectual mentor for two generations of people who wandered westward to make a new start, people who had never been mentored. "All of a sudden there was a guy named Abbey who had come West in the 1940s," says Mike Lacey, "who was a big wild hair, as crazy for life as they were, and who had made it. He'd kept his independence, and he'd written well and lived honorably, and had enjoyed his ass.

"You had a whole bunch of people in the West who received a mentoring by example. They said, 'Well Goddamn, here's at least one guy that didn't sell out, that didn't give up, that still had a voice.'"

Not long after Abbey died, a bright young Navajo woman was taking a course in Southwestern literature at Mesa Community College near Phoenix. She showed up one day, looking disgruntled with her assignment. "This Abbey," she grumped to her instructor, "he really piss me off." So the instructor, Dick Kirkpatrick, gave her another of Abbey's books to read. It was Abbey's own favorite novel, *Black Sun*.

A few days later, she returned to class, looking just a little less grumpy. "Well, Abbey is a good writer," she conceded, "but he still piss me off."

Somewhere in the lilac purple desert, pausing on a pile of mangled ancient rock the color of red iron, Abbey's ghost was surely grinning.

EPILOGUE

As I write this, Ed's been technically dead for a while, and I've had a hard time with what's happened to his career since he died. The guy I knew has become an object, a category, a legend of sorts, and something that almost seems to be spelled in capital letters: EDWARD ABBEY.

I have never really recovered from his death. The day he died was the first time in years I raised my hand in anger at another person. For days, I felt violent, and I was appalled at myself, but it felt good. Why did this happen? I think because of a kind of selfishness and a kind of fear.

I knew I would no longer have anyone to talk to about the words as music. Not that we ever said a hell of a lot. But that's the point. We didn't have to say much because we both felt the same way. I think of him a lot. Not in any concrete way, remembering a moment or some stunning pronouncement, but in a vague way, like he's a friendly ghost watching over me.

And judging me! I can give you a dime-store version of what he gave me: Don't write just for money; don't write anything you don't believe; don't listen to others; don't quit, don't ever quit. And don't believe the good things they say about you. You see? It's all rather obvious. But I still think of him, because even though these thoughts, these admonitions, are common; to live them and practice them is very uncommon.

I have a hunch Abbey is delighted at this new change in his status. As they said of Elvis's death, "good career move." But this new guy, he's not the one I knew or would ever want to know.

The Abbey I knew, an anarchist, a quiet loner addicted to classical music, bouts of solitude, and strict work habits, hardly knew the creature he had created and admitted as much in his essay "Confessions of a Literary Hobo." But then there were a lot of Abbeys, and different people knew different men parading about under that name.

I still remember that hotel squatting by the Los Angeles airport, the corridors clogged with magazine people in full rut at an industry convention. I was an editor at that time, and my major investor was sweating blood as he stood before me. He told me he had just talked to his office and discovered that it was going to be picketed by Mexican-Americans, that there might be violence, that some fabled end was near. There had been angry phone calls, he sputtered. All because of Abbey, because of what Abbey wrote—an attack on Hispanic culture as anti-nature, anti-democratic, as patron-ridden—and what I had decided to print . . . ah, the power of words.

Then I fielded a call from a Mexican-American leader in the community who wanted to talk to Abbey, wanted to correct in an honest discussion the errors of his way. I said I'd call Ed (the phone number by that time in his life was a minor secret, unlisted and known to only a few thousand people here and there) and have him call back. So I did.

It was early in the morning and overcast, the kind of half-rainy day where cars sing on the asphalt as they roll past, and Abbey's voice was slow, soft, and with wide spaces between his words.

That was normal. He often was not much of a talker. I told him of the tempest he'd created and of the man who wanted to talk to him. I said the man deserved to be answered. So he said he'd give him a call. Then he paused and sighed, and continued that he wished he'd never written that piece, that it had hurt too many people and raised too much bad feeling for whatever value the ideas in it might have. Words can do that, too.

Words, that is really a lot of whatever friendship existed between Ed Abbey and me, words, the mystery of words. Abbey could be wrong-headed, angry, vicious at times, but not careless when it came to words. He delighted in their exact value, the same way a gunfighter was into the ballistics of various cartridges . . . at times he seemed to favor magnum loads.

I'll tell you about the Abbey I knew. He'd promised to write about a kind of standoff with a local developer-car dealer for a newspaper where I worked in Tucson. And when it was due, I called him and he'd forgotten all about it. So I drove out to his house to get it, while he typed out a piece in a semi-panic. When I got there it was finished, the pages were full of pen marks moving sentences, scratching out words, adding new thoughts. The damn thing looked like a snake pit packed with writhing serpents and he was still at it with his pen as I pried it out of his hands.

Or, there was the Abbey I was having lunch with once when I happened to mention a passage in John Steinbeck's novel *The Log of the Sea of Cortez*, a few paragraphs describing Bahia Concepcion. He'd read the book years before and started quoting the description from memory.

This is the man who was my friend and whom I remember. A guy who sweat blood over words and never by his own standards got it right. The man who never rested on his laurels, who constantly read other writers, who every single time I met him was shoving books into my hands and insisting that I read them, telling me in that flat, soft voice that I had to read this or that.

Basically, a hillbilly from Appalachia who mainlined the English language and never recovered from his love for it. That feeling is very rare, at least it has been in my life. I have by accidents of employment been around a lot of people who write down words, and sell them, but Abbey was about the only person I ever knew who shared my own passions for the language.

We were both essentially children, semi-dolts, in awe of the sound of words. I must emphasize the sounds because Abbey was a product of spoken language, of the music of words. I think of this sense of language as music, as rhythm, resulting from his early rearing in the hills.

In my case, I remember a childhood of people talking in the kitchen: of men sitting there with quarts of beer and talking, telling tales, commanding attention through their sense of editing of quirky words, of comedy mixed with pain; of women at the sink or bustling about the stove and counters and telling tales of their life with men; of vocabulary being a chest of tools for constructing narratives of life as a song, the words as notes, the people or characters being melodies. For me, and I suspect for Ed, reading books came later, and by that time we could not alter this sense of language as music.

Basically, he thought writing was a moral task dedicated to moral issues and if it were not, then it was a bunch of bullshit. Hence, his endless rage at the Henry Jameses and John Updikes of the world. He also believed that writing was to be read.

The students he taught could not get an A unless their work in class was accepted by some publication—I know because they would show up at my editorial office door with his recommendation for immortality.

I happened to agree with him on these matters, and so, while our conversations tended to be about writing, we didn't say a lot because we agreed. We carried on more of a wink-and-nod sentence-fragment kind of conversation.

Anyone who wonders how he felt about words should simply read a couple of pages of him, then pick a paragraph and try to remove a sentence. Then take a sentence and try to scratch out a word. Or change a word. It's not easy to do.

Abbey wrote in the vernacular style, the words sounding as though they were coming out of his mouth as he sat on the bar stool next to you. And this makes his writing look offhanded. But it is tight, very tight.

I can't recall asking him a direct question about what someone should do and say and write. I'm not sure I cared. People ask me things now as if I had been keeping detailed notes, making tape recordings of penetrating talks with the Master. Well I didn't. I'm not that kind of person.

I know people who dream about him. Some of them never met him, but they still dream about him. I don't, but I believe they do. I'm now living in Mexico, that place and culture that Abbey skewered so harshly and yet efficiently in an essay that temporarily ignited the magazine I once worked for.

I never agreed with the essay or Ed about Mexico or Mexicans. But I loved the way he constructed a demolition job on the culture, and I don't doubt he believed every word of it. So I live in Mexico, and that's just one more thing Ed Abbey technically disagreed about.

From time to time in the press now, I read attacks on Abbey as being racist, sexist, rednecked, and having other failings. I never feel any need to respond to these attacks. I don't think they are entirely fair, but I don't care. Any writer who is dead and still raises hackles must have done his work properly.

In a way, I hope I never have to write about him again. Oh, well, the hell with it. Abbey can take care of himself. He always has.

Chuck Bowden
Alamos, Sonora
Mexico

BIBLIOGRAPHY

Austin, Mary. *The Land of Journey's Ending*. New York: Century Company, 1924.

————. *The Land of Little Rain*. Boston: Houghton Mifflin, 1934.

Billington, Ray Allen. *The Far Western Frontier: 1830–1860*. New York: Harper, 1956.

Clark, William, and Meriwether Lewis: *The Journals of Lewis and Clark*. Ed. Bernard DeVoto. Boston: Houghton Mifflin, 1953.

Clissold, Stephen. *The Seven Cities of Cibola*. London: Eyre and Spottswoode, 1961.

Colorado River Storage Project: Congressional Subcommittee Hearings. Washington, D.C. U.S. Government Printing Office, 1954.

DeVoto, Bernard. "Let's Close the National Parks." *Harper's Magazine* 207 (October 1953): 49–52.

————. *Across the Wide Missourri*. Boston: Houghton Mifflin, 1947.

————. *The Course of Empire*. Boston: Houghton Mifflin, 1952.

Douglas, Kirk. *The Ragman's Son*. New York: Pocket Books, a division of Simon & Schuster Inc., 1988.

Fergusson, Erna. *Our Southwest*. New York: Alfred A. Knopf, 1940.

Graham, Frank, Jr. *Man's Dominion: The Story of Conservation in America*. New York: M. Evans, 1971.

Jeffers, Robinson. *Not Man Apart*. San Francisco: Sierra Club Books, 1965.

Krutch, Joseph Wood. *The Best Nature Writing of Joseph Wood Krutch*. New York: Morrow, 1969.

Lawrence, D. H. *Mornings in Mexico*. London: Martin Secker, 1927.

Leopold, Aldo. *A Sand County Almanac*. New York: Oxford University Press, 1949.

McPhee, John. *Encounters with the Archdruid*: New York: Farrar, Straus & Giroux, 1971.

Nash, Roderick. *Wilderness and the American Mind*. New Haven: Yale University Press, 1967.

————. *The Call of the Wild 1900–1916*. New York: George Braziller, 1970.

————. *The Rights of Nature: A History of Environmental Ethics*. Wisconsin: The Univeristy of Wisconsin Press, 1989.

Porter, Eliot. *The Place No One Knew: Glen Canyon on the Colorado*. San Francisco: Sierra Club Books, 1962.

Powell, John Wesley. *Canyons of the Colorado*. New York: Flood and Vincent, 1895.

————. *Report on the Lands of the Arid Lands of the United States*. Washington D.C.: U.S. Government Printing Office, 1978.

Priestly, J. B. *Midnight on the Desert*. New York: Harper Brothers, 1937.

Reisner, Marc. *Cadillac Desert: The American West and Its Disappearing Water*. New York: Viking, 1986.

Robbins, Roy. *Our Landed Heritage: The Public Domain, 1776–1970*. 2nd rev. ed. Lincoln: Univeristy of Nebraska Press, 1976.

Ronald, Ann. *The New West of Edward Abbey*. The University of Nevada Press, 1988.

Roosevelt, Theodore. *Theodore Roosevelt: An Autobiography*. New York: Macmillan, 1913.

Ruess, Everett. *On Desert Trails*. El Centro, CA: Desert Magazine Press, 1940.

Sibley, George. "The Desert Empire." *Harper's Magazine* 255 (October 1977): 49–56, 61–68.

Smith, Henry Nash. *Virgin Land: The American West as Symbol and Myth*. Cambridge, MA: Harvard University Press, 1950.

Stegner, Wallace. *Beyond the Hundredth Meridian*. Boston: Houghton Mifflin Co., 1953.

Thoreau, Henry David. *Walden and Civil Disobedience*, ed. Owen Thomas. New York: W. W. Norton & Company, 1966.

Turner, Frederick Jackson. *The Frontier in American History*. New York: Henry Holt and Company, 1920.

Udall, Stewart. *The Quiet Crisis*. New York: Holt, Rinehart and Winston, 1963.

————. *1976—Agenda for Tomorrow*. New York: Harcourt, Brace and World, 1968.

Van Dyke, John C. *The Desert: Further Studies in Natural Appearances*. New York: Charles Scribner's Sons, 1901. Reprint. Tucson: Arizona Historical Society, 1976.

Wild, Peter. *Pioneer Conservationists of Western American*. Missoula, MT: Mountain Press Publishing Co., 1979.

STUDIES OF EDWARD ABBEY

Haslam, Gerald. Introduction to *Fire on the Mountain* by Edward Abbey. Albuquerque: University of New Mexico Press, Zia Books, 1978.

Herndon, Jerry. "Moderate Extremism": Edward Abbey and

"The Moon-Eyed Horse." *Western American Literature* 16 (August 1981): 97–103.

Lambert, Neal E. Introduction to *The Brave Cowboy* by Edward Abbey. Albuquerque: University of New Mexico Press, Zia Books, 1977.

McCann, Garth. *Edward Abbey*. Boise State University Writers Series, no. 29. Boise, Idaho: Boise State University, 1977.

Pilkington, William T. "Edward Abbey: Southwestern Anarchist." *Western Review* 3 (Winter 1966): 58–62.

————. "Edward Abbey: Western Philosopher, or How to be a 'Happy Hopi Hippie.'" *Western American Literature* 9 (May 1974): 17–31.

Powell, Lawrence C. "A Singular Ranger." *Westways*, March 1974, 32–35.

Rawlings, Donn. "Abbey Essays: One Man's Quest for Solid Ground." *Living Wilderness*, June 1980.

————. "Anarchic Dreams in Ed Abbey's Wild Southwest." *Living Wilderness*, June 1980.

Standiford, Les. "Desert Places: An Exchange with Edward Abbey." *Western Humanities Review* 24 (Autumn 1970): 395–98.

Wylder, Delbert E. "Edward Abbey and the 'Power Elite'." *Western Review* 6 (Winter 1969): 18–22.

INDEX